ANGLO-AMERICAN
RELATIONS SINCE 1939

MANCHESTER
UNIVERSITY PRESS

ANGLO-AMERICAN RELATIONS SINCE 1939

THE ENDURING ALLIANCE

Edited by
JOHN BAYLIS

Manchester University Press
Manchester and New York
Distributed exclusively in the USA by Palgrave

Copyright © John Baylis 1997

Published by Manchester University Press
Oxford Road, Manchester M13 9NR, UK
and Room 400, 175 Fifth Avenue, New York, NY 10010, USA
www.manchesteruniversitypress.co.uk

Distributed exclusively in the USA by
Palgrave, 175 Fifth Avenue, New York NY 10010, USA

Distributed exclusively in Canada by
UBC Press, University of British Columbia, 2029 West Mall,
Vancouver, BC, Canada V6T 1Z2

British Library Cataloguing-in-Publication Data
A catalogue record for this book is available from the British Library

Library of Congress Cataloging-in-Publication Data
A catalog record for this book is available from the Library of Congress

ISBN 0 7190 4779 X *paperback*

First published 1997

First digital, on-demand edition produced by Lightning Source 2003

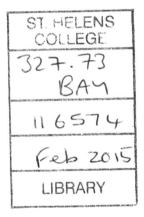

Contents

Acknowledgements		*page* vi
Chronology of events		viii
Introduction		1
A brief note on sources		17
1	The wartime relationship	18
2	The search for a new relationship, 1945–50	38
3	Cooperation and friction, 1950–56	68
4	Rebuilding the alliance, 1957–59	84
5	Challenges to the nuclear partnership, 1960–63	118
6	The 'close relationship', 1964–70	146
7	The 'natural relationship', 1970–79	168
8	The 'extraordinary' alliance restored, 1979–89	197
9	The post-Cold War era	223
	Guide to further reading	253
	Bibliography	255
	Index	261

Acknowledgements

Part of the research for this book was made possible by financial assistance provided by the Higher Education Funding Council for Wales. I am very grateful for the council's support. I wish to thank Dr Len Scott, Dr Stephen Twigge, Professor Mick Cox, Alan Macmillan, Kerry Longhurst and Mark Smith for their help and advice with various aspects of the book. I am also grateful to Elaine Lowe, who shouldered the burden of word-processing it with her usual efficiency, patience and good humour. Thanks are also due to the staff of the Hugh Owen Library, at the University of Wales, Aberystwyth, and the staff of the National Library of Wales, Aberystwyth. I also wish to record my thanks to the following for permission to cite copyright material: the Controller of Her Majesty's Stationery Office for Crown copyright material held in the Public Record Office, London; parliamentary and Crown copyright material is reproduced with the permission of the Controller of HMSO; British American Newspapers Ltd; Curtis Brown Ltd, London, on behalf of the estate of Sir Winston S. Churchill, for permission to reproduce material from *The Second World War*, Vol. 3, copyright Winston S. Churchill; Harper Collins *Publishers* Ltd for permission to quote from James Callaghan *Time and Chance* and Margaret Thatcher The *Downing Street Years*; Anthony Hartley; Macmillan General Books in respect of *Riding the Storm* by Harold Macmillan; the New York Times Company for material by Dean Acheson, copyright © 1962, reprinted by permission; Penguin Books Ltd; Peter Riddell; R. G. H. Seitz; Times Newspapers Ltd; the US Government Printing Office; the US Department of State. Finally, I owe an enormous debt to my wife, Marion, to my brother, Brian, to my in-laws, Margaret and Joe Brockhurst, and to my parents, for their love and support.

J.B.

In Memory of my father-in-law
Joe Brockhurst

Chronology of events

1940

September   Britain and the United States conclude the 'destroyers for bases' agreement.

1941

December   Japan attacks Pearl Harbor, bringing the United States into the war as a full belligerent ally. At the Arcadia conference British and American Chiefs of Staff plan for a combined war effort.

1943

January   The Casablanca conference.
August   The Quebec agreement.

1944

June   The Declaration of Trust is issued.
July   The Bretton Woods agreement.
September   The Hyde Park agreement.

1945

February   The Yalta conference.
April   Harry S. Truman becomes President of the United States following the death of Roosevelt.
July–August   The Potsdam conference.
July   A Labour government is elected in Britain with Clement Attlee as Prime Minister.
The world's first atomic bomb is detonated in New Mexico.

August	The US Congress ends Lend Lease to Britain.
December	Britain secures a loan from the United States.

1946

March	Churchill makes his 'Iron Curtain' speech at Fulton, Missouri. He also refers to the 'special relationship' between Britain and the United States.
May	The Anglo-American Committee of Enquiry on Palestine produces its final report.
August	The McMahon Act becomes law in the United States.
September	Montgomery meets US Joint Chiefs of Staff on the USS *Sequoia*, laying plans for the continuance of Anglo-American military co-operation after the war.

1947

January	It is decided that Britain should build its own atomic bomb.
March	The 'Truman doctrine' is passed by Congress.
April	Britain hands her mandate in Palestine over to the United Nations.
May	The United States begins to take over British commitments in Greece.

1948

March	The US Congress approves the Marshall Plan.
April	The Organisation for European Economic Co-operation (OEEC) is founded.
May	The independent state of Israel is created.
June	The Soviet Union imposes a blockade of Berlin which is to last for almost a year.
July	The US National Security Council agrees to dispatch B-29 'atomic bombers' to Britain.
August	The signing of the Burns–Templer agreements (involving cooperation in conventional weapons).

1949

April	The North Atlantic Treaty is signed.

May	The Berlin blockade ends.
	The Federal Republic of Germany is established from the British, American and French occupation zones.
August	The first Soviet atomic bomb is successfully exploded.
October	The People's Republic of China is established.
	The Soviet Union establishes the German Democratic Republic.

1950

January	Britain and the United States sign a Mutual Defence Agreement.
June	North Korea invades South Korea.
July	Coalition forces (under US command) with a UN mandate fight North Korea.
December	The Truman/Attlee 'understandings' are reached on the control of US nuclear forces on British soil.

1951

May	Iranian Prime Minister Mossadeq nationalises the Anglo-Iranian Oil Company.
October	Churchill returns as Prime Minister.

1952

October	Britain conducts its first atomic bomb test, at Monte Bello.
November	The US tests its first hydrogen bomb.

1953

January	Dwight D. Eisenhower ('Ike') becomes President of the United States.

1954

February	President Eisenhower requests Congress to amend the McMahon Act.
April	At the Geneva meeting the final settlement leads to the partition of Vietnam.
July	The Cabinet decides that Britain should acquire a hydrogen bomb.

1955

April Anthony Eden becomes Prime Minister following the resignation of Winston Churchill.

May A rearmed West Germany enters NATO.

June Revisions of the McMahon Act are signed.

1956

October British and French forces (in collusion with Israel) launch an attack on Egypt in response to Colonel Nasser's nationalisation of the Suez canal.

1957

January Harold Macmillan becomes Prime Minister following the resignation of Anthony Eden.

March President Eisenhower and Prime Minister Macmillan meet in Bermuda in an attempt to restore Anglo-American relations after the Suez debacle.
The Treaties of Rome setting up the European Economic Community (EEC) and Euratom are signed by the six countries.

May The first British hydrogen bomb test takes place on Christmas Island.

October The Declaration of Common Purpose is issued.

1958

January The Treaties of Rome come into force.

February Agreements are reached for the stationing of Thor intermediate-range ballistic missiles in the United Kingdom.

July Joint Anglo-American landings take place in Jordan and the Lebanon.
The US Atomic Energy Act greatly opens up areas of Anglo-American atomic cooperation previously curtailed by the McMahon Act of 1946.

1960

March Macmillan and Eisenhower agree on the provision of the US Skybolt missile and the stationing of US Polaris submarines at Holy Loch in Scotland.

Chronology of events

1961

January   John F. Kennedy becomes President of the United States.

August   East German authorities begin the construction of the Berlin wall.

1962

October   The United States and Soviet Union clash over the stationing of Soviet missiles in Cuba.

December   Macmillan succeeds in acquiring Polaris in place of the Skybolt missile system cancelled by the United States in November.

Dean Acheson offends the British government with his claim that Britain has lost an empire but not yet found a role.

1963

January   General de Gaulle announces his veto of the British application to join the EEC.

October   Alec Douglas- Home becomes Prime Minister following the resignation of Harold Macmillan.

November   President Kennedy is assassinated; Vice-president Lyndon Johnson takes over.

1964

October   Labour returns to power in Britain with Harold Wilson as the new Prime Minister.

1965

February   The United States intensifies its bombing of North Vietnam.

1966

February   The British government announces that it will pull out of Aden over the next two years but will remain in the Gulf region and the Far East.

1967

July   It is announced that Britain will withdraw from East of Suez by the mid-1970s.

November	Devaluation of sterling.
December	France displays its continued opposition to British membership of the EEC.

1968
January	An acceleration of Britain's East of Suez withdrawal is announced for the end of 1971.
October	Anti-Vietnam War protests take place in Britain.

1969
January	Richard M. Nixon becomes President of the United States.
December	Plans are released for the establishment of an Anglo-American base in the Indian Ocean.

1970
June	Edward Heath becomes Prime Minister as the Conservatives are returned to power in Britain. A period of strained Anglo-American relations ensues.

1973
January	The United States launches its 'Year of Europe' project.
	Britain joins the EEC.
April	The British decide to proceed with the Polaris improvement programme.
October	Egypt attacks Israel on the day of Yom Kippur.

1974
February	Harold Wilson returns as Prime Minister.
August	Gerald Ford becomes President of the United States following Nixon's resignation.

1975
	The United States pulls out of Vietnam.
June	In a referendum the British people choose to stay in the EEC.

1976
April	James Callaghan becomes Prime Minister after the resignation of Harold Wilson. Signs of some improvement in Anglo-American relations ensue.

1977
January   Jimmy Carter becomes President of the United
               States.

1978
April   President Carter cancels the neutron bomb project.

1979
May   Margaret Thatcher becomes Prime Minister as
               the Conservatives are returned to power in
               Britain.
December   The Nato 'dual track' decision is taken.

1980
July   Prime Minister Thatcher announces the
               government's decision to purchase the US Trident
               I (C4) missile system.

1981
January   Ronald Reagan becomes President of the United
               States.

1982
March   It is agreed that Britain will buy the Trident II
               (D5) missile system from the United States.
April   Britain goes to war with Argentina over the
               Falkland Islands. The conflict ends in June with
               British victory. Important military assistance is
               provided by the United States.

1983
March   Reagan announces his Strategic Defense Initiative
               or 'Star Wars' project.
October   The United States invades Grenada, to overthrow
               its 'Marxist' government.

1984
January   US cruise missiles begin to be deployed in
               Britain.

Chronology of events

1985
March   Mikhail Gorbachev comes to power in Moscow.
November   Gorbachev and Reagan meet in Geneva.

1986
April   Using British bases, US bombers attack Libya in retaliation for terrorist activity.
June   The Westland affair and competition between the US Sikorsky group and a European consortium lead to the resignation of two Cabinet Ministers.
October   Gorbachev and Reagan meet at Reykjavik.

1987
December   The INF treaty is signed.

1989
January   George Bush becomes President of the United States.
            Reformist revolutions sweep through the former Eastern Bloc.

1990
October   The reunification of Germany takes place as the former GDR is absorbed into the Federal Republic.
            John Major becomes Prime Minister in Britain.

1991   The disintegration of Yugoslavia begins.
            The United States declares that it is to leave the Poseidon base at Holy Loch and that the F-111 bombers will also be withdrawn.
January   Britain and the United States join ranks in the coalition against Iraq after the invasion of oil-rich Kuwait in August 1990.
February   The Warsaw Pact is disbanded.

1992
February   In the 'Maastricht treaty' the EC puts forward plans for the creation of political, economic and

monetary union. The former includes ideas for the development of common foreign and security policies.

1993

January   Democrat Bill Clinton becomes President of the United States.
Disagreements arise between Britain and the United States over a strategy for Bosnia.

1994

January   NATO announces its 'Partnership for Peace' initiative.

September   Sinn Fein leader Gerry Adams is granted a visa to visit the United States for fund-raising, much to the annoyance of the British government.

1995   The ongoing war in the former Yugoslavia together with the Northern Ireland issue leads many commentators to conclude that the 'special relationship' is no more.

July   The United Nations decides to end the arms embargo imposed on the Bosnian Muslims.

November   Clinton visits Northern Ireland and signs of improvement emerge in Anglo-American relations.

December   Dayton Accord on Bosnia.

1996

January   US troops begin to arrive in Bosnia to implement the Dayton Accord.

Introduction

Issues of epistemology, methodology and ideology

There are a number of problems with undertaking research in the field of diplomatic history which are only rarely addressed by those engaged in this field of scholarly enquiry.[1] The problems centre on three main issues relating to epistemology, methodology and ideology. Epistemology is concerned with theories of knowledge: how we know what we know. In terms of the subject covered by this particular book the question is what we can know with any certainty about the history of Anglo-American relations, much of which, especially on issues of security, has been shrouded in secrecy. Methodology is concerned with the way in which we go about trying to build up our knowledge; the methods we use to find out what we want to know. And ideology concerns the relationship between values and knowledge; how far ideological beliefs get in the way of the search for 'truth' and objectivity.

The study of history suffers from what one writer has described as 'epistemological fragility'.[2] In their pursuit of knowledge historians are faced with a number of difficult problems. The first, and perhaps most obvious, is the problem of hindsight. Historians always have the advantage of knowing more about the past than those who lived through it. Also they have an awareness of how the

[1] There are, however, some notable exceptions. They include E. H. Carr, *What is History?* (London: Penguin, 1964); Marc Bloc, *The Historian's Craft* (Manchester: Manchester University Press, 1954); A. Marwick, *The Nature of History* (London: Macmillan, 1970); J. Tosh, *The Pursuit of History* (London: Longman, 1984); and K. Jenkins, *On 'What is History?' From Carr and Elton to Rorty and White* (London: Routledge, 1995).
[2] K. Jenkins, *Rewriting History* (London: Routledge, 1991), p. 11.

1

'story' developed subsequently. This often leads them to give a coherence and a meaning to events which were not apparent at the time. Lowenthal has pointed out that there is a tendency in historical writing for time to be 'foreshortened, details selected and highlighted, action concentrated, relations simplified, not to (deliberately) alter . . . the events but to . . . give them meaning'.[3] A study of Anglo-American relations written in 1942 is obviously going to be very different from one written in 1947 or 1995. Hindsight and contemporary preoccupations often have a powerful effect on the way that history is written.

Another limitation on the acquisition of knowledge is the difficulty created by research into sensitive areas of government policy. It is not uncommon for documents to be destroyed, for them to be kept classified for long periods (for thirty years, fifty years or even longer), or for them to be written with later scrutiny by the historian in mind. This is something which presents particular difficulties in the field of Anglo-American relations. Getting access to documents relating to nuclear or intelligence relations or persuading those who participated in these fields to talk about their work is often constrained by the Official Secrets Act and unwillingness by officials to take risks when it comes to issues of security. Access to nuclear information varied from country to country during the Cold War period, with the US government being more inclined to release information than the other nuclear powers, especially as a result of the Freedom of Information Act. In contrast, the British government tended to be rather more secretive. Agreements between the two governments meant that, although historians of Anglo-American relations could gain more information from American than from British sources, distinct limitations were placed on access to information about the relationship kept in the US archives. This situation eased somewhat as a result of the end of the Cold War and the Waldegrave initiative in Britain in 1992, which resulted in a steady release of papers on the 1950s and 1960s which had not been available in the past. Important gaps, however, have remained, inevitably affecting interpretations of the past.

How historians deal with this kind of 'epistemological fragility' stems, in part, from their approach to historical method. In general,

[3] D. Lowenthal, *The Past is a Foreign Country* (Cambridge: Cambridge University Press, 1985), p. 218.

2

Introduction

two kinds of historical methodology stand out. They can roughly be
termed the 'empiricist' school and the 'interpretivist' school.[4] 'Empiricist' historians focus on the 'facts'. They believe that it is important to try to uncover the 'absolute truth' about past events through
a rigorous historical methodology. This was the approach adopted
by the German historian Von Ranke, who believed that, even if it
was not possible at present to uncover the truth, the accumulation
of facts would one day reveal 'how things really were'.[5] The role of
the historian was, therefore, to search for the 'facts' as part of the
gradual revelation of an objective truth. This was also the approach
adopted by the British historian, Lord Acton. Writing in October
1896, Acton argued that:

> Ultimate history we cannot have in this generation; but we can dispose
> of conventional history, and show the point we have reached on the
> road from one to the other, now that all information is within reach,
> and every problem has become capable of solution.[6]

According to this view, history consists of 'a corpus of ascertained
facts'. It also reflects a clear distinction which 'empiricists' argue
can be drawn between 'subject' and 'object'. Facts, like sense-
impressions, impinge on the observer from outside and are believed
to be independent of the consciousness of the historian. According
to this view there is a hard core of facts which are the same for all
historians. These facts are available in documents, inscriptions and
so on, 'like fish on the fishmonger's slab'.[7]

This approach to historical method views documents as being of
particular importance. They have been described as the 'Ark of the
Covenant in the temple of facts'. Historians from this school of
thought view documents as sacred sources which cannot justifiably
be questioned. If information is found in the documents, it must be

---

[4] *Within* these two schools there are important differences between historians. See
G. Elton, *The Practice of History* (London: Fontana, 1969); Carr, *What is History?*; Jenkins, *On 'What is History?'*, and E. D. Ermath, *Sequel to History.
Postmodernism and the Crisis of Representational Time* (Princeton: Princeton
University Press, 1992).
[5] L. von Ranke, *Histories of the Latin and German Nations from 1494 to 1514*,
extract translated in G. P. Gooch, *History and Historians in the Nineteenth
Century* (London: Longman, 1952), p. 74.
[6] Lord Acton, *The Cambridge Modern History. Its Origins, Authorship and Production*, quoted in Carr, *What is History?*, p. 7.
[7] Carr, *What is History?*, p. 9.

3

true. The aim of the historian, therefore, should be 'to let the documents speak for themselves'.

Such a view of history and historical method has been the subject of a great deal of debate and criticism over the years. One of the most notable critics, Sir George Clark, pointed to the way that the 'empiricist' school of thought ignored the importance of 'interpretation' in historical writing. Writing in 1957, Clark rejected the idea that 'ultimate history' was possible. Historians, he argued, expected:

> their work to be superseded again and again. They consider that knowledge of the past has come down through one or more minds, has been 'processed' by them, and therefore cannot consist of impersonal atoms which nothing can alter.[8]

The importance of the historian in the process of reconstruction has also been a central theme in the work of the American historian Carl Becker, and in that of the Oxford philosopher and historian R. G. Collingwood. For Becker, 'the facts of history do not exist for any historian till he creates them'.[9] This argument is developed further by Collingwood in *The Idea of History*. Collingwood argues that 'all history is the history of thought'. It is 'the re-enactment in the historian's mind of the thought of those whose history he is studying'.[10]

The central point of this view of history is that the 'facts' can never be recovered 'pure', since they do not and cannot exist in a pure form. They are always 'refracted through the mind of the recorder'. Historical 'facts', therefore, are not like 'fish on the fishmonger's slab', or gold nuggets waiting to be picked up off the ground. They are discovered, partly by chance, and partly by a process of selection. According to this view, interpretation is everything.

This 'interpretivist' school of history sees 'the past' and historical writing as two very different things. The past has already taken place, it has gone for ever, and can never be reproduced in exactly the same form. In that sense, the past is an 'absent subject' which

[8] Sir George Clark, *The New Cambridge Modern History*, I (Cambridge: Cambridge University Press, 1957), pp. xxiv–xxv.
[9] *Atlantic Monthly*, October 1910, p. 528.
[10] R. G. Collingwood, *The Idea of History* (Oxford: Oxford University Press, 1946).

Introduction

can be recreated only by historians, 'working under all kinds of presuppositions and pressures which did not operate on the people in the past'.[11] This distinction between past events and attempts by historians to recreate those events is a crucial one according to historians who stress the importance of interpretation. It implies that *certain* knowledge is not possible because there can be no fully definitive historical study for historians to check their own accounts against. Steven Giles has summed up this argument in the following way: 'what has gone before is always apprehended through the sedimented layers of previous interpretations and through the reading habits and categories developed by previous/current interpretive discourses'.[12]

According to this view, when students of Anglo-American relations read the works of historians like H. G. Nicholas, H. C. Allen or Christopher Thorne, they are reading about events that have filtered through the minds of those particular individuals.[13] Their viewpoints and perceptions have shaped their selection of material and provided a meaning for the events with which they deal. This does not mean that H. G. Nicholas, H. C. Allen and Christopher Thorne made up what they wrote. Their historical writing is not simply a product of their imagination. In each case their work is the result of meticulous research. What is suggested, however, is that, like all historians, the bulk of the material with which they were confronted meant inevitably that they had to be selective. They had to make judgements, from the records and sources that were available to them, about what was important and what was not. They had to interpret the evidence, weighing up what the words in the documents, or the words of those interviewed, actually meant. What they produced, therefore, was not the 'Anglo-American past' but their individual interpretations of that past.

The importance of interpretation has been stressed more recently by 'postmodern' historians. They take the argument a little further, however. For them the importance of the historian in writing his-

[11] See Jenkins, *Rewriting History*, pp. 22–3.
[12] S. Giles, 'Against interpretation', *British Journal of Aesthetics*, 28, 1, 1988.
[13] H. G. Nicholas, *The United States and Britain* (London: University of Chicago Press, 1975); H. C. Allen, *Great Britain and the United States. A History of Anglo-American Relations* (London: Odhams, 1955); Christopher Thorne, *Allies of a Kind. The United States, Britain and the War against Japan* (London: Hamish Hamilton, 1979).

tory tends to rule out the possibility of any objective history at all. Keith Jenkins has argued that what determines interpretation 'lies beyond method and evidence'.[14] It is ideology which establishes the way in which evidence is selected and given meaning. To be meaningful, Jenkins argues, 'facts' have to be embedded in interpretive readings. 'Facts' and 'sources' are not mute. They have to be given 'weight, position, combination and significance' through a process and construction of explanations.[15] It is this *interpretive* process which historians use, regardless of their methodology, to transform the events of the past into patterns of meaning.

Such a view rejects the idea that 'the documents can speak for themselves'. The wording of the documents has to be 'deconstructed' and its meaning has to be fitted into a broader narrative or story which is constructed by the historian to make sense of the events being studied. For 'postmodernist' historians, values and ideology are central to this process of 'deconstruction' and provide the underlying explanation for differences of historical interpretation.

According to historians like Jenkins, the great danger of the 'empiricist' approach is that historians lose sight of their own ideological stance and often claim too great a degree of objectivity, truth and knowledge. In line with this argument, the American pragmatist Richard Rorty has written that 'our culture has a long, dominant tradition wherein *truth* and *certainty* have been held to be found and not created'.[16] The search for certainty, which has deep philosophical roots, gives rise to an historical approach which aims to achieve (true or ultimate) knowledge. Such an approach, 'postmodernists' argue, is unachievable and often leads historians to ignore the crucial values embedded in their empirical studies. Far better to see history as 'inescapably interpretive', as part of a discourse, or of a language game, in which one view is as good as another.

The idea that 'all history is ideological history' leads 'postmodernist' writers to argue that 'history can never be simply for itself', interesting in its own right, without any purpose. Rather,

---

[14] Jenkins, *Rewriting History*, p. 15.
[15] *Ibid.*, p. 33.
[16] R. Rorty, *Contingency, Irony and Solidarity* (Cambridge: Cambridge University Press, 1989), p. 3.

history is 'always for someone'.[17] It is always designed to reinforce particular political positions. This is reflected, it is argued, in the way history is used by governments to establish or maintain a national identity or by sectional interests to legitimise their claims. The key question, therefore, for these historians, is 'Who is history *for?*' What is the (often hidden) agenda that historical writing is designed to achieve?

If there are competing historical interpretations, as there always will be, many 'postmodernists' argue that which interpretation becomes predominant will be determined by power relationships. According to this view, the use of the concept of 'truth' is itself part of a process by which groups attempt to close down the opportunity for competing groups with different interpretations to claim legitimacy for their views. Governments, sectional interests and even historians themselves, therefore, who claim to be seeking the 'truth' and objectivity, are seen as being engaged, in reality, in an effort to maintain their predominant positions – positions which reflect their power and ideology. In the words of Michel Foucault, ' "Truth" is linked . . . with systems of power which produce and sustain it.'[18]

This 'postmodernist' approach, which is sceptical of the idea of 'objective historical truth', is opposed by 'empiricist' historians, even those who accept that interpretation plays a part in historical writing. E. H. Carr in *What is History?* argues forcefully that it does not follow that, because interpretation has a role to play in establishing the facts of history, and because no existing interpretation is wholly objective, one interpretation is as good as another, and the facts of history are, in principle, not amenable to objective interpretation. Carr attempts to find a middle way between the problem created by the traditional 'empiricist' emphasis on revealing the 'ultimate truth' and the danger, emanating from the ideas of historians who emphasise the importance of interpretation, that history can have an infinity of meanings. The task of the historian, Carr argues, is to navigate:

> delicately between the Scylla of an untenable theory of history as an objective compilation of facts, of the unqualified primacy of fact over

---

[17] Jenkins, *Rewriting History*, p. 18.
[18] M. Foucault, *Power/Knowledge*, (New York: Pantheon, 1981), pp. 131–3.

interpretation, and the Charybdis of an equally untenable theory of history as the subjective product of the mind of the historian who establishes the facts of history and masters them through the process of interpretation . . .'.[19]

Carr accepts that historians inevitably select the facts they use. The facts and the interpretation, however, in his view are inextricably linked. History, in his view, is a 'continuous process of interaction between the historian and his facts, and an unending dialogue between the present and the past'.[20] As with other 'empiricists', however, 'facts' remain important in Carr's view of history.

The historiography of Anglo-American relations

The debate between 'empiricist' and 'interpretivist' historians is obviously an important one for historians of Anglo-American relations, as it is for all historians. Are they (we) engaged in seeking the 'ultimate truth' through the pursuit of a particular kind of rigorous historical methodology? Or are they (we) engaged in a discourse on Anglo-American relations which reflects ideological and power positions (and in which there can be an infinity of interpretations)?

This debate raises interesting questions about the historiography of Anglo-American relations, as well as about how the student should view the documents presented in a volume of the present kind. According to one review of the literature on the subject, there are three main approaches which have been adopted by historians of Anglo-American relations: the 'Evangelical', the 'Functional' and 'the Terminal'.[21] The 'Evangelical' mode reflects the writings of those historians, like H. C. Allen and, more specifically, Winston Churchill himself, who have promoted what has been described as 'the hands-across-the sea approach'.[22] This attitude to Anglo-American relations involves 'a sense of mission'. It is characterised by emphasis on the sentimental and cultural dimensions of the relationship. The 'special relationship', according to this view,

[19] Carr, *What is History?*, p. 29.
[20] *Ibid.*, p. 30. For a discussion of differences within the 'empiricist' school see the debate between E. H. Carr and G. Elton in Jenkins, *On 'What is History?'*.
[21] A. Danchev, 'Specialness', *International Affairs* (forthcoming, 1997).
[22] See H. C. Allen, *The Anglo-American Predicament* (London: Macmillan, 1960), and *Great Britain and the United States. A History of Anglo-American Relations* (London: Odhams, 1955).

emerged in the Second World War as the result of a long process of 'coming together' by people of essentially the same stock: a 'fraternal association of English-speaking people' whose common culture, language and institutions set them apart from 'normal' relations between states in the international system. This view of Anglo-American relations is summed up in a statement made by George Ball, a former US Under-Secretary of State, in the late 1960s. In his view:

> to an exceptional degree we [the United States and Britain] look out on the world through similarly refracted mental spectacles. We speak variant patois of Shakespeare and Norman Mailer, our institutions spring from the same instincts and traditions and we share the same heritage of law and custom, philosophy and pragmatic *Weltanschauung*... starting from similar premises in the same intellectual tradition, we recognise common allusions, share many common prejudices, and can commune on a basis of confidence.[23]

For many of the 'Evangelical' group of Anglo-American historians, the purpose of their writing is not simply to tell the story of 'a ripening of friendship' and a 'persistent, even steady progress from mistrust to cordiality' but to emphasise the value of the relationship to both Britain and the United States. The 'special relationship' is seen as 'a good thing', something to be nurtured and preserved not only for the good of Britain and the United States but for international peace and stability as well. This view is clearly summed up in Churchill's famous speech at Westminster College, Fulton, Missouri, on 5 March 1946, when the term 'special relationship' was effectively launched on the world scene. According to the former Prime Minister:

> Neither the sure prevention of war, nor the continuous rise of world organisation, will be gained without what I have called the fraternal association of the English-speaking peoples. This means a special relationship between the British Commonwealth and Empire and the United States. . . . Fraternal association requires not only the growing friendship and mutual understanding between our two vast but kindred systems of society, but the continuance of the intimate relationship between our military advisers, leading to common study of

---

[23] G. Ball, *The Discipline of Power* (London: Bodley Head, 1968), p. 91.

9

potential dangers, the similarity of weapons and manuals of instruction, and to the interchange of officers and cadets at technical
colleges.[24]

Given these views, it is not surprising that in the 1950s, when
Churchill published his histories of the Second World War, he told
President Eisenhower that he had been careful not to include anything which might undermine the 'special relationship' which he
regarded as the cornerstone of world peace.

In contrast to this 'Evangelical' school of historians of
Anglo-American relations, those who have adopted a 'Functional'
approach are less concerned with common culture and more concerned with common interests. According to this view, the close
relationship between the two countries has been developed for a
purpose: firstly to balance the power of Germany and later to
balance the power of the Soviet Union. 'It did not arise naturally
from an existential sense of community. It had to be nurtured and,
above all, negotiated.'[25] Historians, like Christopher Thorne, David
Reynolds and Ian Clark, who adopt this view emphasise that the
'reality' of Anglo-American relations has involved as much disagreement and friction as co-operation and harmony.[26] In a major
study of Anglo-American relations in the Far East in the Second
World War, entitled *Allies of a Kind,* Thorne emphasises the different dimensions and complexities of the relationship which charac-
terise the work of this group of historians. Thorne sees the Far East
as an important exception to the traditional sentimentalised picture
of close harmony between Britain and the United States during the
war. 'Neither militarily, nor politically,' he argues, 'did there exist
as regards the Far East anything like the degree of collaboration
between the two states that was achieved elsewhere.' In his view,
the fact that the relationship between the United Kingdom and the
United States 'was at times a remarkably close one can be established without the need to wander off, however well-meaningly,

[24] Quoted in R. R. James, *Winston Churchill. His Complete Speeches, 1897–1963,*
VII (London: Chelsea House Publishers, 1974), p. 7289.
[25] Danchev, 'Specialness'.
[26] See D. Reynolds, *The Creation of the Anglo-American Alliance, 1937–41. A
Study in Competitive Cooperation* (London: Europa Publications, 1981), and I.
Clark, *Nuclear Diplomacy and the Special Relationship. Britain's Deterrent and
America, 1957–1962* (Oxford: Oxford University Press, 1994).

into mythology'. Thorne's contention is that in the Far East, at least, Anglo-American relations 'were extremely poor'.[27]

This emphasis on the 'mythology' of the 'special relationship' has been taken up by other historians who fit into the 'Functional' category. Max Beloff, writing in 1966, described the 'special relationship as 'a fact, but a fact of a rather peculiar kind; for myths are also facts'. One of Beloff's professed purposes was:

> to enquire further into why it has been found psychologically so necessary to dress up a perfectly honourable relationship as though national self-interest were something which should play no part in this branch of international politics.'[28]

Sentimental interpretations of the 'special relationship', Beloff believed, obscured a perfectly intelligible explanation of close Anglo-American relations: that it was in the interests of both states to cooperate as fully as possible.

A slightly different interpretation of the 'special relationship' has been put forward by David Reynolds. Reynolds accepts that, in terms of *quality* and *importance*, there is some substance in the idea that a 'special relationship' has existed between Britain and the United States for much of the period since 1940. In his view, however, the 'special relationship' should be viewed (functionally) as 'a tradition invented as a tool of diplomacy'.[29] He sees it largely as a deliberate (and quite successful) British creation, designed to shore up Britain's declining world power by linking its destiny with that of the United States.

Those who support this view often emphasise the sense of (patronising) superiority towards the Americans which can be gleaned from British documents. It is reflected in some verses often quoted from an anonymous British official engaged in the difficult loan negotiations with the United States in 1947. According to their anthor, the United States may have been more powerful in economic terms, but Britain was superior in diplomatic wisdom. (see

---

[27] Thorne, *Allies of a Kind*, p. 725.
[28] M. Beloff, 'The special relationship: an Anglo-American myth?' in M. Gilbert (ed.), *A Century of Conflict, 1850–1950. Essays for A. J. P. Taylor* (London: Hamish Hamilton, 1966), pp. 151–71.
[29] D. Reynolds, 'A "special relationship"? America, Britain and the international order since the Second World War', *International Affairs*, 62, 1, winter 1985/6.

p. 45). The sense of superiority can also be seen in the tendency by British statesmen, particularly Harold Macmillan, to refer to Britain and the United States in terms of 'Greeks' and 'Romans'. Macmillan frequently argued that the Americans represented 'the new Roman Empire and we Britons, like the Greeks of old, must teach them how to make it go'.[30] Similarly, he remarked that 'we are the Greeks of the Hellenistic age: the power has passed from us to Rome's equivalent, the United States of America, and we can at most aspire to civilise and occasionally to influence them'.[31]

Whether the 'special relationship', as 'a tool of diplomacy', has been successful or not has been a matter of some disagreement between historians of Anglo-American relations. George Ball, advising President Kennedy in the early 1960s, was in no doubt that the British had used the concept of the 'special relationship' to great effect in their dealings with the United States. Indeed, he believed that American interests had been undermined as a result. Ball argued that this was well illustrated at the Nassau conference in December 1962 when Macmillan used the rhetoric of the 'special relationship' to persuade Kennedy to provide Britain with Polaris missiles, against the advice of State Department officials (like Ball himself). In his view, the President was seduced at the conference by 'the emotional baggage of the special relationship', which got in the way of cooler judgement. Nassau, he believed, was a good example of the way the United States 'yielded to the temptations of a myth'. As a result 'US interests in both a strong and united Europe and the prevention of nuclear proliferation have been harmed by the over-zealous support for the partnership with Britain, especially in the defence field.'[32]

Such an evaluation of the 'special relationship' as a successful tool of British diplomacy is not shared by all commentators on Anglo-American relations. Another former State Department official, Andrew Pierre, has argued that the 'special relationship' has been 'injurious' to Britain's long-term interests 'to the extent that it encouraged Britain to feel that she could avoid Europe'.[33] It helped

---

[30] Quoted in Anthony Sampson, *Macmillan*, (Harmondsworth: Penguin, 1967), pp. 65–6.
[31] *Ibid.*
[32] Ball, *The Discipline of Power*, pp. 93–4.
[33] A Pierre, *Nuclear Politics. The British Experience with an Independent Strategic Force, 1939–1970* (London: Oxford University Press, 1972), p. 316.

to reinforce the image of Britain as a great power, capable of playing an independent world role. The result, Pierre suggests, was that Britain was deflected from coming to terms with her European destiny.

The eminent British historian, Sir Michael Howard, has made much the same point. In his view, the close wartime relationship with the United States had a continuing and detrimental effect on post-war British foreign policy. Although the Second World War was, in some ways, Britain's 'finest hour', Howard argues that the nation 'has continued to re-live it disastrously'.

> Its position at the top table in NATO gave it a sense of superiority to its continental allies – countries which it had either conquered or liberated – who sat below the salt. The significance of their economic recovery was under-rated. Their plans for the creation of a European Community were treated with contempt. The special relationship with the United States prolonged British delusions of grandeur. It took the humiliation of Suez to bring home to the British the reality of their position in the world and to force belated readjustments.[34]

Writing in 1994, Howard goes on to argue that it still remained unclear whether the distortions and delusions associated with the 'special relationship' had finally been overcome. Britain, he suggested, remained ambivalent about Europe partly as a result of the continuing close ties with the United States.

A third approach to Anglo-American relations which takes some of these arguments a stage further has become discernible in the post-Cold War era. The 'Terminal' school of thought, as Alex Danchev describes it, seeks to reveal the mythical nature of the 'special relationship' and to demonstrate the malign power of the concept over British thinking about its role in the world.[35] According to this view, ' "specialness" is, and always was, self-deception'. Thus the 'special relationship' was not simply 'a tool of diplomacy' but a linguistic construct which fostered a damaging national illusion.

If the hollowness of the concept is revealed historically, as well as in contemporary terms, then, some historians argue, Britain can adopt a more realistic and appropriate role in world affairs in the

---

[34] Sir Michael Howard, *The Times*, 28 May 1994.
[35] Danchev, 'Specialness'.

years ahead. This is the theme of John Dickie's study *'Special' No More*, written in 1994.[36] Dickie focuses on the impact of the end of the Cold War on Anglo-American relations, arguing that when there was no longer a communist threat requiring Britain to be the alliance standard-bearer in Europe, the principle *raison d'être* of the relationship ended. From Dickie's point of view, only when the rhetoric changes can Britain finally break free from the illusions created by the concept and adjust to her diminished role as a medium European power.

Conclusions

This brief review of the historiography of Anglo-American relations may seem, on the face of it, to reinforce the arguments of those 'postmodern' historians who emphasise the multiplicity (indeed, infinity) of interpretations available when it comes to studying the past. 'Evangelical' historians of Anglo-American relations emphasise the importance of cultural and sentimental ties, and the need to maintain the relationship as a keystone of world peace. 'Functional' historians, on the other hand, view the 'special relationship' in much less sentimental terms. They chart its ups and downs and emphasise the importance of common interests. Most tend to see it as being more 'special' from Britain's point of view than from America's, and for some it is no more than 'a tradition invented as a tool of diplomacy to shore up the British decline in power'. The 'Terminal' school of thought takes this argument further, focusing on the rhetoric and mythology of the 'special relationship' and its inappropriateness as a conceptual framework for studying Anglo-American relations, especially in the post-Cold War era. Each school offers a very different interpretation of Anglo-American relations and the purposes of their analysis vary considerably.

There is no doubt that the 'postmodernist' historical approach does an important service in pointing to 'epistemological fragility' and the limitations of methodology. The call of such historians for 'reflexive scepticism' which challenges claims to certainty in historical judgement and emphasises the tentativeness of particular inter-

---

[36] J. Dickie, *'Special' No More. Anglo-American Relations: Rhetoric and Reality* (London: Weidenfeld & Nicolson, 1994).

14

pretations is an important contribution to the debate about the nature of history.

At the same time, however, 'empiricists' argued that there are significant dangers associated with this approach. It has been argued that to reduce history, as 'postmodernist' writers tend to do, to a discourse or language game can lead to moral and cognitive nihilism. John Mearsheimer has argued that for supporters of 'postmodernism' there are 'no constants, no fixed meanings, no secure grounds, no profound secrets, no final structures or limits of history . . . there is *only* interpretation. History is grasped as a series of interpretations, imposed upon interpretation.'[37] If history is merely the result of interpretation, and no one can ever know the truth, all explanations may be regarded as equally valid. If everything is relative and anything goes, what is the point of historical discourse? If the *search* for objectivity and truth is discarded and ideological interpretation is given full rein, what results may be regarded as an unscholarly polemical dialogue. Rigorous historical methodology in this context has no real meaning. Far better, 'empiricists' would argue, to search as objectively as possible for the facts about the evolution of Anglo-American relations.

Whether an objective understanding of the past can ever be achieved or is worth seeking is at the heart of the debate between 'empiricist' and 'postmodern' historians. It is not the purpose of this introductory chapter, however, to close off the debate by coming down firmly on one side or the other. It is for the student to make up his or her mind which of these approaches is the most acceptable to them. Whichever approach is adopted, however, it is the author's belief that it remains an important scholarly objective to try to understand the past through a reasoned appeal to the best sources of information which are available. Documents are obviously not the only sources of information which historians use but as a contemporary record they provide a useful insight into what people at the time thought was happening. As such they are of considerable value to the historian in his attempt to understand and re-create the past.[38]

---

[37] J. Mearsheimer, 'The false promise of institutions', *International Security*, 19, 3, winter 1994/5 (emphasis added).

[38] For a discussion of the debate on the role of documents in historical research see Elton, *The Practice of History*, and Jenkins, *Rewriting History*.

In the pages that follow, readers will find a range of documents and contemporary commentaries on Anglo-American relations from the Second World War onwards which inevitably reflect the biases of the author. Choice involves exclusion, as well as inclusion. Choice is also constrained by the documents and other sources available, and by those the author has actually seen. There is no pretence, therefore, that what follows is, in any sense, a definitive list of documents which will provide a comprehensive understanding of Anglo-American relations from 1939 to the present day. It has been chosen as a representative sample of documents from both sides of the Atlantic which reflect the harmony as well as the friction inherent in Anglo-American relations and which highlight different perspectives of the concept of the 'special relationship'. A summary at the beginning of each chapter sets the documents in a wider context and a brief analysis highlights the significant issues in each document. It is hoped, however, that readers will go beyond the summaries and analysis to come to their own conclusions about the 'meaning' of the documents. Equally, the purpose of this book is to whet the appetite for further documentary research into Anglo-American relations, which, for this author at least, are an exciting and stimulating area of study.

A brief note on sources

The material contained in this book has been taken from a variety of sources. Some comes from government archives and published government documents. Other material has been taken from the memoirs of key political leaders involved in the conduct of Anglo-American relations. A third source has been contemporary opinion on both sides of the Atlantic contained in newspaper articles and journals, written by government officials, academics and journalists. It should be stressed that this material has not been chosen to present any particular view of Anglo-American relations. The aim is to show the harmony as well as the friction which has characterised the relationship at various times during the Second World War and since. To the extent that there is a single theme, some effort has been made to focus attention on the 'special relationship' and how contemporary observers have dealt with the concept both within government and outside.

1

The wartime relationship

Although the roots of what is called the 'special relationship' between Britain and the United States can be traced back to the origins of the United States itself, it was only during the Second World War that a partnership was developed between the two countries which became so close, intimate and informal in such a wide spectrum of political, economic and especially military fields that the term 'special' can really be applied. It was during this period that the two countries became so intertwined that traditional state sovereignty was eroded and a common Anglo-Saxon identity and purpose developed in their joint war effort against the Axis powers.

In the early stages of the war, before Pearl Harbor, what became known as a common-law alliance was established between the two countries. During that period a 'gradual mixing-up process' took place, with close co-operation involving such things as the exchange of destroyers for bases, the sharing of information about atomic energy, joint Staff Talks and the beginnings of intelligence collaboration, all of which laid the foundations of the 'full marriage' which followed. It involved the formation of a joint war machine after the US entry into the war. This was initiated at the Arcadia Conference in December 1941 with the adoption by the United States of a 'Germany first' strategy and was followed by the creation of a range of Combined Boards which played a crucial role in the direction and co-ordination of the joint war effort over the following four years. The war against Germany and Japan, and the two specific areas of Anglo-American co-operation in the fields of atomic energy (the Manhattan Project) and intelligence, in different ways highlighted the extraordinary degree of collaboration which was achieved. It was summed up in General George C. Marshall's claim that Anglo-American combined planning between 1941 and 1945 represented 'the most complete unification of military effort ever achieved by two allied states' in the history of warfare.

Despite the remarkable nature of the partnership, however, it is also true that various differences and strains arose in certain areas (especially in the

war against Japan). 'Special' the relationship may have been, but that
should not be allowed to obscure the fact that Britain and the United States
retained interests which could and did differ and conflict as well as coincide. Manipulation of the concept of a 'special relationship' as a tool of
diplomacy remained a feature of Anglo-American relations during the
Second World War.

1.1 'A matter of life or death'

In June 1940, with the United States neutral and French resistance to Germany faltering, Britain faced the prospect of standing alone against Germany yet lacking the naval strength to
protect its coast and crucial trade routes. The crucial objective
of British policy was to involve the United States in the war on
Britain's side. Here Prime Minister Winston Churchill, iden-
tifying himself as a 'Former Naval Person' in reference to a
previous posting as First Lord of the Admiralty, brings this
situation to President Roosevelt's attention. He asks for assistance in the form of destroyers to enable Britain to survive: a
matter of life and death for Britain, but essential also, Churchill argues, to the security of the United States.

Secret and Personal for the President from Former Naval Person
I am grateful to you for your telegram and I have reported its
operative passages to Reynaud to whom I had imparted a rather
more sanguine view. He will I am sure, be disappointed at non-
publication. I understand all your difficulties with American public
opinion and Congress, but events are moving downward at a pace
where they will pass beyond the control of American public opinion
when at least it is ripened. Have you considered what offers Hitler
may choose to make to France. He may say, 'surrender the fleet
intact and I will leave you Alsace Lorraine', or alternatively 'if you
do not give me your ships I will destroy your towns'. I am personally convinced that America will in the end go to all lengths but this
moment is supremely critical for France. A declaration that the
United States will, if necessary, enter the war might save France.
Failing that in a few days French resistance may have crumbled and
we shall be left alone.

Although the present government and I personally would never
fail to send the fleet across the Atlantic if resistance was beaten
down here, a point may be reached in the struggle where the present

ministers no longer have control of affairs and when very easy terms could be obtained for the British islands by their becoming a vassal state of the Hitler empire. A pro-German government would certainly be called into being to make peace and might present to a shattered or a starving nation an almost irresistible case for entire submission to the Nazi will. The fate of the British fleet as I have already mentioned to you would be decisive on the future of the United States because if it were joined to the fleets of Japan, France, and Italy and the great resources of German industry, overwhelming sea power would be in Hitler's hands. He might, of course, use it with a merciful moderation. On the other hand he might not. This revolution in sea power might happen very quickly and certainly long before the United States would be able to prepare against it. If we go down you may have a United States of Europe under the Nazi command far more numerous, far stronger, far better armed than the new [world].

I know well, Mr President, that your eye will already have searched these depths but I feel I have the right to place on record the vital manner in which American interests are at stake in our battle and that of France.

I am sending you through Ambassador Kennedy a paper on destroyer strength prepared by the naval staff for your information. If we have to keep, as we shall, the bulk of our destroyers on the east coast to guard against invasion, how shall we be able to cope with a German–Italian attack on the food and trade by which we live? The sender [sic] of the 35 destroyers as I have already described will bridge the gap until our new construction comes in at the end of the year. Here is a definite practical and possibly decisive step which can be taken at once and I urge most earnestly that you will weigh my words.

Since beginning of war Britain and France have lost 32 destroyers with displacement of 47,380 tons which were complete losses. Out of these 25, with displacements of 37,637 tons, were lost since 1st February.

There is always a large number of destroyers out of action for repairs to damage caused by enemy action and hard service. From outbreak of war up to Norwegian invasion approximately 30 per cent of British destroyers in home waters were in this condition but since then the percentage has greatly increased and for instance, out of 133 destroyers in commission in home waters today, only 68 are

20

fit for service, which is lowest level since war started. In 1918 some 433 destroyers were in service.

The critical situation which has arisen in land operations has unfortunately made less apparent the grave difficulties with which we are faced on the sea.

The seizure of the Channel ports by the enemy has provided him both with convenient bases and stepping off ground for descents on our coast. This means that our east coast and Channel ports will become much more open to attack and in consequence more shipping will have to be concentrated on west coast ports. This will enable the enemy to concentrate their submarine attacks on this more limited area, the shipping lanes of which will have to carry the heavy concentration of shipping.

This alone is a serious enough problem at a time when we know that the enemy intend to carry out the bitter and concentrated attack on our trade routes, but added to our difficulties is the fact that Italy's entry into the war has brought into the seas another 100 submarines many of which may be added to those already in the German U-boat fleet, which at a conservative estimate numbers 55.

The changed strategical situation brought about by the possession by the enemy of the whole coast of Europe from Norway to the Channel has faced us with a prospect of invasion which has more hope of success than we had ever conceived possible. While we must concentrate our destroyers on protecting the vital trade, we must also dispose our naval forces to meet this threat.

If this invasion does take place, it will almost certainly be in the form of dispersed landings from a large number of small craft and the only effective counter to such a move is to maintain numerous and effective destroyer patrols.

To meet this double threat we have only the 68 destroyers mentioned above. Only 10 small type new construction destroyers are due to complete in next four months.

The position becomes still worse when we have to contemplate diverting further destroyer forces to the Mediterranean as we may be forced to do when the sea war there is intensified.

We are now faced with the imminent collapse of French resistance and if this occurs the successful defence of this island will be the only hope of averting the collapse of civilization as we define it.

We must ask therefore as a matter of life or death to be reinforced with these destroyers. We will carry out the struggle whatever the odds but it may well be beyond our resources unless we receive every reinforcement and particularly do we need this reinforcement on the sea.

Message from Churchill to Roosevelt, London (via US embassy), 15 June 1940. *Foreign Relations of the United States, 1940*, Vol. III, pp. 53–5. Quoted in Warren F. Kimball (ed.), *Churchill and Roosevelt. The Complete Correspondence*, Vol. I, *Alliance Emerging, October 1933–November 1942* (Princeton, New Jersey: Princeton University Press, 1984), pp. 49–51.

1.2   Roosevelt's *quid pro quo*

Acceding to Churchill's request, Roosevelt stresses that domestic American opinion would have to be satisfied that it was in the interests of American, and not merely British, national security. One means which he suggests of ensuring that this would be so was for the British to make available to the United States some of their imperial possessions in the Caribbean and elsewhere for the establishment of military bases.

From the President to the Former Naval Person
I have been studying very carefully the message transmitted to me through the British Ambassador in Washington on August 8, and I have also been considering the possibility of furnishing the assistance in the way of releases and priorities contained in the memorandum attached to your message.

It is my belief that it may be possible to furnish to the British Government as immediate assistance at least 50 destroyers, the motor torpedo boats heretofore referred to, and, insofar as airplanes are concerned, five planes of each of the categories mentioned, the latter to be furnished for war testing purposes. Such assistance, as I am sure you will understand, would only be furnished if the American people and the Congress frankly recognized that in return therefor the national defense and security of the United States would be enhanced. For that reason it would be necessary, in the event that it proves possible to release the materiel above mentioned, that the British Government find itself able and willing to take the two following steps:

1. Assurance on the part of the Prime Minister that in the event that the waters of Great Britain become untenable for British ships of war, the latter would not be turned over to the Germans or sunk, but would be sent to other parts of the Empire for continued defense of the Empire.

2. An agreement on the part of Great Britain that the British Government would authorize the use of Newfoundland, Bermuda, the Bahamas, Jamaica, St Lucia, Trinidad and British Guiana as naval and air bases by the United States in the event of an attack on the American hemisphere by any non-American nation; and in the meantime the United States to have the right to establish such bases and to use them for training and exercise purposes with the understanding that the land necessary for the above could be acquired by the United States through purchase or through a 99-year lease.

With regard to the agreement suggested in point 2 above, I feel confident that specific details need not be considered at this time and that such questions as the exact locations of the land which the United States might desire to purchase or lease could be readily determined upon subsequently through friendly negotiation between the two Governments.

With regard to your reference to publicity concerning the contingent destination of the British fleet, I should make it clear that I have not had in mind any public statement by you but merely an assurance to me along the lines indicated, as for example, reiteration to me of your statement to Parliament on June 4.

I should welcome a reply as soon as may be possible.

Roosevelt to Churchill, Washington (via US embassy), 13 August 1940. *Foreign Relations of the United States, 1940*, Vol. III, pp. 65–6. Quoted in Warren F. Kimball (ed.), *Churchill and Roosevelt. The Complete Correspondence*, Vol. I, *Alliance Emerging, October 1933–November 1942* (Princeton: Princeton University Press, 1984), pp. 58–9.

1.3 'The achievement of our common purpose'

Exactly one year to the day before the Japanese attack on Pearl Harbor on 7 December 1941 brought the United States into the war, Churchill updates Roosevelt on Britain's position, pointing out that even at that stage of the war Britain's ability to pay for military equipment supplied by the United States

23

was all but exhausted. Asking Roosevelt not to deny Britain assistance because of this, Churchill underlines the US interest, moral and military, in sustaining Britain in its opposition to fascism, and notes that a bankrupt Britain after the war would be unable to import goods from the United States: in helping Britain, America was helping itself.

My Dear Mr President,
As we reach the end of this year I feel that you will expect me to lay before you the prospects for 1941. I do so *strongly and confidently* because it seems to me that the vast majority of American citizens have recorded their conviction that the safety of the United States as well as the future of our two democracies and the kind of civilisation for which they stand are bound up with the survival and independence of the British Commonwealth *of Nations*. Only thus can those bastions of sea-power, upon which the control of the Atlantic and the Indian Oceans depends, be preserved in faithful and friendly hands. The control of the Pacific by the United States Navy and of the Atlantic by the British Navy is indispensable to the security of the trade routes of both our countries and the surest means to preventing the war from reaching the shores of the United States. . . .

17. . . . The more rapid and abundant the flow of munitions and ships which you are able to send us, the sooner will our dollar credits be exhausted. *They are already as you know very heavily drawn upon by payments we have made to date. Indeed as you know orders already placed or under negotiation, including expenditure settled or pending for creating munitions factories in the United States, many times exceed the total exchange resources remaining at the disposal of Great Britain. The moment approaches* when we shall no longer be able to pay cash for shipping and other supplies. While we will do our utmost and shrink from no proper sacrifice to make payments across the exchange, I *believe that you will agree that it would be wrong in principle and mutually disadvantageous in effect if, at the* height of this struggle, *Great Britain were to be divested of all saleable assets* so that after victory was won with our blood, civilisation saved and time gained for the United States to be fully armed against all eventualities, we should stand stripped to the bone. Such a course would not be in the moral or economic interests of

24

either of our countries. We here would be unable after the war
to purchase the large balance of imports from the United States
over and above the volume of our exports which is agreeable to
your tariffs and domestic economy. Not only should we in Great
Britain suffer cruel privations but widespread unemployment in the
United States would follow the curtailment of American exporting
power.

18. Moreover I do not believe the Government and people of the
United States would find it in accordance with the principles which
guide them, to confine the help which they have so generously
promised only to such munitions of war and commodities as could
be immediately paid for. You may be assured that we shall prove
ourselves ready to suffer and sacrifice to the utmost for the Cause,
and that we glory in being its champion. The rest we leave with
confidence to you and to your people, being sure that ways and
means will be found which future generations on both sides of the
Atlantic will approve and admire.

19. If, *as I believe*, you are *convinced*, Mr President, that the
defeat of the Nazi and Fascist tyranny is a matter of high consequence to the people of the United States and to the Western
Hemisphere, you will regard this letter not as an appeal for aid, but
as a statement of the minimum action necessary to *the achievement
of* our common purpose.

I remain, Yours very sincerely, Winston S. Churchill.

Churchill to Roosevelt, letter as telegram, London, 7 December 1940.
(Emphasis contained in the original document.) *Foreign Relations of the
United States, 1940*, Vol. III, pp. 18–26. Quoted in Warren F. Kimball
(ed.), *Churchill and Roosevelt. The Complete Correspondence*, Vol. I,
Alliance Emerging, October 1933–November 1942 (Princeton: Princeton
University Press, 1984), pp. 102–9.

1.4   The common-law alliance

Evidence of the increasing closeness of the relationship between Britain and the United States can be found in the Atlantic Charter of August 1941. This was a statement of common
purpose agreed even though the United States had yet to enter
the war. It has been described as the basis of a 'common-law
alliance' between the two countries.

The President of the United States of America and the Prime Minister, Mr Churchill, representing His Majesty's Government in the United Kingdom, being met together, deem it right to make known certain common principles in the national policies of their respective countries on which they base their hopes of a better future for the world.

First, their countries seek no aggrandisement, territorial or other.

Second, they desire to see no territorial changes that do not accord with the freely expressed wishes of the peoples concerned.

Third, they respect the right of all peoples to choose the form of government under which they will live; and they wish to see sovereign rights and self-government restored to those who have been forcibly deprived of them.

Fourth, they will endeavour, with due respect for their existing obligations, to further the enjoyment by all states, great or small, victor or vanquished, of access, on equal terms, to the trade and to the raw materials of the world which are needed for their economic prosperity.

Fifth, they desire to bring about the fullest collaboration between all nations in the economic field, with the object of securing for all improved labour standards, economic advancement, and social security.

Sixth, after the final destruction of the Nazi tyranny they hope to see established a peace which will afford to all nations the means of dwelling in safety within their own boundaries, and which will afford assurance that all the men in all the lands may live out their lives in freedom from fear and want.

Seventh, such a peace should enable all men to traverse the high seas and oceans without hindrance.

Eighth, they believe that all the nations of the world, for realistic as well as spiritual reasons, must come to the abandonment of the use of force. Since no future peace can be maintained if land, sea or air armaments continue to be employed by nations which threaten, or may threaten, aggression outside of their frontiers, they believe, pending the establishment of a wider and permanent system of general security, that the disarmament of such nations is essential. They will likewise aid and encourage all other practicable measures which will lighten for peace-loving peoples the crushing burden of armaments.

Franklin D. Roosevelt and Winston Churchill, *The Atlantic Charter*, 12 August 1941. Winston S. Churchill, *The Second World War*, Vol. 3, *The Grand Alliance* (London: Cassell, 1950), pp. 385–6.

1.5 The French connection

The capitulation of the French government and American entry into the war left Britain, the United States and the Soviet Union as the main allies. However, French resistance was maintained by some individuals, most notably Charles de Gaulle. A difficult ally to manage, de Gaulle provoked this stinging criticism, expressed by Roosevelt in correspondence with Churchill. We see here some of the origins of later Franco-American and Franco-British difficulties.

To the Former Naval Person from the President.
Secret and Personal.
I am fed up with De Gaulle and the secret *personal and political* machinations of that Committee in the last few days indicates that there is no possibility of our working with De Gaulle. If these were peace times it wouldn't make so much difference but I am absolutely convinced that he has been and is now injuring our war effort and that he is a very dangerous threat to us. I agree with you that he likes neither the British nor the Americans and that he would doublecross both of us at the first opportunity. I agree with you that the time has arrived when we must break with him. It is an intolerable situation. I think the important thing is that we act together and my thinking regarding the whole matter runs about as follows:

We must divorce ourselves from De Gaulle because, first, he has proven to be unreliable, uncooperative, and disloyal to both our Governments. Second, he has more recently been interested far more in political machinations than he has in the prosecution of the war and these machinations have been carried on without our knowledge and to the detriment of our military interests. One result of this scheming on the part of De Gaulle has been that Eisenhower has had to give half his time to a purely *local* political situation which De Gaulle has accentuated. The war is so urgent and our military operations so serious and fraught with danger that we cannot have them menaced any longer by De Gaulle.

Our two countries have solemnly pledged that they will liberate the French Republic and when we drive the Germans out, return that country to the control of the sovereign French people. This pledge we renew.

All of the above can be put by us in language which will be mutually agreeable. Above all I am anxious that the break be made on a basis and for reasons which are identical with both our governments. There are plenty of emotional and dissident people throughout the world who will try to separate England and the United States in this matter and we must stand shoulder to shoulder, identically and simultaneously through this miserable mess. My affirmative thought is that we should go ahead and ... *encourage the creation* of a committee of Frenchmen made up of people who really want to fight the war and are not thinking too much about politics. I am sure we can find such a group. During the formation period we can continue to deal with the military authorities as in the past.

Roosevelt to Churchill, Washington (via US Navy), 17 June 1943. *Foreign Relations of the United States, 1943*, Vol. II, pp. 155–7. Quoted in Warren F. Kimball (ed.), *Churchill and Roosevelt. The Complete Correspondence*, Vol. II, *Alliance Forged, November 1942–February 1944* (Princeton: Princeton University Press, 1984), p. 255.

1.6 The Quebec agreement, 19 August 1943

Fear of German research in the atomic energy field led to a suggestion by Britain to the United States in 1941 that a joint effort should be made to develop atomic weapons. For a time, however, little was achieved. Eventually, British participation in the Manhattan Project, which would produce the first atomic bombs, was secured by the Quebec agreement of August 1943. Each party promised not to use an atomic bomb against the other, nor to use it against any other state without the other's consent. Britain agreed also that the US President should determine after the war the extent to which Britain could exploit commercially the knowledge which it accrued from the joint project on Tube Alloys (the code name by which atomic energy was known).

Whereas it is vital to our common safety in the present War to bring the Tube Alloys project to fruition at the earliest moment; and whereas this may be more speedily achieved if all available British and American brains and resources are pooled; and whereas owing to war conditions it would be an improvident use of war resources to duplicate plants on a large scale on both sides of the Atlantic and therefore a far greater expense has fallen upon the United States;

It is agreed between us

First, that we will never use this agency against each other.

Secondly, that we will not use it against third parties without each other's consent.

Thirdly, that we will not either of us communicate any information about Tube Alloys to third parties except by mutual consent.

Fourthly, that in view of the heavy burden of production falling upon the United States as the result of a wise division of war effort, the British Government recognise that any post-war advantages of an industrial or commercial character shall be dealt with as between the United States and Great Britain on terms to be specified by the President of the United States to the Prime Minister of Great Britain. The Prime Minister expressly disclaims any interests in these industrial and commercial aspects beyond what may be considered by the President of the United States to be fair and just and in harmony with the economic welfare of the world.

And fifthly, that the following arrangements shall be made to ensure full and effective collaboration between the two countries in bringing the project to fruition:

(a) There shall be set up in Washington a Combined Policy Committee composed of:

The Secretary of War	(United States)
Dr Vannevar Bush	(United States)
Dr James B. Conant	(United States)
Field-Marshal Sir John Dill, G.C.B., C.M.G., D.S.O.	(United Kingdom)
Colonel the Right Hon. J. J. Llewellin, C.B.E., M.C., M.P.	(United Kingdom)
The Honourable C. D. Howe	(Canada)

The functions of this Committee, subject to the control of the respective Governments, will be:

(1) To agree from time to time upon the programme of work to be carried out in the two countries.

(2) To keep all sections of the project under constant review.

(3) To allocate materials, apparatus and plant, in limited supply, in accordance with the requirements of the programme agreed by the Committee.

(4) To settle any questions which may arise on the interpretation or application of this Agreement.

(b) There shall be complete interchange of information and ideas on all sections of the project between members of the Policy Committee and their immediate technical advisers.

(c) In the field of scientific research and development there shall be full and effective interchange of information and ideas between those in the two countries engaged in the same sections of the field.

(d) In the field of design, construction and operation of large-scale plants, interchange of information and ideas shall be regulated by such *ad hoc* arrangements as may, in each section of the field, appear to be necessary or desirable if the project is brought to fruition at the earliest moment. Such *ad hoc* arrangements shall be subject to the approval of the Policy Committee.

The Quebec agreement: Articles of Agreement governing Collaboration between the Authorities of the USA and the UK in the matter of Tube Alloys, 19 August 1943. A copy of this agreement can be found in John Baylis, *Anglo-American Defence Relations 1939–1984. The Special Relationship* (London: Macmillan, 1984, second edition), pp. 23–4.

1.7 The Combined Chiefs of Staff

> To co-ordinate the military effort of Britain and the United States during the war, the Combined Chiefs of Staff Committee was established. In this speech to an American audience in 1943 Churchill praises the effectiveness of this unprecedented venture, and makes the case for its continuation in the post-war world.

At the present time, Mr President, we have in continual vigorous action the British and United States Combined Chiefs of Staff Committee which works immediately under the President and myself as representative of the British War Cabinet. This Committee, with its elaborate organisation of staff officers of every grade, disposes of all our resources, and, in practice uses British and

30

American troops, ships, aircraft and munitions just as if they were the resources of a single state or nation.

I would not say there are never divergences of view among these high professional authorities. It would be unnatural if there were not. That is why it is necessary to have plenary meetings of principals every two or three months. All these men now know each other; they trust each other; they like each other, and most of them have been at work together for a long time. When they meet they thrash things out with great candour and plain, blunt speech. But after a few days the President and I find ourselves furnished with sincere and united advice.

This is a wonderful system. There was nothing like it in the last war. There never has been anything like it between two allies. It is reproduced in an even more tightly knit form at General Eisenhower's headquarters in the Mediterranean, where everything is completely intermingled and soldiers are ordered into battle by the Supreme Commander or his Deputy, General Alexander, without the slightest regard as to whether they are British or American or Canadian, but simply in accordance with the fighting needs.

Now in my opinion it would be a most foolish and improvident act on the part of our two governments, or either of them, to break up this smooth running and immensely powerful machinery the moment the war is over. For our own safety, as well as for the security of the rest of the world, we are bound to keep it working and in running order after the war, probably for a good many years, not only till we have set up some world arrangement to keep the peace, but until we know that it is an arrangement which will really give us that protection we must have from danger and aggression – a protection we have already had to seek across two vast world wars.

I am not qualified, of course, to judge whether or not this would become a party question in the United States, and I would not presume to discuss that point. I am sure, however, that it will not be a party question in Great Britain. We must not let go of the securities we have found necessary to preserve our lives and liberties, until we are quite sure we have something else to put in their place which will give us an equally solid guarantee.

Extract from text of an address by Mr Winston Churchill, at a convocation of Harvard University, Monday 6 September 1943. Public Record Office, PREM 3/465/4.

1.8   'Difficulties and shortcomings'

Despite Churchill's attempts to play down the 'divergences of view' (mentioned in the last document) disagreement between the two allies was a constant feature of Anglo–American relations behind the scenes. In a private communication to Roosevelt, Churchill expresses reservations about the co-ordination of military policy between the two states, and voices opposition to the appointment of a Supreme Commander of their military forces. He points out the impossible situation into which such a commander would be placed as he tried to satisfy the differing strategic views of the two states. In particular, the British preference for a focus on Mediterranean operations would clash with Overlord, the planned opening of a second front in France, favoured by the Americans.

1. The difficulties and shortcomings in our conduct of the war since the Battle of Salerno have arisen from divergencies of view between our two Staffs and Governments. It is not seen how these divergencies would be removed by the appointment of a Supreme Commander working under the Combined Chiefs of the Staff and liable to have his decisions reversed by them. The divergencies, which are political as much as military, would still have to be adjusted by the present methods of consultation between the Combined Staffs and the Heads of the two Governments. Thus the Supreme Commander, after being acclaimed as the world war-winner, would in practice find his functions restricted to the narrow ground between the main decisions of policy and strategy which can only be dealt with by the present methods, and the spheres of the two chief regional Commanders.

2. This would certainly not be sufficient to justify arousing all the expectations and setting up all the apparatus inseparable from the announcement of a 'Supreme Commander for the defeat of Germany.'

3. On the other hand, if the power of decision is in fact accorded to the Supreme Commander, the work of the Combined Chiefs of the Staff would be virtually superseded and very great stresses would immediately arise between the Governments and the Supreme Commander. Without going into personalities, it is greatly to be doubted whether any single officer exists who would be capable of giving decisions over the vast range of problems now dealt with

by the Heads of Government assisted by the Combined Chiefs of the Staff.

4. The principle which should be followed as far as possible between Allies of equal status is that the Command in any theatre should go to the Ally who has the largest forces deployed or about to be deployed there. On this it would be natural that the Command in the Mediterranean should be British and that the Command of Overlord should be American. Such Commands would also correspond with the outlook of the two Governments, the Americans regarding Overlord of overwhelming importance, while the British believe that the greatest and most immediate results can be obtained in the Mediterranean and that Overlord is a knock-out blow, the timing of which must be settled in relation to the condition and dispositions of the enemy.

5. If the two Commands are merged under a Supreme Commander, the British would have available against Germany in May decidedly larger forces than the United States. It would therefore appear that the Supreme Command should go to a British officer. I should be very reluctant, as Head of His Majesty's Government, to place such an invidious responsibility upon a British officer. I have very little doubt that he would concentrate his main effort on the Mediterranean and treat the Overlord sphere as a highly important but none the less residuary legatee. This point of view would certainly not be accepted by the Government or Staff of the United States. If, on the other hand, disregarding the preponderance of forces involved, the Supreme Command was given to a United States officer and he pronounced in favour of concentrating on Overlord irrespective of the injury done to our affairs in the Mediterranean, His Majesty's Government could not possibly agree. The Supreme Commander, British or American, would therefore be placed in an impossible position. Having assumed before the whole world the responsibility of pronouncing and being overruled by one Government or the other, he would have little choice but to resign. This might bring about a most serious crisis in the harmonious and happy relations hitherto maintained between our two Governments.

6. It is not seen why the present arrangement should not continue, subject to any minor improvements that can be suggested. Under this arrangement, an American Commander would conduct the immense Operation Overlord and a British Commander would

conduct the war in the Mediterranean, their action being concerted and forces assigned by the Combined Chiefs of the Staff working under the Heads of the two Governments. Regular periodic conferences should be held at Gibraltar between the two Commanders, at which they could adjust minor differences about the movement of units, landing-craft etc., so as to help each other as much as possible, and they should also prepare together the timing and concert of their respective operations. More frequent meetings of the Combined Chiefs of Staff should also be arranged, and possibly visits of one week's duration by the Chairman of each Chiefs of Staff Committee alternately to London and Washington.

Memorandum from Churchill to Roosevelt, Cairo, 25 November 1943. *Foreign Relations of the United States, Teheran Conference*, pp. 407–8. Quoted in Warren F. Kimball (ed.), *Churchill and Roosevelt. The Complete Correspondence*, Vol. II, *Alliance Forged, November 1942–February 1944* (Princeton: Princeton University Press, 1984), pp. 613–15.

1.9 'Essentials of an American policy'

This internal Foreign Office paper of March 1944 makes plain the belief that Britain and the United States were so closely linked as barely to constitute separate, sovereign states. At the same time, it discusses the means by which American power must be manipulated in the post-war period so as to further the realisation of British national interests in relation to the Commonwealth, the Empire and Europe. Here we see the idea of 'the special relationship' as a tool of future British foreign policy.

Recent events have suggested that the work of the Foreign Office and other Government Departments would be greatly facilitated if it were possible to redefine the principles of our policy towards the United States. The need for such a policy, and for a general understanding of it, has become evident, particularly in connexion with the tentative exploration of Commonwealth relations which has been going on during the last few months, and with developments concerning a number of subjects in which British and American interests are more and more involved – civil aviation, telecommunications, relief, and so forth. The latest and most pressing example of the need is the exchange of views over the future of oil reserves.

2. Leaving aside consideration of the extent to which the Dominions, and particularly Canada, *can* work closely with us if we are not working with the United States, it is essential to recognise the relationship which exists between the United States and this country. The special quality of this relationship can no more be denied than can the nature of our relations with Soviet Russia, which justified the making of the Anglo-Soviet Treaty. It has been so well illustrated in the Prime Minister's Harvard and Guildhall speeches that it should need no detailed exposition. Its essence is in the degree to which the two peoples form one community, within which the relations of individuals and organisations to one another are similar to those which exist within one national community; they are, that is to say, 'domestic' rather than 'external' in character. But this connexion brings with it no automatic guarantee of immediate unity or solidarity between the two nations; on the contrary, the complexity and all-pervading quality of the relationship makes it, on the national plane, a source of endless irritation.

3. Nevertheless, in the long run, the nature of the relationship does compel national collaboration between ourselves and the Americans, no matter what friction may occur. And it should be noted that more often than not this means that the Americans follow our lead rather than that we follow theirs. Fortunately, we are not confronted with the alternatives of pleasing them or standing up to them; we also have the opportunity and the capacity to guide and influence them. They have enormous power, but it is the power of the reservoir behind the dam, which may overflow uselessly, or be run through pipes to drive turbines. The transmutation of their power into useful forms, and its direction into advantageous channels, is our concern.

4. Many Americans are now thinking for the first time about taking part in world affairs, and to most of them this means collaborating with us. America is increasingly conscious of the need for alliance and support . . . It must be our purpose not to balance our power against that of America, but to make use of American power for purposes which we regard as good. The process of calling in the new world to redress the balance of the old is still incomplete, and the ability to evoke the new world's immense resources is stronger in these islands than elsewhere. We should be throwing away one of our greatest assets if we failed to evoke it, or if we were

to credit the people of the United States with having developed their own ideas of the world's future to such a point of clarity that they were uninfluenced by ours. If we go about our business in the right way we can help to steer this great unwieldy barge, the United States of America, into the right harbour. If we don't, it is likely to continue to wallow in the ocean, an isolated menace to navigation.

5. A strong American policy must therefore be based not on a determination to resist American suggestions or demands, but on an understanding of the way in which their political machinery works, and a knowledge of how to make it work to the world's advantage – and our own. Instead of trying to use the Commonwealth as an instrument which will give us the power to outface the United States, we must use the power of the United States to preserve the Commonwealth and the Empire, and, if possible, to support the pacification of Europe. In any event, we cannot afford, within the next ten or fifteen years, to face the sort of tension which grew up after the last war, which was apparent in the Disarmament Conference, the Manchurian affair, the war debt dispute and the Hawley–Smoot tariff, and which played so great a part in causing the economic collapse of 1929–34 and the whole sorry failure of the security system. Nor can we afford to face the risks of post-war Europe without the maximum of American support.

AN 1538/16/45, 'The Essentials of an American Policy', 21 March 1944. Public Record Office, FO 371/38523.

1.10 Full post-war nuclear collaboration guaranteed

Concerned that the Quebec agreement of 1943 limited British post-war development of atomic energy in the commercial sphere to that allowed by the US President, Churchill tackled Roosevelt on the subject as they relaxed at the President's Hyde Park retreat in September 1944. Without reference to advisers, the two agreed that full collaboration should continue after the war and initialled an *aide-mémoire* to that effect. The agreement was misfiled and became a source of considerable controversy after Roosevelt's death and Churchill's defeat in the 1945 general election.

The suggestion that the world should be informed regarding tube alloys, with a view to an international agreement regarding its control and use, is not accepted. The matter should continue to be regarded as of the utmost secrecy; but when a 'bomb' is finally available, it might perhaps, after mature consideration, be used against the Japanese, who should be warned that this bombardment will be repeated until they surrender.

2. Full collaboration between the United States and the British Government in developing tube alloys for military and commercial purposes should continue after the defeat of Japan unless and until terminated by joint agreement.

3. Enquiries should be made regarding the activities of Professor Bohr and steps taken to ensure that he is responsible for no leakage of information particularly to the Russians.

Aide-mémoire of conversation between the President and the Prime Minister at Hyde Park, 19 September 1944. Reproduced in John Baylis, *Anglo-American Defence Relations 1939–1984. The Special Relationship* (London: Macmillan, 1984, second edition), p. 28.

2

The search for a new relationship, 1945–50

In the immediate post-war period there was initially a rapid cooling of the close wartime relationship. This was exemplified by the break-up of the integrated war machine in 1945–46, with the abrupt cancellation by the United States of the Lend Lease arrangements, the winding up of the Combined Wartime Boards, growing differences over Palestine, and the unilateral ending of nuclear cooperation by the United States, despite wartime agreements that it should continue. There were also suspicions in the United States of British socialism, which were reflected in the difficulties that arose in post-war negotiations over a loan to see Britain through the immediate economic crisis bequeathed by the war. Britain regarded the terms offered by the United States as unnecessarily hard, reflecting a failure by the Truman administration to recognise the effort the British people had put into the war, initially alone.

As the Cold War gathered momentum, however, there was clear recognition in both military and political circles in Britain that security considerations required a restoration of the close military partnership with the United States. The object of overcoming the traditional policy of isolationism and entangling the United States in Western European security became the central tenet of Ernest Bevin's foreign policy from January 1948 onwards. The Brussels Pact of March 1948 and the concept of a Western Union were seen by the Foreign Secretary as a 'sprat to catch a whale'. British leadership in Western Europe and a demonstration that the European states were prepared to help themselves in the struggle against communism were perceived as an essential prerequisite of American involvement in a North Atlantic Pact.

In March 1949, shortly before the North Atlantic Treaty was signed, a major review was undertaken in the Foreign Office of Anglo-American relations. Britain, it was argued, had a choice between a 'Third Power' grouping or a close partnership with the United States. The choice, it was felt, should not be dictated by 'ties of common feelings and tradition' but by 'a cold estimate of advantage'. It was decided that the 'Third Power' concept should be rejected because the partnership with the United States was seen as essential to British security. The best policy for Britain, the Foreign Office felt, was to be closely related to the United States but independent enough to influence US policy. It would require Britain to remain a major European and world power and to sustain its own independent military capacity. Britain must be the partner, not a poor relation, of the United States. This reflected the British view at the time that there was no contradiction between a European policy and a 'special relationship' with the United States. Indeed, the two were complementary. Playing a leading role in Europe would reinforce British influence with the United States and close ties with the United States would strengthen Britain's position on the Continent.

In general this was a view that was accepted in the United States itself. Britain was seen as America's leading ally, and close ties were believed to be in the interest of the United States. Some disagreement, however, took place amongst American officials over whether the 'special' nature of the relationship should be acknowledged. For some, any attempt to single out the partnership with Britain would undermine US relations with other West European states. For others, the 'special relationship' was a reality which had to be acknowledged.

2.1 The poison of Palestine

Relations between Britain and the United States cooled considerably in the immediate aftermath of the Second World War. Strains were particularly evident in certain areas, one of which was the Middle East. With its powerful Jewish lobby, the United States took great interest in the future of Palestine, mandated by the United Nations to British rule. The United States often took issue with British policy. This document from the Foreign Secretary, Ernest Bevin, to the British embassy in Washington shows British concern about the state of affairs but also the difficulties which Palestine caused in Anglo-American relations after the war.

Private and Personal from Secretary of State
I am sending you herewith an official telegram with proposals for policy relating to Palestine (see my immediately following telegram).

2. This problem has been giving us very serious concern. We are particularly anxious to remove everything we can which poisons the

relations between the United States and ourselves. I regard this as very vital having regard to the turn of events arising out of the Council of Foreign Ministers. It is impossible to foresee which way things are going to turn. . . .

5. . . . [I]n the middle of all this is Palestine. I feel that the United States have been thoroughly dishonest in handling this problem. To play on racial feeling for the purpose of winning an election is to make a farce of their insistence on free elections in other countries. On the other hand the Jews have suffered terribly and this throws up a number of problems which President Truman and others in America have exploited for their own purposes.

(a) Should we accept the view that all the Jews or the bulk of them must leave Germany? I do not accept that view. They have gone through, it is true, the most terrible massacre and persecution, but on the other hand they have got through it and a number have survived. Now what succour and help should be brought to assist them to re-settle in Germany and to help them to get over the obvious fears and nerves that arise from such treatment.

(b) Here comes another difficulty. I am told that the Zionist Organisation and the Jewish Agency are using every possible form of intimidation to stop Jews leaving Palestine in order to go back to Europe, which rather indicates that there are many Jews who believe that their place is in Europe playing their part in its reconstruction and in its future trade. The extent of the truth of this of course I cannot prove without very close examination. Therefore it seems to me that the first thing to do is to ascertain what is the view of the Jews in Europe. Are they going to survive and under what conditions? I am not satisfied with Earl Harrison's report which looks to me like a device to put pressure on England. I should be very sorry to have to say these things in the House of Commons but I cannot go on submitting to intimidation.

(c) No doubt when we have settled the problem of what their future in Europe is going to be there will still be many Jews who want to go to Palestine. Then arises the question, what can Palestine absorb? Figures have been submitted to me that seem just fantastic. Arguments have been advanced that the south can be developed and that great opportunities out of that desert are possible. That is a specific question. Let United States Government join with us in investigating and let us obtain impartial evidence. Also there is the question of the Jordan scheme which has been advocated by

Lowdermilk. What are its possibilities? I would like to have an enquiry in order to put it to the test.

(d) The point I am leading up to is that I do not think it is right to go on asserting that there are these great opportunities unless we can show to the Arabs that they are practicable, and that the admission of more Jews will not necessarily increase the pressure on the land.

(e) This being the problem how should we handle it? I think that to fly in the face of the Arabs after all the undertakings that have been given would cause a breakdown at the beginning. We have therefore confined ourselves to continuing the present arrangement for a limited immigration, but the whole plan is a clear indication of our desire for a settlement without waiting until the United Nations Organisation is ready to deal with it. . . .

7. My only fear of bringing the United States into the picture at this stage is this: the propaganda in New York has destroyed what looked to me a few weeks ago a reasonable atmosphere in which we could get Jews and Arabs together, because obviously we must have a conference with Arabs and Jews in the same room somewhere.

Telegram from Foreign Secretary Ernest Bevin to the British embassy, Washington, 12 October 1945. Public Record Office, PREM 8/627.

2.2 Fraternal association and special relationship: Churchill's Fulton speech

Despite the difficulties there was clear recognition in Britain of the continuing importance of close Anglo-American relations. This is reflected in Winston Churchill's 1946 speech at Fulton, Missouri, which popularised two phrases that remain famous today. The first was 'Iron Curtain', an emblem of the Cold War. The second was 'special relationship', the fraternal association between Britain and the United States which he believed necessary to wage the Cold War. Here Churchill sets out his view of what such a relationship entailed.

. . . When American military men approach some serious situation they are wont to write at the head of their directive the words, 'over-all strategic concept'. There is wisdom in this as it leads to clarity of thought. What, then, is the over-all strategic concept which we should inscribe today? It is nothing less than the safety and welfare, the freedom and progress of all the homes and families of all the men and women in all the lands. . . .

To give security to these countless homes they must be shielded from the two gaunt marauders – war and tyranny. We all know the frightful disturbance in which the ordinary family is plunged when the curse of war swoops down upon the breadwinner and those for whom he works and contrives. The awful ruin of Europe, with all its vanished glories, and of large parts of Asia, glares in our eyes. When the designs of wicked men or the aggressive urge of mighty states dissolve, over large areas, the frame of civilized society, humble folk are confronted with difficulties with which they cannot cope. For them all is distorted, broken or even ground to pulp. . . . Our supreme task and duty is to guard the homes of the common people from the horrors and miseries of another war. . . .

I now come to the second danger which threatens the cottage home and ordinary people, namely tyranny. . . . It is not our duty at this time, when difficulties are so numerous, to interfere forcibly in the internal affairs of countries whom we have not conquered in war, but we must never cease to proclaim in fearless tones the great principles of freedom and the rights of man, which are the joint inheritance of the English-speaking world and which, through Magna Carta, the Bill of Rights, the habeas corpus, trial by jury and the English common law, find their most famous expression in the Declaration of Independence.

All this means that the people of any country have the right and should have the power by constitutional action, by free, unfettered elections, with secret ballot, to choose or change the character or form of government under which they dwell, that freedom of speech and thought should reign, that courts of justice independent of the executive, unbiased by any party, should administer laws which have received the broad assent of large majorities or are consecrated by time and custom. Here are the title deeds of freedom, which should lie in every cottage home. Here is the message of the British and American peoples to mankind. Let us preach what we practise and practise what we preach. . . .

Neither the sure prevention of war, nor the continuous rise of world organization will be gained without what I have called the fraternal association of the English-speaking peoples. This means a special relationship between the British Commonwealth and Empire and the United States. This is no time for generalities. I will venture to be precise. Fraternal association requires not only the growing friendship and mutual understanding between our two vast but kindred systems of society but the continuance of the intimate relationships between our military advisers, leading to common study of potential dangers, similarity of weapons and manuals of instruction and interchange of officers and cadets at colleges. It should carry with it the continuance of the present facilities for mutual security by the joint use of all naval and air-force bases in the possession of either country all over the world. This would perhaps double the mobility of the American Navy and Air Force. . . .

A shadow has fallen upon the scenes so lately lighted by the Allied victory. Nobody knows what Soviet Russia and its Communist international organization intend to do in the immediate future, or what are the limits, if any, to their expansive and proselytizing tendencies. I have a strong admiration and regard for the valiant Russian people and for my wartime comrade, Marshal Stalin. . . . We understand the Russians' need to be secure on her western frontiers from all renewal of German aggression. We welcome her to her rightful place among the leading nations of the world. Above all we welcome constant, frequent and growing contacts between the Russian people and our own people on both sides of the Atlantic. . . .

[Nevertheless] From Stettin in the Baltic to Trieste in the Adriatic, an iron curtain has descended across the Continent. Behind that line lie all the capitals of the ancient states of central and eastern Europe. Warsaw, Berlin, Prague, Vienna, Budapest, Belgrade, Bucharest, and Sofia, all these famous cities and the populations around them lie in the Soviet sphere and all are subject in one form or another, not only to Soviet influence but to a very high and increasing measure of control from Moscow. . . .

In front of the iron curtain which lies across Europe are other causes for anxiety. In Italy the Communist party is seriously hampered by having to support the Communist trained Marshal Tito's claims to former Italian territory at the head of the Adriatic. Nevertheless the future of Italy hangs in the balance. Again one cannot imagine a regenerated Europe without a strong France. All my public life I have worked for a strong France and I never lost faith in her destiny, even in the darkest hours. I will not lose faith now.

However, in a great number of countries, far from the Russian frontiers and throughout the world, Communist fifth columns are established and work in complete unity and absolute obedience to the directions they receive from the Communist center. Except in the British Commonwealth and in this United States, where Communism is in its infancy, the Communist parties or fifth columns constitute a growing challenge and peril to Christian civilization. . . .

The outlook is also anxious in the Far East and especially in Manchuria. The agreement which was made at Yalta, to which I was a party, was extremely favorable to Soviet Russia, but it was made at a time when no one could say that the German war might not extend all through the summer and autumn of 1945 and when the Japanese war was expected to last for a further eighteen months from the end of the German war. . . .

On the other hand I repulse the idea that a new war is inevitable; still more that it is imminent. It is because I am so sure that our fortunes are in our own hands, and that we hold the power to save the future, that I feel the duty to speak out now that I have an occasion to do so. I do not believe that Soviet Russia desires war. What they desire is the fruits of war and the indefinite expansion of their power and doctrines. But what we have to consider here today, while time remains, is the permanent prevention of war and the establishment of conditions of freedom and democracy as rapidly as possible in all countries. Our difficulties and dangers will not be removed by closing our eyes to them. They will not be removed by merely waiting to see what happens; nor will they be relieved by a policy of appeasement. What is needed is a settlement and the longer this is delayed the more difficult it will be and the greater our dangers will become. From what I have seen of our Russian friends and allies during the war, I am convinced that there is nothing they admire so much as strength, and there is nothing for which they have less respect than military weakness. For that reason the old doctrine of a balance of power is unsound. We cannot afford, if we can help it, to work on narrow margins, offering temptations to a trial of strength. If the Western democracies stand together in strict adherence to the principles of the United Nations Charter, their influence for furthering these principles will be immense and no one is likely to molest them. If, however, they become divided or falter in their duty, and if these all-important years are allowed to slip away, then indeed catastrophe may overwhelm us all. . . .

If the population of the English-speaking commonwealth be added to that of the United States, with all that such cooperation implies in the air, on the sea and in science and industry, there will be no quivering, precarious balance of power to offer its temptation to ambition or adventure. On the contrary, there will be an over-whelming assurance of security. . . .

Winston Churchill, speech at Fulton, Missouri, 5 March 1946. Barton J. Bernstein and Allen J. Matusow (eds), *The Truman Administration. A Documentary History* (New York: Harper & Row, 1966). Quoted in Ian S. McDonald, *Anglo-American Relations since the Second World War* (London: David & Charles, 1974), pp. 34–8.

2.3 'Money bags and brains'

Despite the Fulton speech there were important differences between the United States and Britain in the economic field. In the very difficult loan negotiations between the two countries in 1947 an anonymous British official expressed the feeling of superiority towards America which existed in parts of White-hall in the following terms:

In Washington Lord Halifax
Once whispered to Lord Keynes,
'It's true they have the money bags
But we have all the brains.'

Poem by anonymous British official, 1947. Quoted in R. N. Gardner, *Sterling–Dollar Diplomacy in Current Perspective* (New York: Columbia University Press, 1980), p. xiii.

2.4 'America's best bet': British withdrawal from Greece

Economic difficulties in the early post-war period placed a question mark against British ability to sustain worldwide commitments. Withdrawing forces from foreign theatres, how-ever, had implications for Anglo-American relations and had to be handled with delicacy if the Americans were to continue to regard Britain as a reliable and important partner in the defence of the free world.

Withdrawal of troops in Greece and Italy

At a time when His Majesty's Government are considering drastic cuts in dollar expenditure in order to eke out our slender reserves of hard currency, I think it right to point out that, unless carefully presented beforehand, there is a distinct danger that whatever emergency measure we may shortly find it necessary to take for this purpose will be regarded here as a desperate eleventh-hour abandonment of our international responsibilities rather than as part of a considered plan to facilitate our ultimate recovery. This is particularly true in the military field. In his private talk with me yesterday about our decision to withdraw our remaining troops from Greece, the counsellor of the State Department was also at particular pains to express the hope that His Majesty's Government would not (repeat not) reduce their forces in Germany without giving reasonable advance notice to the Administration. Mr Bohlen implied that, in that event, the United States Government would appreciate details about the timetable and extent of the withdrawal.

2. In this context it should not be forgotten that, as this Embassy has from time to time pointed out, the special position which Britain tends to occupy in American eyes has until now largely derived from the belief that she can be counted upon to share with the United States the responsibility of defending the democratic position in the world. If we are not to run the risk of altogether forfeiting our claim to be so regarded, it seems important that, in the enforced process of partially liquidating our military commitments, we should give this country the impression that we have a considered plan which will enable us to halt our tactical retreat before it assumes the proportions of a rout.

3. With this major consideration in mind, it would appear desirable, if at all possible, that we should at some early appropriate moment take the Administration into our confidence through the intermediary of the Joint Staff Mission and the Embassy about all the overseas theatres where contractions are necessitated and about the time and extent of the reduction envisaged in each instance if only because our action may call for adjustments in American military and diplomatic plans. It would seem reasonable that the United States Government should be given such information as far as possible in advance. In respect of certain features of our programme, you might even think it expedient to invite the comments of the United States Government before we irrevocably commit

ourselves to reduce our forces in one theatre rather than another, or on a specific date. It would in any case serve to maintain confidence in Britain as an effective partner, if we were able to demonstrate in each instance that the saving in manpower and foreign exchange had been carefully balanced against Anglo-American as well as purely British materialistic interests.

4. In their general approach to this problem His Majesty's Government will doubtless keep constantly in mind that the presence of British forces in many parts of the world constitutes an indirect but important bargaining counter in any Anglo-American negotiations. Were responsible Americans to become convinced of what is unfortunately already a growing impression here that Britain can be permanently written off as an important world power capable of sharing with the United States the burdens of world leadership, we should lose whatever advantages we now possess over other nations in search of assistance from this country. In sum, whether in the political, military, or economic fields, we should do our best to inspire confidence that, come what may, we shall remain America's best bet as we proved ourselves to be in the darkest days of the war.

Telegram from the British embassy, Washington, to the Foreign Office, 31 July 1947. Public Record Office, FO 371/61003.

2.5 'The Secretary of State resents . . .': Anglo-American frictions

This document testifies to the friction which could be generated between British and American leaders. Bevin's thoughts on a number of criticisms levelled at the British by Americans are recorded in this document, as are his suggested responses.

The Secretary of State is a little troubled by the tone of this letter [from the British embassy in Washington] in so far as it does not show that Sir J. Balfour refuted all these insinuations which from time to time are advanced by the Americans. I assured him that Sir J. Balfour certainly had, but he gave me some notes for a reply to him. He is most anxious that our Embassy in Washington should immediately knock down this sort of talk by Americans.

The Secretary of State resents the suggestion that we use 'shock tactics' with the Americans. As regards the question of the withdrawal of our troops from Greece, this was discussed in Paris a year ago. It was again discussed with the State Department and then with Mr Marshall in Moscow in March. The Secretary of State believes the trouble is that until we take definite action, the State Department do not take us seriously. In order to make them realise that we mean business, we have had to come to a decision, and show ourselves prepared to take the action we have all along told the Americans we were contemplating.

The Americans knew for months in advance of the withdrawal from Greece and Turkey what our intentions were. The Secretary of State wishes to point out that the deadlines are imposed by the dollar. Our deadlines have been fixed and advanced to earlier than we had expected by Mr. Truman's decision to take off controls. This reduced the value of the dollar 40 per cent, and in taking this action the President went back on all the pledges given at the time of the signature of the Loan Agreement.

As regards Greece, we can also make it plain to the Americans that we have now been there three years. When we first went in no one intended that we should stay there more than a few months. Moreover, when we went in there, we received no support from the US and certainly no kind words from them. We were tilted at and pulled to pieces in the US on all sides.

It must be made clear on all occasions that we do nothing under Left-Wing pressure. HMG do not conduct their policy under pressure from any particular section or pressure group. As regards Greece, the feeling that we should remove our troops is widespread – almost as widespread on the Right as on the Left.

As regards the question of demobilisation, there is a clear answer. In proportion to her population, financial position and responsibilities, the demobilisation of the US has been infinitely greater than ours.

As regards curtailment of our garrisons overseas, one has only to read our correspondence with the Americans over the Egyptian question to see how very hard it has been to get the US Administration to support us in our dispute with Egypt. Their attitude at first appeared to show that they would have welcomed a decision from us to evacuate Egypt completely. This was despite the fact that we had discussed the question of Egypt with the American Administration on several occasions and given them an indication of what our attitude would be.

As regards resistance to Communism, the Secretary of State feels that no one – and certainly no US Statesman – has shown as firm and consistent a resistance to Communism as he has, himself.

'Tactics with the United States Administration', memorandum by a Foreign Office official, 19 August 1947. Public Record Office, FO 371/61003.

2.6 'Natural allies': objectives of US policy toward Britain

This statement of US policy towards Britain in 1948 describes the common values which are believed to underpin the alliance. It also makes clear, however, that the partnership with Britain was a requirement of American national interest and that it required effort and thought to maintain it in smooth working order.

A. Objectives

The basic objectives of US policy toward Britain are to obtain maximum British cooperation in the establishment and maintenance of a just and lasting peace and in the protection of our national interest. It is our dual objective that peace shall be maintained by cooperation with other like-minded nations, of which Britain is the outstanding example, through the United Nations or other broad international machinery, and that we shall have informal working arrangements with the United Kingdom which can be immediately implemented, if necessary, for defensive purposes to maintain the peace and protect our national interest.

British friendship and cooperation is not only desirable in the United Nations and in dealing with the Soviets; it is necessary for American defense. The United Kingdom, the Dominions, Colonies and Dependencies, form a world-wide network of strategically located territories of great military value, which have served as defensive outposts and as bridgeheads for operations. Subject to our general policy of favoring eventual self-determination of peoples, it is our objective that the integrity of this area be maintained; that the United Kingdom retain control of her outlying possessions; that any retrenchment which she may have to make shall take place in an orderly manner; and that territory over which she may relinquish control shall not fall into less friendly hands.

As a defensive measure, it is our object to continue to develop, on an informal basis, wartime cooperative military arrangements with the United Kingdom, particularly as they relate to the exchange of information, the exchange of officers' training, arms standardization, and the mutual use of each other's naval and air ports.

The United Kingdom, with its Labour Government and its respect for individual liberty, is well fitted to counteract Soviet propaganda and, because of its historic position, is suited to take a leading part in the unification of Western Europe into a prosperous whole. It is our objective that the peoples of the UK shall continue to be devoted to the democratic ideals of life and that the UK shall continue to take a leading part in the Western European Union.

The policies and actions of no other country in the world, with the possible exception of the USSR, are of greater importance to us. It is our objective that the United Kingdom shall have a viable economy and adequate standard of living and with sufficient margin to permit her to play her full part in maintaining overseas commitments, either individually or jointly with the United States or in accord with the United Nations, to maintain the peace.

Our general policies with respect to the United Kingdom are implemented with the realization that when working closely together with unity of purpose, the United States, the United Kingdom, and the Commonwealth constitute a presently unequalled force in international affairs. Their people have a common language, heritage, and legal system, devotion to the concepts of liberty and human rights, and paramount interests in the maintenance of peace. America and Britain, as presently constituted, are natural allies. Cooperation between the two governments in achieving coordination should be on a basis of equality. The bargaining power which its greater strength gives the United States must be used with restraint and tact since that course is better calculated to achieve our fundamental objectives.

While Anglo-American friendship is based on solid foundations, its maintenance and development require constant attention. This is especially true at present in view of the often expressed fear and resentment of the US in Britain, and similar feelings toward Britain in the United States. We seek to eradicate adverse British attitudes toward us and misconceptions about the US through a wide exchange of information, and by giving due weight to this factor in formulating American policies which affect British interests.

Department of State policy statement, Washington, 11 June 1948. *Foreign Relations of the United States, 1948*, Vol. III, pp. 1091–2.

2.7 The question of a third world power

In the bipolar post-war international system Britain found itself in between the two superpowers. Ideologically opposed to and perceiving itself threatened by the Soviet Union, it could ally itself with the United States for security. A further option, however, was also discussed. It involved trying to form a Third World Power bloc.

The question of a third world power

Nevertheless, despite the ties of common feelings and traditions, the choice between the two courses must be based on a cold estimate of advantages. It is possible to concede that a Third World Power could be organised to hold its own, if necessary, against either of the other two power-systems or to extract such concessions as it could by maintaining neutrality between them. But, even if this could be done, a mere policy of neutrality would not suffice to hold the component countries together, especially as it must be assumed that these countries would contain a number of Soviet sympathisers. A Third Power, by its very weakness, then, might be an invitation to the Soviet Government to swallow its opponents one by one. In essence, therefore, the problem is whether a strong and independent Third World Power can be created. The answer depends on:

(a) The countries or groups of countries which would compose a Third World Power.

(b) The chances of such a Power, however composed, maintaining its cohesion and its independence in the political, economic and military spheres.

Foreign Office memorandum, 'Third World Power or Western Preponderance', provisional summary, 25 March 1949. Public Record Office, FO 371/76384.

2.8 Anglo-American relations: present and future

This survey of the current and projected state of Anglo-American relations, prepared by senior officials in the Foreign Office, dismisses the idea of Britain becoming part of a third power standing between the superpowers. It looks at how Britain can ensure that it continues to be the principal ally of the United States, and the danger that declining British power poses to that role.

Anglo-American relations

Introduction

1. The Committee has already reached the conclusion (PUSC.22) that the United States of America is an essential component of any group of nations, excluding Russia, which would be strong enough to retain its independence in the future. In arriving at this conclusion the Committee has discarded as either impracticable or undesirable the alternative of a union comprising Western Europe, or Western Europe with the Commonwealth, as a self-sufficient 'Third World Power'. A review of Anglo-American relations is therefore likely to involve consideration of many aspects of the foreign policy of both countries.

Present situation

2. Because of their victorious wartime alliance, collaboration between the USA and the United Kingdom since the war has been closer than ever before and closer than the relations maintained by the USA with any other country. Canada has been associated in specially close military and economic relations with the partnership.

(a) Military

In the military field, the continued existence of the combined Chiefs of Staff organisation has hitherto kept alive an effective United Kingdom–United States partnership. The USA has in fact hitherto assumed that the principal partner and ally on which, from the military point of view, she may rely is the United Kingdom.

(b) Economic

Although the American Loan to Britain was the first great new departure in United States post-war foreign economic policy, and although the United Kingdom led the response to the European Recovery programme, collaboration in the formulation of economic policy has been less close. The prosperity of the USA and the United Kingdom's economic difficulties have made the relationship somewhat one-sided. The dollar shortage has acted as a barrier between the two economies.

(c) Political

Political collaboration is largely a function of economic or military collaboration, but is facilitated by the fact that the United Kingdom shares with the USA not only a common language but also, to a

52

great extent, a similar political, cultural and religious heritage. The two countries are also bound together by their instinctive dislike of Russian expansion and communist penetration.

Relations between the United States of America and the United Kingdom

(a) *United States reliance on Britain*

10. As has been said, the USA has, since the war, assumed that the principal ally on whom she may rely in any conflict with Russia will be the United Kingdom, with the support of the Commonwealth. Relations with Russia on the one hand and with the United Kingdom and Commonwealth on the other naturally influence United States policies in many part of the world.

12. American policy in China may have been too narrowly conceived on account of inexperience and the treatment of Japan is an instance of the somewhat unimaginative tendency of the Americans to graft their own way of life on to rather improbable stock. Moreover, their insistence on restoring the Japanese low-cost economy on multilateral principles takes little account of British economic interests. But an American stake in the region is of great importance for the consolidation of Western influence. Here is another opportunity for the United Kingdom, with her longer experience, to guide the policy of the USA. The United States government will certainly maintain some line of strategic defence in the Pacific and have indicated that they may be willing to consider some pact or agreement extending to the Western fringe of the Pacific. Much may therefore turn upon the extent to which the United Kingdom and other members of the Commonwealth find themselves able to contribute.

15. The problem of Israel occupies a special place in Anglo-American relations. There are about 10 million Jews in the world. Some 5 million of them live in the USA, many of whom are concentrated in the politically key state of New York. The sympathy of the strong zionist element of American Jewry for the establishment of Israel and the political pressure which this element has been able to exert on the White House have imposed a considerable strain on relations with the United Kingdom, whose position in the Middle East would be fatally compromised if she were to lose entirely the friendship of the Moslem world. Now that Israel has come into

being, pressure in the United States is likely to diminish. Divergences of view over Palestine between the two governments have now been narrowed and since the British and American views about the Middle East are, apart from this issue, virtually identical, it may be hoped that major difficulties will not recur.

16. Among political issues which in the past have darkened relations between the United Kingdom and the USA have been the Irish question, India and colonial policy. Events have now either removed or largely diminished their force. There is, however, a persistent remnant of anti-British feeling among the older generation of Irish Americans. There is also apt to be anti-British feeling among the Catholics in America, partly perhaps owing to Irish Americans among them, and partly to the fact that the United Kingdom is the largest Protestant power. Positive anti-British feeling among the sections of the population of German and Italian origin has never manifested itself decisively. Prejudice arising from the traditions of the American Revolution and the teaching of the history of that period is a stronger source of ill-feeling but is diminishing.

(e) *Economic relations*

17. The economic relations of the two countries may bring these issues to a head. The United States Government and His Majesty's Government are equally pledged to the conception of multilateral trading with fully convertible currencies, in accordance with the provisions of the ITO Charter and the statutes of the International Monetary Fund. These international instruments carry with them complementary requirements in the field of domestic policy, such as the maintenance of full employment and tariffs no higher than are consistent with the general objectives. There is thus no difference between the USA and the United Kingdom in their conception of the sort of economic world which is wanted.

18. There has, however, been increasing friction resulting from the slow pace which the United Kingdom has so far found herself compelled to take in moving towards these objectives. The Americans are beginning to doubt whether the United Kingdom really wishes, or could even if she wished to, attain these objectives in view of her economic policies, both internal and external. Progress appears to many Americans to have been impeded by restrictionist policies and methods which have robbed the British economy of its

competitive strength and sapped the will to work of the British people. They consider that, apart from any question of Government policy, British business methods are unsuited to modern conditions. Moreover, an official policy based on controls and bilateral trading, with an eye always fixed on the level of reserves, seems to them selfish caution, out of keeping with the spirit of adventure which made Britain great and on which American free enterprise has prospered. The widespread suspicion of Socialism, which is often a by-product of American opposition to governmental interference, arouses antagonism to measures which appear to be introduced for political reasons, although their practical effects are largely economic. The most recent and striking example of this point of view is the attempt to introduce into the E[uropean]R[ecovery]P[rogramme]. Appropriation Bill a veto on further nationalisation by recipient countries (clearly directed against the UK). But there has been for some time growing criticism of the alleged extravagance of a Welfare State supported by excessive Government expenditure, especially on the ground that high government expenditure means high taxes and, in effect, a ceiling on free enterprise. There are effective replies to all these lines of criticism, but any analysis of present Anglo-American relations must take into account the fact that adverse opinions of the various kinds listed above are being held with increasing strength.

19. American suspicion of 'colonialism' also inspires a feeling that the United Kingdom, through the sterling area machinery, is exploiting the resources of the Commonwealth and Colonial Empire for her own benefit. There is a reluctance to deal with the sterling area as a whole through the United Kingdom as intermediary.

20. If this friction is allowed to increase, or even to continue, it may threaten the basis upon which strategic and political collaboration with the USA rests. Many Americans agree with President Coolidge that the business of the United States is business. They are therefore beginning to wonder whether Britain is still a good commercial risk. Is the path which she has chosen a reflection of a fundamental change for the worse in the national character, a tacit withdrawal from the ranks of Great Powers? If these doubts are justified, is Britain more of an asset or a liability to the United States as a long-term partner in international affairs?

Summary
21. The preceding paragraphs suggest the conclusion that there need be no fundamental conflict of interests between the USA and the United Kingdom in any part of the world, provided that the United Kingdom can achieve a position, closely related to the USA and yet sufficiently independent of her to be able to influence American policy in the directions desired. If, on the other hand, the UK were forced to embark upon policies which entailed so sharp a contraction of British influence and responsibilities that it became clear that she was ceasing to exist as a leading world power, there would be a risk of a major divergence. The USA would be likely to withdraw from any commitments in the Middle East, the Mediterranean and Africa. She might also decline to accept any responsibility in South and South-East Asia and might limit her responsibilities in the Far East and the Pacific.

(b) *Danger of a retreat into isolationism*
29. The very fact that the USA has been thrust into a position of world leadership before she had developed fully the experience and political and economic philosophy necessary for the role, entails the danger of a retreat into isolationism should the general venture into world affairs appear to be a failure. There is no doubt that in the post-war world American official circles have enjoyed the widespread support of public opinion in their policy of collaboration with like-minded countries in the ordering of world affairs. But isolationist sentiment is still latent in the USA and could be revived in many sections of the population if conditions were favourable. Individuals, groups, and in particular, newspapers which have supported and encouraged isolationist movements in the past (e.g. America First) still exist and are ready to go into action again. Indeed, a school of thought is already developing on the lines that the American taxpayer has supported Bretton Woods, British loans, the United Nations, the European Recovery Programme, etc. and has subscribed billions to put the world right economically. In this way the US Government has done all that should be expected of it, and more. The lack of success of these efforts must be due to the shortcomings of the recipient countries, and the US should therefore be slow in adding to its existing commitments until foreign countries have proved themselves worthy, by their own efforts, of further support. This new line of thought has a powerful attraction,

since it allows for natural inclination, for an assumption of the inability to make mistakes and for a dislike of the acceptance of responsibility and the consequences of power. It would prove particularly attractive to American opinion if Russian pressure were to appear to relax at the same time as disappointment with Europe was growing.

30. Any retreat into isolationism has obvious dangers for the United Kingdom, which with Western Europe would be left on the Russian side of a dividing line drawn down the Atlantic and separating the world between the two great power blocs of the United States and the Soviet Union.

Conclusions

43. (a) Although British and American political interests coincide in most parts of the world, they rest on the assumption that the United Kingdom is the principal partner and ally on whom the USA can rely.

(b) If the USA were to reach the conclusion that the United Kingdom's position no longer justified this assumption, she might gradually turn to one or more of the following courses of action, none of which would favour British interests:

(i) Adoption of Germany or France as the pivot of United States policy in Europe.

(ii) A retreat into isolationism.

(iii) An accommodation with Russia.

(c) The United States may be dissuaded from such courses if the United Kingdom can show enough strength of national will and retain enough initiative to maintain her position as a leading world power, and as such, influence United States policy, but the British position is at present weakened by the economic crises affecting the United Kingdom and the sterling area.

(d) It is clear, in fact, that far the best solution from our point of view would be the attainment of an equilibrium between the dollar and the sterling areas at a high level of trade.

(e) If, for any reason, however, this is not attainable except as part of some wider plan, then it seems quite conceivable that the idea may emerge of some solution along the lines of a closer financial union between the United States and the United Kingdom.

(f) If such a proposal were seriously considered by the United States it would seem desirable that it should not be rejected out of hand by the United Kingdom, since the solutions, other than (d) above, would appear to be highly undesirable.

PUSC (51) Final, 'Anglo-American Relations: Present and Future', Report of the PUSC, 24 August 1949. Public Record Office, FO 371/76385.

2.9   A special relationship, but not overtly

From the US point of view also close cooperation with Britain was desirable. However, the Americans were keen that it should not be to the detriment either of their own or of Britain's wider relations with the rest of Europe, and were therefore keen to avoid too explicit a stress on the special relationship, as this State Department paper shows.

2. No other country has the same qualifications for being our principal ally and partner as the UK. It has internal political strength and important capabilities in the political, economic and military fields throughout the world. Most important, the British share our fundamental objectives and standards of conduct. Linked to the UK, and a source of much of its strength, is the Commonwealth. Much of that grouping, in particular the other dominions, share the same objectives and standards. The area of the Commonwealth is of greater importance, economically, strategically and politically than any other existing grouping. The US can find its most important collaborators and allies in the UK and the Commonwealth, just as the UK and the Commonwealth are, in turn, dependent upon us.

II.   *Variety of roles we expect the British to play*

1. We expect and depend upon the British to play a variety of roles on the world scene, including the following: (a) a leader (with France) in the movement toward closer European unity, (b) the cement which holds the Commonwealth together, (c) our principal partner in strategic planning, (d) a major force in ensuring political and economic stability in the Near and Middle East, (e) a collaborator in the resistance to Communist expansion in the Far East, (f) a willing collaborator in promoting the development of an expanding multilateral world trade, (g) a leader in furthering the development and emergence of dependent areas, and (h) a principal supporter of the UN. Even if there were not internal inconsistencies

between these roles, they would tax the capacities of any country. While these roles may correspond to the capabilities of the British Empire of 50 years ago, when that Empire was the major world power, the British do not now have the capacity to fulfill all these various functions without the closest support and collaboration of the US.

(c) The British attach great importance to the continuance of an especially close relationship with the US. This coincides with our own policy. The British, however, are inclined to wish to make this relationship more overt than we feel desirable. This manifests itself in various efforts to reestablish openly the relationship which existed during the last war when, in substance, the British and ourselves managed the resources of all the Western powers. The British react strongly against being treated as 'just another European power'.

It should be our line with the British to assure them that we recognize the special relationship between our two countries and that we recognize their special position with regard to the Commonwealth. We should insist, however, that these relationships are not incompatible with close association in a European framework. In fact, the close US–UK relation and the Commonwealth today find their significance in their ability to contribute to the attaining of other ends, including the strengthening of Western Europe and resistance to Soviet expansion everywhere. We should insist, moreover, that the British recognize that it is necessary for us, when we are dealing with a generalized European problem, not to make overt distinctions between them and other European countries. Any such overt distinctions could only have the effect of seriously upsetting the Continental countries, particularly France, adding to the ever present fear that both we and the British will abandon them in case of an emergency.

5. *Differences of Economic Philosophy*. The divergencies of economic and social philosophy between the US and UK lead to differences between us, particularly in the economic and financial fields. Aside from giving a general policy priority to domestic welfare expenditures over external responsibilities, the dominant socialist creed of the Labor Party undoubtedly encourages the maintenance of economic controls in line with the theory that a planned managed economy is desirable. While it is claimed by the British Government that there is no inconsistency between the

maintenance of a socialist state and progress towards non-discriminatory multilateral expanding world trade, it is undoubtedly true that there is no theoretical aversion on their part to managed bilateralism. Further, the belief that state economic management is necessary to achieve social and economic welfare leads to the practice of trying to protect the economy against adverse economic developments in the outside world. This practice, in fact, leads to attempts to insulate the economy from outside competitive economic forces, thus limiting the ability of the British economy to adapt itself to changing world conditions.

It is also undoubtedly true that the more doctrinaire of the British socialists are personally affected by a reaction against what they believe to be the antagonistic philosophy of competitive capitalism. In extreme cases that leads to a personal distrust of American motives and in many cases it leads to an insistence on insulating British economic planning from any chance of intervention by Americans (e.g. British resistance to the idea of US point IV activities in their colonies).

6. *Temperamental Differences.* A last point which should be mentioned is both traditional and temperamental. We are apt to be impatient, urging fast action, specific commitments and definite plans. The British are much more cautious and favor the gradual approach of expediency and step-by-step pragmatic action, an approach which has traditionally been known as 'muddling through'. While it is certainly true that we may be too impatient, and dogmatic, the pressure of events and the tempo of the Cold War are not such as to permit leisure.

IV. Conclusions

1. The forces and attitudes which have been described above are realities which cannot be ignored. There is no alternative to facing up to them and trying to work out an accommodation which will permit the full development of the essential US–UK partnership and the application of that partnership to the necessities of the world today. There will have to be flexibility and compromise on both sides. The interplay of these factors and forces is such that it is deceptive to believe that clear-cut policy decisions can emerge in any conversation or set of conversations with British representatives. The best that can be achieved is agreement upon ultimate objectives, the allaying of suspicions and doubts, and agreement on

the necessity of working out solutions. The last may include the establishment of special procedures for continuing consultations comparable to the continuing talks after the September 1949 meetings. One thing is sure, that there can be no accommodations unless there is established a framework within which both countries feel free to discuss and make recommendations with regard to policies and actions which may seem to be of purely domestic concern. Furthermore, it must be realized on both sides that governmental leaders can at best only agree on what policies they will seek to have their government follow. On neither side can binding long-range commitments be made.

2. The salient points to bear in mind in determining our relations with the British are as follows.

(a) To achieve our foreign policy objectives we must have the cooperation of allies and friends. The British and with them the rest of the Commonwealth, particularly the older dominions, are our most reliable and useful allies, with whom a special relationship should exist. This relationship is not an end in itself but must be used as an instrument of achieving common objectives.

(b) We cannot afford to permit a deterioration in our relationship with the British. We must strive to get agreement on the identity of our objectives and reaffirm the fundamental identity of our interests.

(c) British capabilities are limited by the British financial position. We are affected as well by limits on our financial and other capabilities. The British appear to be giving an overriding priority to these steps which will terminate their need for outside aid and reestablish sterling as a strong international currency by mid-1952. Concentration on this financial goal may be seriously prejudicing other more important world objectives. If we urge the British to change their emphasis, we must ourselves face the probable necessity of some form of continued US aid after 1952, the necessity for each to take difficult internal actions, and the necessity of doing something to lessen the pressure of the sterling balances.

(d) We should reassure the British that we do not advocate their political merger with the Continent, but that we are convinced that closer economic and political, as well as military, ties between them and the Continent are essential. In this connection we would be glad to support British leadership (in conjunction with the French), and we must face the implication for us, i.e. what action must be taken to enable closer UK–Continent association to develop.

(e) While we recognize and support the British in their role as leader of the Commonwealth and their attempts to strengthen it, we do not believe that, except in very special cases, this role is incompatible with close association with the US or with Europe.

(f) We recognize the special close relations between us and it is one of the premises of our foreign policy. It is not, however, a substitute for but a foundation under closer British (and perhaps US) relations with the Continent. In dealing with other Europeans, however, we cannot overtly treat the British differently and they should recognize that the special US–UK relation underlies US–Europe relations, and that we do not consider close UK–European relations as prejudicial to the US–UK relations.

(g) There is no future for the British apart from close collaboration with the US. They will have to rely on our record, which is good, and we each have to continue to recognize that public debates and domestic political antics are an essential and fundamentally useful part of the democratic process.

(h) Both the UK and ourselves must strive to temper our domestic programs to the realities of the Cold War. Since we have greater economic latitude, this will be harder on the British. Their economy needs to be made more adaptable to the economic facts of life. There is no future in economic isolationism, for the UK or the Commonwealth or the sterling area.

(i) The traditional British preference for the gradual step-by-step approach is too leisurely for the pace of Cold War.

Paper prepared in the Department of State, 19 April 1950. *Foreign Relations of the United States, 1950*, Vol. III, pp. 870–9 *passim*.

2.10 The special relationship: cornerstone or millstone?

Seen from the point of view of the US ambassador to France, however, there were serious dangers in promoting the special relationship as the cornerstone of US foreign policy. It could turn into a millstone when it came to building a European community of which the United States hoped Britain would be a key member.

The search for a new relationship

For Jessup from Bruce
Both Harriman and I had similar concern in regard to the results of the Bilateral Subcommittee meeting with the British reported in Secto 56 April 30. However, since talking with Bohlen we understand that it is the report of an informal Sub-committee meeting which does not in any way commit the US to the positions set forth in this cable and will be subject to review on a higher level before presentation to the Secretary. With this in mind I am giving you my views as to the possible dangerous consequences which the formal adoption of the policy suggested in the cable might have on our general European policy.

1. If the special relationship on a world-wide basis implied in this cable becomes established US policy, I believe the consequences in regard to our other partners in the Atlantic community will be extremely harmful. A special relationship of this kind, which would in effect mean that the US and UK would formulate their policies bilaterally on a world-wide basis, could not under any circumstances be concealed from other countries. I believe it would be regarded on the continent as the abandonment by the US of any serious attempt at European or even Atlantic community integration in favor of an Anglo-American world alliance as the cornerstone of US foreign policy.

2. From past experience we could be certain that the British in their dealings with other European countries would make full use of this 'special relationship' in order to develop the point of view that they are in effect an intermediary between the other European countries and the US.

3. I think we should recognize that the British desire for a special relationship with the US is in fact indissolubly linked with their unwillingness with respect to greater participation in European affairs and will inevitably be so interpreted by continental European Powers.

I know from Bohlen's report that these considerations are very much in your mind in London and I am therefore sending them to you rather than to the Dep in order to avoid what might appear to be divided counsel to the Secretary. Should however the question of confirming the report of the Subcommittee as definite US policy arise before the Secretary's departure, I would appreciate your transmitting my views and in general those of Harriman to him on this point.

Telegram from David Bruce, the US ambassador in France, to Phillip Jessup, head of the United States delegation at the tripartite preparatory meetings, Paris, 4 May 1950. *Foreign Relations of the United States, 1950,* Vol. III, pp. 960–1.

2.11 Acknowledging the special relationship

In response to the above report by the US ambassador to France, his counterpart in Britain gives his own view of the relationship and discusses the extent to which the United States should acknowledge its existence, given the difficulties that this could cause in America's relations with Britain and with other allies.

For the Secretary, Bruce, Harriman, Jessup, Perkins, and Bohlen

1. I am taking this occasion to comment on Bruce's cable to Jessup (Paris Embtel 590 to London May 4 and Jessup's reply London Embtel 752 to Paris). This is not intended to be a full discussion of the issue which these cables raise. It is merely a brief summary of what appear to be inescapable facts and conclusions that flow from them.

2. There are it seems to me, two issues. The first issue is whether there is in fact a peculiar relationship which exists between the US and the UK. The second is whether, assuming that such a peculiar relationship does exist, we should disclose our realization of this relationship to the British, and if so, the extent to which it should be disclosed and, by agreement, used as a basis of combined foreign policy.

(a) Dealing with the first issue – there is no country on earth whose interests are so wrapped around the world as the UK. Among her Crown Colonies she is in more vitally strategic areas than any other nation among the community of Western nations. She is the center of a great commonwealth. The US enjoys the benefits of being a neighbor to the most important member of this Commonwealth whose relationships with the UK can no more be disguised or eliminated at the moment, or in the immediate future, than can the relationship between the Hawaiian Islands and the US. She is the center of the sterling area in which a particular monetary unit known as the pound circulates and enjoys common usage as a common medium of exchange. This area is held together not alone by the circulation of an identical currency or other currencies easily convertible into it. It is held together also by an intricate and complicated system of commercial and financial arrangements built up tediously by the British with the natives and the Colonials of this vast area throughout the course of 300 years. There is no substitute for the sterling area and none can be erected in any short period of time. But beyond all of these considerations the UK is the only Power, in addition to ourselves, west of the Iron Curtain capable of wielding substantial military strength. This assembly of facts, though some may disagree with a few of them, makes a special relationship between the US and the UK as inescapable as the facts themselves. And no amount of dialectical argument can erase either the facts or the conclusion.

(b) The above does not imply that a special relationship between the US and UK is necessarily exclusive of, or precludes, special arrangements with other countries, or excludes or prohibits the inclusion of other countries in any peculiar arrangements which, on more than a bilateral basis with the UK, may be made. I suggest that there are certain areas in respect of which the peculiar US–UK relationship should be expressed in terms of bilateral arrangements. There is for example the Near East. There is sub-Asia and there are the Crown Colonies of Africa. Some of these areas, because of their remoteness from other Powers and because of our intimate concern with them, belong naturally among the category of areas susceptible to treatment by US–UK arrangements. There are other areas which may best be dealt with by a broader multilateral policy toward Colonial areas. There are certain financial and economic relations which are peculiar to the US and UK but which, because they bear also a relationship to other Powers, lend themselves not only in the first instance to US–UK discussion and negotiation, but also to multilateral consideration. There are certain military questions, certain matters of defense which are peculiar to the US and UK. Thus as a matter of practical international politics we must acknowledge the existence of a special relationship between the UK and the Commonwealth on one hand and ourselves on the other.

3. To what extent should this peculiar relationship be admitted to the British as a basis for policy? The great danger of a too extensive acknowledgement of our peculiar association is that this Govt, or indeed any British Govt, while Britain is in straitened circumstances, might lean too heavily upon us in order (a) to

perpetuate the protectionist program which the present Govt considers to be essential, or (b) to relieve a strain to which UK resources might be put. There is too the danger that an indiscreet and too extensive acceptance of this relationship in dealing with some specific questions in advance of, or without appropriate preparatory explanations to, some of the Continental Powers might give rise to the view that a US–UK alliance was, by design, being substituted for the North Atlantic community. Therefore a certain amount of caution in acknowledging the existence of the relationship, and a certain amount of discretion in dealing with specific questions which arise out of this special relationship are required. But to say that in the face of UK's and the Commonwealth's interests all over the world, and US interests all over the world, we should not recognize a special relationship solely because it might possibly interfere with the smooth working of the North Atlantic community, however important this community is to the world, is to ignore, it seems to me, the fundamental position of both the UK and the US in all quarters of the globe. The issue is not whether we should deny this relationship but rather how to acknowledge it without injuring the NA community.

4. It may be that the British will use a too extensive acknowledgement of this relationship by us for the purpose of establishing, or attempting to establish, her position as an intermediary between the US and the Continent. If she would become a good intermediary and exert the sort of leadership we want, what harm would this do? In fact our major criticism of HM Government has been that she has not exerted leadership on the Continent and has in fact refused to be an American intermediary. The issue is not whether the UK would attempt to be Mr Bones in a minstrel show but whether the UK would be a good Mr Bones. Throughout our discussions of this subject everyone I believe has agreed to the proposition that there cannot be any substantial progress toward a closer association of European nations either in an economic or political sense without UK leadership, participation where it is compatible with UK's other relationships, and active encouragement in matters in which, because of other obligations, the UK cannot become a participant.

5. I dissent from the view expressed in the third paragraph of the subject cable from Paris. I do not believe that the principal reason the UK desires a special relationship with the US is to avoid, as this

paragraph implies, greater participation in European affairs. Surely the UK did not ask us to assume responsibilities in Greece, which we accepted because of a peculiar relationship with the UK, for the reason that she wanted to avoid a more intimate participation in European affairs. The Marshall Plan had not even then been launched upon an unwitting world. Surely the UK didn't press us to buy raw materials from her Crown Colonies and from the members of the Commonwealth in 1949 because she wanted thereby to establish a closer relationship with us which would enable her to avoid a more cozy association with European countries.

I do not for a moment imply that the UK's desire to have a special relationship with the US is as pure as Castile Soap and as clean as Snow White. Her motives are often no worse than ours, and no better, but I do not agree with the view that the primary reason which moves her to attempt to establish a special US–UK relationship is because of her unwillingness to join in molding a more closely knit Western Europe. Her principal motive is to buy insurance.

The ambassador in the United Kingdom, Lewis Douglas, to the embassy in France, London, 7 May 1950. *Foreign Relations of the United States, 1950*, Vol. III, pp. 972–4.

3

Cooperation and friction, 1950–56

The period from 1950 to 1956 saw important movements in Anglo-American relations towards even greater cooperation but also difficulties, which at the end of the period shook the bilateral alliance to its foundations.

In the early 1950s the pattern of progress towards greater intimacy in the range of defence fields, established in the late 1940s, was continued. The most notable of the areas of cooperation occurred in the nuclear field. In 1954 the McMahon Act, which had been signed in 1946 (excluding Britain from nuclear collaboration with the United States), was amended. The amendment opened up, to a much greater extent than before, the flow of information on the characteristics of nuclear weapons and laid the foundations of more far-reaching legislation later.

At the same time, however, problems arose in various areas of Anglo-American relations, with difficulties over the recognition of China, nuclear issues during the Korean war, different interpretations of the Indochina war, the European Defence Community, and misgivings about the Baghdad Pact on the defence of the Middle East. The worst of these difficulties came with the traumatic clash over the Anglo-French invasion of Suez in November 1956. Such was the hostility generated by the crisis that the alliance between Britain and the United States which had been so carefully built up since the Second World War came close to collapse.

3.1 'Pallid allies': an American view of British thinking about America

Gauging the state of the Anglo-American relationship during the Korean War, the US ambassador to Britain here reports that, while they do not question the need for close relations, the British are going through a phase of irritation and exasperation with the United States. He highlights the causes of this.

1. As Department aware, British attitude towards US follows fluctuating pattern. Periods when American prestige is high are followed by lows generally occasioned by divergence of views over specific political or economic issues. Effect of disagreement is however aggravated by psychological intangibles stemming from fact that despite many similarities, we are two different peoples with different reactions, different methods of operation and at times transitory differences in interest although long-term objectives are same. US prestige in British eyes reached high at time Inchon landings [15 September 1950] but subsequent UN reverses in Korea gave such a jolt that period of low commenced which now appears to be at nadir. This condition does not reflect anti-Americanism in sense of unfriendliness toward US or US people. On contrary anti-Americanism of this nature is to all intents and purposes quiescent if not in fact moribund except among (I) Communists, (II) handful labor left-wingers who have always been suspicious of and even hostile to US, and (III) hard core of empire-fired Tories who wield negligible influence. Moreover present low does not presage any weakening of Anglo-American partnership which British continue to be convinced is indissoluble rock upon which future of free world must be based. It does however reflect strong undercurrent exasperation and irritation towards US and distrust of certain of our policies which prevail among practically all sectors British community. Unlike situation at time sterling devaluation in 1949 and previous differences over economic questions, this feeling is not voiced in press except for sharp criticisms of our FE policy. Nevertheless it is in our view possibly more intense and widespread today than at any time in past five years.

2. Following analysis seeks to bring up to date earlier assessments of causation current British attitude and insofar as possible to explain why British feel this way. As will be noted attitude contains certain contradictions, illogicalities and even blind spots since it combines disagreements on specific issues with instinctive and emotional reactions.

3. Basic causes present British attitude are fear that UK may have lost control over own destiny, that US may go beyond 'point of no return' and chain of events may ultimately result in war with Soviet Union in which UK would necessarily become involved and that US will squander its resources in hopeless war with China which would leave Europe, key to security of West, defenceless. These fears are

69

intensified by reports highly excited state of American public opinion and exaggerated idea of power and influence of General MacArthur and of his alleged proclivity to take political decisions on his own authority.

4. Most immediate motivation of present British attitude is concern over what they consider absence of realism in our FE policy and questionable wisdom some of our actions there. British views toward FE in general and China in particular have not been in accord with our own ever since war. This divergence did not however become of primary importance until British recognized CPG and did not in their eyes take on acute aspect until Chinese Communists intervened in Korea. British feel we are supporting Chiang and Syngman Rhee and that this 'support' indicates that we are confusing fundamental social upheavals in Asia with Soviet machinations. Constantly bearing in mind vulnerability of Hong Kong, British place second only to relationship with US continued solidarity of Commonwealth and avoidance any action which might alienate India as potential leader non-Communist Asia. In present crisis continuance MacArthur in key political as well as military position tends to aggravate their concern that US actions will be guided by emotional and prestige considerations in defiance of Asiatic opinion. In many instances there is no disagreement re importance specific issues. For example British Government but not public is probably awake to necessity of keeping Formosa for time being in friendly hands or neutralized but there is belief that this could be accomplished more realistically than by army of discredited Chiang regime. British feel some accommodation to Asiatic viewpoint principally as expressed by Nehru is justifiable especially since they have not yet given up hope of eventual conflict between Peking and Moscow.

British Government and public seemingly unable to grasp facts that future of collective security depends as much on events in FE as in Europe and that failure UN to continue to resist aggression there could be as disastrous for UN as breakdown of sanctions against Italy was for League.

5. Contributing factors to present British attitude include

(a) Weaknesses in US diplomacy. Although British people do not in general mistrust US motives or intentions and indeed feel that our postwar foreign policy has furnished remarkable evidence that America is rising to great and new responsibilities, they still lack full confidence in our ability to handle delicate international issues. They feel US methods sometimes unnecessarily put them and others publicly on spot and that purpose could be better achieved by other means. They also believe that we are prone to act without adequate prior study of possible implications of a move and to make piecemeal decisions. They are consequently disturbed by what they regard as our impulsiveness and tendency to plunge ahead, sometimes in anger. At same time they are concerned by what they feel is our proneness to decide matters with minimum prior consultation with them and to insist that courses of action which we propose are the only practicable ones. They regard these methods as high pressure tactics incompatible with real leadership and are surprised that nation our stature feels need to use them. Britain realizes that power tactics have place in diplomatic tools of trade but believe we are inclined to employ them to exclusion other means of suasion. As instance US diplomatic shortcoming, British cite approach used in Washington September discussions on German rearmament. They feel we broached subject without sufficient advance spadework with respect to French and maintain that if this had been done, wranglings in following months would not only have been avoided by also that we would be much further ahead today with German rearmament.

(b) Failure to capitalize on British experience. British believe that we fail to make use of their experience in diplomacy and government gained over decades when UK was dominant world power. They realize that its position in West is definitely second to that of US but still feel that they have much practical knowledge to offer which could be advantageously employed in formulation and execution of Western policy. British feel their long association with and skill in handling peoples of Europe exceeds our own and, in fact, regard themselves as natural leaders of Western Europe. They therefore believe that greater use should be made of these assets in stimulating continent to greater defense effort. British maintain that much that is practical in European cooperation since war has been achieved because of their contribution and close their eyes to fact that their prestige and consequently influence in Western Europe is at low ebb as result negative attitude they have adopted towards European integration.

(c) Concern re inconsistency US policy. British feel that their early misgivings re implications US election for Europe have been

71

borne out by Hoover in speech and more recently and far more seriously by Taft's statements. They have already been alarmed by attacks on the Secretary who is highly respected here for his foresight and judgement and fact that 'McCarthyism' made such an impression on American people. They are concerned at possibility US public may forget our commitments under NAT and at prospect of increased neo-isolationism with all it connotes for future security of UK and Europe. These fears are further deepened by current controversy over constitutional authority executive to send US forces abroad.

(d) Alleged negative US approach to talks with Soviet. British sentiment is strongly in favor talks between Western Powers and Soviet. Latest Gallup poll showed 76 per cent would like meeting between President, Attlee and Stalin. This desire does not mean that British would be prepared to appease Soviet. Memory of Munich is still green. However, with spectre of war looming large in their minds British feel we should overlook no opportunity to explore every reasonable avenue settlement East–West differences and therefore West is morally bound to take part in talks. They are consequently disturbed by impression that US overly negative in its approach to proposed meeting four Foreign Ministers, that we feel talks would be unproductive and hence no purpose would be served by holding them, that US emphasizing military factor to contain Soviet without parallel political offensive. British recognize that West cannot hope to gain from talks unless in position of strength. They are inclined feel however that our position has been strengthened by Soviet fears at prospect German rearmament and because of this there is a chance talks may have some beneficial results, and at very least West will gain time.

(e) Failure US to appreciate UK contribution to common defense. British are irritated at apparent failure US to appreciate importance their contribution to cause of West and are resentful tendency to regard them as 'pallid allies'. They point to facts that they have almost 40,000 troops plus large armed police forces in Malaya who have been fighting Communist guerrillas long before aggression in Korea, that on per capita basis size UK forces comparable to our own, that military service universal and term longer, and that until Korea percentage UK gross national production devoted to defense was higher than that in US and that since Korea British have substantially increased proportion GNP allocated to defense and will shortly up it still further. British themselves primarily at fault for having failed to publicize importance their contribution. Nevertheless they tend to overlook this and to blame US public for being misinformed. We also sense some feeling of guilt on part British that despite relatively creditable showing to date it does not at present time compare with US defense effort and feel that from this standpoint their self-esteem will be raised when details accelerated defense program are announced.

(f) Envy of US. Consciously or unconsciously British people tend to be envious of US. They are envious of our standard of living and luxurious way of life as portrayed in movies and other media, of our economic and industrial strength, of our relative geographic security, and of fact that we have replaced them as the leading world power. In summary, feeling of superiority towards US which characterized British in past is on way to developing into one of inferiority. As is usual in such cases, sense of disparity is expressed in criticism of object of envy. Such criticism is particularly sharp here at present time because of fear that we may be dragging UK into war.

6. Factors contributing to British attitude towards US which have diminished in importance since previous assessments (Embtels 3043, November 24, 3241, December 3 and 3664, December 29) are (1) 'junior partner' role, (2) A-bomb, (3) raw materials. Suspension Marshall aid and Attlee's visit to Washington where British voice raised have done much to remove British feeling of being 'a dependent' and all sections British public believe UK now in better position to deal on more equal basis with US. Growing self-confidence among British takes form wider public demand for UK actively to influence US rather than merely follow in US wake. On A-bomb, fears have quieted since Attlee visit, and evidence that scare stories from Washington about US willingness to make immediate use weapon were not based on fact. British worries re effect on UK economy of US stockpiling have also tended to decline as result President's talk with Attlee and plans to provide for equitable distribution of commodities in short supply.

7. While we are naturally disturbed by British attitude described above, past experience teaches us that Anglo-American disagreements can be eased if not removed by real effort on both sides to appreciate other's position. We must also bear in mind fact that maintenance closest possible ties with US is basic objective UK

foreign policy and therefore that British will seek to avoid any step which might seriously jeopardize their relations with US. As our present divergencies stem in large measure from FE situation, on which no basic understanding was apparently reached in Attlee–Truman conversations, we suggest you consider possible advantage in having high-ranking official Department such as Jessup or Rusk who can speak authoritatively on US-FE policy, come to London in very near future to discuss subject with Bevin and Fonoff officials concerned, in light of admitted advantages derived from similar exchanges of view on NE and other questions in past.

The US ambassador in the United Kingdom, Walter Gifford, to the Secretary of State, London, 20 January 1951. *Foreign Relations of the United States, 1951*, Vol. IV, pp. 894–9.

3.2 Unique but not affectionate: Dean Acheson's view

Dean Acheson, US Secretary of State, gives his views in his memoirs on the nature of the special relationship, noting that it was unique but not always affectionate. Pro-British himself, he nevertheless objects to the existence of a paper proclaiming the special nature of the relationship, for if publicised it would prejudice American relations with other allies.

The latter of these special relationships had created a problem for me almost on the moment of my arrival in London. It took the form of a paper on the special nature of Anglo-American relations that had come out of staff talks between some of my colleagues and Foreign Office officials while I had been in Paris. My immediate and intense displeasure with this document caused its origin to become obscure. It was not the origin that bothered me, but the fact that the wretched paper existed. In the hands of troublemakers it could stir up no end of hullabaloo, both domestic and international, within the alliance. Of course a unique relation existed between Britain and America – our common language and history insured that. But unique did not mean affectionate. We had fought England as an enemy as often as we had fought by her side as an ally. The very ease of communication caused as many quarrels as understandings. Mayor Thompson of Chicago had found the key to success at the polls in his proclaimed eagerness to 'hit King George on the snout'. Before Pearl Harbor, Communists and 'America Firsters' had joined in condemning Britain's 'imperialist' war. Sentiment was reserved for our 'oldest ally', France.

My own attitude had long been, and was known to have been, pro-British. At the beginning of the Roosevelt administrations, I had urged F.D.R. to relieve Britain of the intolerable and impossible burden of repaying the war debts of 1914–18. In 1939–40 I had preached that the renewal of the European Civil War involved us, and I played a part in the destroyers-for-bases deal that followed Dunkirk. My annoyance with the staff paper produced in London was not caused by doubt about the genuineness of the special relationship, or about the real identity of British and American interests in Europe and elsewhere, however diverse they might appear to particular individuals or governments at the moment. This had been true since Canning had supported the Monroe Doctrine against the Holy Alliance, and Britain after wavering swung to the northern side in our Civil War, while Napoleon III occupied Mexico. My annoyance came from the stupidity of writing about a special relationship, which could only increase suspicion among our allies of secret plans and purposes which they did not share and would not approve, and would give the Mayor Thompsons, McCarthys, McCarrans, and Jenners proof that the State Department was the tool of a foreign power. So all copies of the paper that could be found were collected and burned, and my colleagues, after a thorough dressing-down for their naiveté, were urged to channel their sentimental impulses into a forthcoming speech of mine before the Society of Pilgrims, which by tradition was granted dispensation for expressions of this sort.

Memoirs of Dean Acheson, Secretary of State during the Truman administration. Dean Acheson, *Present at the Creation. My Years in the State Department* (London: Hamish Hamilton, 1970), pp. 387–8.

3.3 A covert relationship: the British view

Discussing the state of the Anglo-American relationship, senior Foreign Office officials show sensitivity to the American desire to maintain it on a covert basis. They also refer to tensions in the relationship.

At the request of Sir Oliver Franks, Sir W. Strang held a meeting on March 20th with him, Sir R. Makins and Sir P. Dixon, at which the

Ambassador raised the broad question of our future relationship with the USA.

Sir O. Franks explained that a series of recent developments had gone far towards leading the Americans to re-establish the old partnership relationship at least on a covert basis. Chief among these developments had been our rearmament programme, our ready response to the American request for a British contribution to the forces in Korea and the fine fighting quality of our forces there, the fact that we were now not receiving Marshall Aid, and finally the exposition of the British point of view by Sir G. Jebb. The question in the Ambassador's mind was whether we ought to work towards converting this covert relationship of partnership into an overt partnership, possibly on the basis of an overt Anglo-American–French relationship. He was not confident that we should be able to do so. The Americans, while showing greater readiness to treat us behind closed doors as equal partners, might find difficulty in openly acknowledging the relationship. Some of the factors he had mentioned were however favourable, in particular the fact that we were no longer petitioners and the Americans donors in the matter of aid.

Sir R. Makins doubted whether it was possible to accept the view that the Americans were now treating us on a partnership basis, even of a covert character. For instance, there was a number of current cases in which they were behaving in an inconsiderate and unco-operative way. In his view, we could expect this attitude to persist and even to increase as the American rearmament programme got under way, since, although Great Britain no doubt expected to speak with greater authority as her own strength increased, American strength would increase much faster and in a few years the disparity in the strengths of the two countries would be even greater than now.

Sir P. Dixon thought that however much the Americans might be prepared to treat us as equals in isolated cases, their general attitude remained that of the strong big brother who in the last resort had the power of decision. This attitude seemed to permeate Anglo-American relations generally. He also had the uncomfortable feeling that the United States Government were not taking us into their confidence in regard to their long term plans. It might sound farfetched but it was not altogether unlikely that the American grand strategy might be based on a conception of strategic air offensive launched from island and forward bases. This would not necessarily suit us at all.

Sir W. Strang thought that there might be something in the theory that the Americans were concealing their long term aims from us. Their behaviour created serious difficulties for the Government in the domestic sphere.

Sir O. Franks doubted whether any long term secret American policy existed. He did not think that policy was made that way in the American administration. It was much more a question of *ad hoc* decisions worked out under the stress of American domestic policies. At the same time he was far from denying that a sentiment did exist in the American administration that the power of decision rested with them. They were constitutionally prone to overlook the reaction of foreign countries.

The meeting then turned to consider what tactics might be adopted in order to assert ourselves more effectively with the Americans. It was generally agreed that we had few economic arrows in our quiver. Sir P. Dixon suggested that we might from time to time make use of appeals of an emotional or sentimental character. Our tendency was to rest our contacts with the Americans on a friendly and intimate basis and not, so to speak, to make scenes with them. Might it sometimes be worth our while to turn awkward and prickly? Sir W. Strang commented that the Fechteler incident, although an accident, had in fact had a remarkable effect on the Americans and there might be something to be said for the technique suggested, provided of course that it carried Parliamentary and public opinion behind it.

It was finally agreed that we were likely to gain more by steadily promoting the partnership relationship with the Americans on a covert basis than by working for the conversion of this relationship into something more overt. It was also thought that, except in specific instances, it would be better not to push too hard the conception of the three Powers – USA, Great Britain and France – working together; we were likely to gain more by maintaining our own special relationship with the USA.

Annexed report, Discussion involving Foreign Office officials, Sir William Strang, Permanent Under-Secretary of State; Sir Pierson Dixon, Deputy Under-Secretary of State; Sir Roger Makins, Deputy Under-Secretary of State; and Sir Oliver Franks, British ambassador to the United States, 20 March 1951. Public Record Office, FO 371/90931.

3.4 The purpose of the special relationship

The newly re-elected Prime Minister Winston Churchill was determined to renew the special relationship he had enjoyed during World War II. In advance of his planned visit to the United States in January 1952, therefore, American officials considered the nature and purpose of the special relationship.

The Nature of the US–UK Relationship

1. We have, in fact, at the present time a special relationship with the U.K. which involves consultation between us on a wide range of matters of joint concern.

2. It can be assumed that one of the major reasons for Churchill's visit is his desire to develop what he regards as a US–UK partnership.

3. It is important for us to consider what we regard as the purpose of this special relationship or partnership with the UK.

(a) There is, of course, the general purpose of maintaining the leadership of the free world in the hands of those closest to us in tradition and outlook. Through our relationship with the UK, we and the British Commonwealth of Nations have been able to maintain such leadership.

(b) Another purpose of our close association is our desire for the use of British bases generally, and specifically the use of British facilities for our strategic air force. The most effective way of assuring that these bases and facilities will be available to us at such time as we may wish to use them will be to secure a concert of views between the two countries.

(c) The other major purpose of our relationship is to make the most effective and efficient use of our respective total capabilities. Here also we require the same objectives, as far as possible, in order to achieve our purpose.

4. In some areas of the world the US carries the major responsibility and therefore exercises the predominant leadership. In Korea, for instance, we would expect the British to support our policies to the greatest possible extent. In Egypt, where the British carry the major responsibility, they would expect the same of us. It is clear that neither country can give a blank check to support the other's policies, but to the extent the alliance or partnership functions successfully the areas of disagreement will be thereby minimized.

5. It is in our interest to take such measures as we can to strengthen the British position generally and in specific areas, so that they can carry out a large share of the overall responsibility.

6. If it develops that the British are not capable of continuing to exercise responsibility in a given area, we will have to decide the strategic importance of the area and whether we will be willing to substitute ourselves (as in the case of Greece), or whether there is some other alternative to British responsibility. Obviously our efforts should be directed toward reducing the number of instances in which British capabilities are unequal to the responsibilities they have undertaken. in [sic] any case, one of the advantages of a partnership is that it can facilitate the shifting of responsibilities to accord with capabilities.

Paper prepared by the Policy Planning Staff, 'Outline for discussion at JCS meeting: US–UK Alliance', Washington, 20 November 1951. *Foreign Relations of the United States, 1951*, Vol. IV, pp. 980–1.

3.5   Anglo-American nuclear collaboration

Following the 1946 McMahon Act, which ended the wartime nuclear collaboration between Britain and the United States, post-war British governments gave a high priority to reopening nuclear cooperation. The first step was taken in 1948 with the so-called Modus Vivendi and was followed by a more significant agreement in 1955. This was an important step towards the full repeal of the McMahon Act in 1958.

The Government of the United Kingdom of Great Britain and Northern Ireland and the Government of the United States of America,

Recognising that their mutual security and defence requires that they be prepared to meet the contingencies of atomic warfare,

Recognising that their common interests will be advanced by the exchange of information pertinent thereto,

Believing that the exchange of such information can be undertaken without threat to the security of either country, and

Taking into consideration the United States Atomic Energy Act of 1954, which was prepared with these purposes in mind.

Agree as follows:

Article I

1. While the United Kingdom and the United States are participating in international arrangements for their mutual defence and security and making substantial and material contribution thereto, each Government will from time to time make available to the other Government atomic information which the Government making such information available deems necessary to:

(a) the development of defence plans;

(b) the training of personnel in the employment of and defence against atomic weapons; and

(c) the evaluation of the capabilities of potential enemies in the employment of atomic weapons.

2. Atomic information which is transferred by either Government pursuant to this agreement shall be used by the other Government exclusively for the preparation and implementation of defence plans in the mutual interests of the two countries.

Article II

1. All transfers of atomic information to the United Kingdom by the United States pursuant to this agreement will be made in compliance with the provisions of the United States Atomic Energy Act of 1954 and any subsequent applicable United States legislation. All transfers of atomic information to the United States by the United Kingdom pursuant to this agreement will be made in compliance with the United Kingdom Official Secrets Acts, 1911–1939, and the United Kingdom Atomic Energy Act of 1946.

2. Under this Agreement there will be no transfers by the United Kingdom or the United States of atomic weapons or special nuclear material, as these terms are defined in Section 11 d. and Section 11 t. of the United States Atomic Energy Act of 1954.

Article III

1. Atomic information made available pursuant to this Agreement shall be accorded full security protection under applicable security arrangements between the United Kingdom and the United States and applicable national legislation and regulations of the two countries. In no case shall either Government maintain security standards for safeguarding atomic information made available pursuant to this Agreement lower than those set forth in the applicable

security arrangements in effect on the date this Agreement comes into force.

2. Atomic information which is exchanged pursuant to this Agreement will be made available through channels existing or hereafter agreed for the exchange of classified defence information between the two Governments.

3. Atomic information received pursuant to this Agreement shall not be transferred by the recipient Government to any unauthorised person or, except as provided in Article V of this Agreement, beyond the jurisdiction of that Government. Each Government may stipulate the degree to which any of the categories of information made available to the other Government pursuant to this Agreement may be disseminated, may specify the categories of persons who may have access to such information, and may impose such other restrictions on the dissemination of such information as it deems necessary.

Article IV
As used in this Agreement, 'atomic information' means:

(a) so far as concerns the information provided by the United States, Restricted Data, as defined in Section II r. of the United States Atomic Energy Act of 1954, which is permitted to be communicated pursuant to the provisions of Section 144 b. of that Act, and information relating primarily to the military utilisation of atomic weapons which has been removed from the Restricted Data category m accordance with the provisions of Section 142 d. of the United States Energy Act of 1954;

(b) so far as concerns the information provided by the United Kingdom, information exchanged under this Agreement which is either classified atomic energy information or other United Kingdom defence information which it is decided to transfer to the United States in pursuance of Article I of this Agreement.

Article V
Nothing herein shall be interpreted or operate as a bar or restriction to consultation and cooperation by the United Kingdom or the United States with other nations or regional organisations in any fields of defence. Neither Government, however, shall communicate atomic information made available by the other Government pursu-

ant to this Agreement to any nation or regional organisation unless the same information has been made available to that nation or regional organisation by the other Government in accordance with its own legislative requirements and except to the extent that such communication is expressly authorised by such other Government.

Article VI
This Agreement shall enter into force on the date on which each Government shall receive from the other Government written notification that it has complied with all statutory and constitutional requirements for the entry into force of such an agreement, and shall remain in effect until terminated by mutual agreement of both Governments.

Agreement between the Government of the United Kingdom of Great Britain and Northern Ireland and the Government of the United States of America for cooperation regarding atomic information for mutual defence purposes. Signed at Washington on 15 June 1955. Reproduced in John Baylis, *Anglo-American Defence Relations 1939–1984. The Special Relationship* (London: Macmillan, second edition, 1984), pp. 85–7.

3.6 Darkening skies: the Suez crisis

The crisis in Anglo-American relations caused by the British intervention in Egypt in 1956 was severe. It disturbed Winston Churchill sufficiently for him to write direct to President Eisenhower counselling the need not to let Suez undermine the relationship.

There is not much left for me to do in this world and I have neither the wish nor the strength to involve myself in the present political stress and turmoil. But I do believe, with unfaltering conviction, that the theme of the Anglo-American alliance is more important today than at any time since the war. You and I had some part in raising it to the plane on which it has stood. Whatever the arguments adduced here and in the United States for or against Anthony's action in Egypt, it will now be an act of folly, on which our whole civilisation may founder, to let events in the Middle East come between us.

There seems to be growing misunderstanding and frustration on both sides of the Atlantic. If they be allowed to develop, the skies will darken and it is the Soviet Union that will ride the storm. We should leave it to the historians to argue the rights and wrongs of all that has happened during the past years. What we must face is that at present these events have left a situation in the Middle East in which spite, envy and malice prevail on the one hand and our friends are beset by bewilderment and uncertainty for the future. The Soviet Union is attempting to move into this dangerous vacuum, for you must have no doubt that a triumph for Nasser would be an even greater triumph for them.

The very survival of all that we believe in may depend on our setting our minds to forestalling them. If we do not take immediate action in harmony, it is no exaggeration to say that we must expect to see the Middle East and the North African coastline under Soviet control and Western Europe placed at the mercy of the Russians. If at this juncture we fail in our responsibility to act positively and fearlessly we shall no longer be worthy of the leadership with which we are entrusted.

I write this letter because I know where your heart lies. You are now the only one who can so influence events both in UNO and the free world as to ensure that the great essentials are not lost in bickerings and pettiness among the nations. Yours is indeed a heavy responsibility and there is no greater believer in your capacity to bear it or well-wisher in your task than your old friend

Winston S. Churchill.

Letter from Winston Churchill to President Eisenhower following the Suez invasion. Harold Macmillan, *Riding the Storm, 1956–1959* (London: Macmillan, 1971), pp. 175–6.

4

Rebuilding the alliance, 1957–59

The Suez crisis of 1956 was a traumatic shock to Britain's great-power pretensions and to its policy of pursuing a 'special relationship' with the United States. Faced with American opposition, the government was forced to back down in humiliating fashion, demonstrating the reality of British dependence on, rather than influence over, the United States. For the French, the lesson of Suez was to seek greater independence and a greater role in Europe. For the British, however, the lesson was the need to develop even closer interdependence with the United States and to avoid the growing integration that was taking place on the Continent at the time. Interdependence became one of the major themes, therefore, in Anglo-American relations in the late 1950s.

Reflecting this theme, from 1957 to 1959, the Macmillan government put considerable effort into re-creating an intimate and harmonious relationship with the United States. Echoing past policy, the Prime Minister believed that Britain could 'play Greece to America's Rome', 'civilising and guiding the immature giant'. This was particularly important, in Macmillan's view, in the nuclear field. At the Bermuda and Washington conferences in 1957 he sought to build on his close wartime friendship with Eisenhower to create a climate of trust at the highest level of government. The renewal of the 'special relationship' which resulted was reflected in the deployment of Thor missiles in Britain, joint strategic planning between the air forces of both countries and the achievement of Britain's long-term objective of seeing the repeal of the 1946 McMahon Act (which had prohibited full nuclear co-operation between the two countries). As a result of the last of these agreements, Britain was to receive preferential treatment in the form of information from the United States on the design and production of nuclear warheads, as well as fissile material. This set the scene for the intimate nuclear relationship which was to follow.

Rebuilding the alliance

4.1   Surviving Suez: repairing the relationship

Ensuring that the special relationship survived the rift caused
by the Suez crisis was a crucial British aim. This paper offers
suggestions on how the British should go about repairing the
damage.

The Gallup poll published on November 10 shows that 45 per cent
of those polled disapproved of the Anglo-French intervention in
Egypt, 31 per cent approved and 24 per cent did not know. These
rather surprising figures mean that opinion in the States may not be
much more divided than it is here. It also means that, as the
Administration and the press and radio seem to be much more
solidly against us than these figures would indicate, our campaign
ought to be concentrated on a comparatively narrow target.

2. We have reason to believe, however, that, sore though the
Administration may be, it too is divided and uncertain in its attitude. Furthermore, the American Foreign Service staff in Europe, so
we have learned from a good source, are puzzled and dissatisfied by
the lack of clear guidance from Washington about the State Department's attitude. All this seems to show that our best hope, apart
from the vigorous campaign which BIS are doubtless already conducting right through America, is to concentrate on securing a
favourable lead from those at the top in Washington:

(a) President Eisenhower's personal prestige being what it is, a
clear lead from him towards restoring so far possible the previous
intimacy and confidence will be more important than anything else
we can hope to achieve. Our best means of getting him to give such
a lead lies in the Prime Minister's and the Secretary of State's
personal contacts with him while they are in America.

(b) A frank approach should be made by Sir H. Caccia, at the
highest possible level, to use the present crisis as a means of thrash-
ing out the fundamental problems underlying the Anglo-American
alliance which the present crisis has brought to the top, and which
we have never had to face up to before. He might take the line that
in both countries perhaps too much has been taken for granted in
their relationship. We must recognize that it is inevitable that between two great, independent allies a situation like the present one
will arise from time to time. It nearly arose two years ago over
Quemoy; only then the Americans would have been in the dock. We
must therefore reach agreement on some fundamental facts about

85

our alliance if it is to continue. We are glad to see that the American Government still intend that the alliance should remain a pillar of their foreign policy in spite of the strong feelings which have been aroused. But the whole episode shows that in an alliance of this kind each party must retain its independence and, as a natural corollary, if the alliance is to survive each party must also conserve sufficient confidence and loyalty in the actions of the other to prevent a break-up of the alliance when urgent events demand immediate action in a part of the world where only one party is in a position to take it. Thus, in the Middle East, at the outbreak of the Egyptian–Israel conflict our interests were vitally involved; fighting had to be stopped as soon as possible; we knew from bitter experience that even unanimous resolutions by the Security Council could have no effect and that unanimity could not be achieved anyway; our forces were available; the Americans were intimately involved in their election. Had we received from the Americans the measure of confidence and support which our hitherto intimate relationship would presuppose, the operation would probably have been more successful than it has been and Nasser might well by now have been out of power and the whole Middle East situation transformed. We should hope the United States could count on the necessary loyalty from us should they ever be involved in a similar crisis in another part of the world. An approach on these lines might conclude with pressure for general guidance to be given so far as possible through the State Department calculated to heal the breach, to recognize frankly that a situation of this kind cannot be avoided from time to time in such a peculiar relationship as exists between the two main, and indeed all the, great English-speaking peoples, and to appeal to all concerned to sink their personal feelings in recognition of the obvious fact that whatever may have happened in the past it is still in the interests of America herself and the West as a whole that the United States/United Kingdom alliance should survive intact.

Memorandum by H. A. A. Hankey, head of American Department, Foreign Office, 'Restoration of Confidence in United States/United Kingdom Relations', 15 November 1956. Public Record Office, FO 371/120342.

4.2 'The end of an era': the special relationship after Suez

In this telegram to the Foreign Secretary, Selwyn Lloyd, the British ambassador in Washington, Sir Harold Caccia, discusses whether the nature of Britain's relationship with the United States has changed in the aftermath of the Suez crisis, as suggested by his predecessor, Sir Roger Makins. The trust and sentiment created by the war years had disappeared. He believes the relationship should be put on a new footing and urges the government to be patient.

Sir Roger Makins concluded his valedictory despatch of the 27th of November with some particularly interesting remarks on Anglo-United States relations and he quoted the prophetic words of his Canadian colleague that his departure marked 'the end of an era'. It did and we should ask ourselves, 'what ended' on the 29th of October when we decided to go it alone in the Middle East without the Americans.

2. Was it the general feeling towards the British people in the United States which Sir Roger Makins reported to have improved steadily? I should say not. In so far as it is possible to talk about the United States as a whole, all our evidence goes to show that the generally friendly feeling towards Britain has not fundamentally changed for the worse. . . .

6. If the American public has not changed, has the Administration? Not, apparently, in its aim of maintaining the United Kingdom–United States alliance. From the beginning the President said his intention was to strengthen it.

7. Yet something has ended, and, in my view, three things: first, the sentimental attachment, in the Administration, created by our wartime experience as crusaders in arms; second, the innate trust in our longer experience of international affairs and our reputation for dependability; third, our largely unquestioned right to a special position.

8. Ever since the beginning of World War II, America has taken an increasingly active part in world affairs. We have profited both from sentiment and reputation for judgement and trustworthiness to build an exclusive machine of co-operation which has enabled us to exercise far more influence on the United States Government than our physical strength alone would have warranted. There have been setbacks, largely the result of Congressional action (*e.g.* the McMahon Act); but, broadly speaking, we had continued to perfect this co-operation until very recently.

9. Now the position is different. I doubt whether we lose much by the snapping of the sentimental ties with the Administration

alone. It is true that consultation will become more difficult with them, and we shall not easily know how much we are being taken into their confidence. But in any case the hard-headed businessmen who lead the present Administration would hardly be moved to do anything which they did not calculate was in their own interests, sentiment or no sentiment. Indeed, I doubt whether that would be within their interpretation of what was their duty to their country or party.

10. On the other hand, I do think that, where our judgements differ, we shall find it much harder to convince them that our view is right and therefore in their own interests. This goes not only for the Administration, but also for the country at large. To them the acid test of our action on the 30th of October was success and rightly or wrongly they do not think that it succeeded. . . .

14. I assume it to be our object to re-establish our relations on their previous footing and to recover all of our special position. While the Communist threat remains, nothing else makes sense, in dealing with a country whose power is likely to increase in relation to our own.

15. We should not find any insuperable difficulties in attaining this objective. The Americans will remain convinced that Communism is their principal enemy and challenge. They will need Allies and on the whole they like doing business with us, provided that we talk in plain and blunt business terms. We should avoid at all costs appealing to emotion and old associations when doing business. We should let them do that, if they want to; and sooner or later they probably will, at least out of business hours.

16. We should not run after them. We should not expect the American constitutional machine to be able to do things for which it was not constructed. We should not expect more of the American President and his Secretary of State than hard experience has taught us they are able to perform.

17. Mr Dulles has asked us to be patient. We will certainly have to be that. I hope that we shall also be plain spoken; that we shall show that we are dealing with our problems, particularly our financial problems, realistically; and that we shall ask for no favours. I hope also that we shall for the time being avoid trying to do business by dramatic means, such as meetings at high levels. I would far rather leave it to the Americans to suggest such meetings than that we should propose them. In any case, there will be a number of

opportunities during the year for you, Sir, to talk to the United States Secretary of State directly at meetings of NATO and SEATO. . . .

19. I therefore see no reason for despondency. The Administration, with whom our chief quarrel lies, is mainly composed of old men. It will disappear before too long, and will in the meantime be diluted or strengthened by new blood. In the lower levels, feelings have been less ruffled, and habits of co-operation and trust have been fairly well implanted and in all the Service and technical fields are now working just as before. Finally, there is no other country with world interests which could take our place as a 'chosen ally'; and most countries, like individuals, feel the need of a confidant.

20. This may take time and we shall not help ourselves by angling for favours. We must also profess to appear to be a logical and inescapable necessity. If we try to thrust ourselves into the councils of the Administration for reason of prestige, we shall merely produce the same pitiful impression the French have so often made.

21. In a sentence the new era of United Kingdom–United States relations should hold no terrors so long as we keep and use our heads.

22. I am sending a copy of this despatch to the United Kingdom High Commissioner, Ottawa.

AU 1051/53, 'The Present State of Anglo-United States Relations', Sir Harold Caccia to Mr Selwyn Lloyd, Washington, 28 December 1956 (received 1 January 1957). Public Record Office, PREM 11/2189.

4.3   Rekindling the relationship: the Bermuda summit, 1957

The new Prime Minister, Harold Macmillan, sought to rebuild relations with the United States, and the Bermuda summit of March 1957 offered an early opportunity to make progress. An important outcome of the meeting was the agreement in principle to make US Thor missiles available to Britain. This agreement in the defence field symbolised a new period of even closer Anglo-American relations.

The President of the United States and the Prime Minister of the United Kingdom, assisted by the United States Secretary of State and the British Foreign Secretary and other advisers, have exchanged views during the past three days on many subjects of mutual concern. They have conducted their discussions with the freedom and frankness permitted to old friends. In a world of growing interdependence they recognize their responsibility to seek to coordinate their foreign policies in the interests of peace with justice.

Among the subjects discussed in detail were common problems concerning the Middle East, Far East, NATO, European Cooperation, the reunification of Germany, and Defense.

The President and the Prime Minister are well satisfied with the results of this Conference, at which a number of decisions have been taken. They intend to continue the exchange of views so well begun.

The agreements and conclusions reached on the main subjects discussed at the Conference are annexed.

Annex I

1. Recognition of the value of collective security pacts within the framework of the United Nations, and the special importance of NATO for both countries as the cornerstone of their policy in the West.

2. Reaffirmation of common interest in the development of European unity within the Atlantic Community.

3. Agreement on the importance of closer association of the United Kingdom with Europe.

4. Agreement on the benefits likely to accrue for European and world trade from the plans for the common market and the Free Trade Area, provided they do not lead to a high tariff bloc; and on the desirability that all countries should pursue liberal trade policies.

5. Willingness of the United States, under authority of the recent Middle East joint resolution, to participate actively in the work of the Military Committee of the Baghdad Pact.

6. Reaffirmation of intention to support the right of the German people to early reunification in peace and freedom.

7. Sympathy for the people of Hungary; condemnation of repressive Soviet policies towards the peoples of Eastern Europe, and of Soviet defiance of relevant United Nations resolutions.

8. Agreement on the need for the speedy implementation of recent resolutions of the United Nations General Assembly on the Gaza Strip and the Gulf of Aqaba.

9. Agreement on the importance of compliance both in letter and in spirit with the Security Council Resolution of October 13 concerning the Suez Canal, and on support for the efforts of the Secretary-General to bring about a settlement in accordance with its provisions.

10. Joint declaration on policy regarding nuclear tests (see Annex II).

11. Agreement in principle that, in the interest of mutual defense and mutual economy, certain guided missiles will be made available by the United States for use by British forces . . .

Communiqué on the talks between President Eisenhower and Prime Minister Harold Macmillan, 24 March 1957. *US Department of State Bulletin*, 8 April 1957, p. 561. Quoted in Ian S. McDonald, *Anglo-American Relations since the Second World War* (London: David & Charles, 1974), pp. 132–4.

4.4   America expects: US objectives for the United Kingdom

This memorandum shows the mood of the United States after Suez. Preferring now to deal with Britain (and France) through the machinery of NATO, American officials spell out their hard-headed expectations of the United Kingdom.

The Suez Affair caused the United States to review its relationship with United Kingdom and with France and as a consequence tripartite consultation was quietly abandoned and replaced by bilateral consultation within the NATO framework.

The United States has the following objectives with respect to the United Kingdom:

1. To encourage the United Kingdom to maintain a substantial military effort.

2. The United States would expect prompt assistance from the United Kingdom in the event of war with the Soviet Union.

3. We expect continued support from the United Kingdom in our dealings with the Soviet Union and the Communist bloc.

4. We expect British support on such questions as Disarmament, European security and German reunification.

5. We would like to see British support for European integration and some association with the organizations developing on the continent in the field of integration.

6. We support the maintenance of the British position in the Persian Gulf, but we would hope that they would refrain from the use of force.

7. We seek continued British support for the UN Moratorium on the question of Chinese representation.

8. In the event of a resumption of Communist aggression in Korea or elsewhere in the Far East, we would hope for British support.

9. The United States continues to support the Commonwealth and the United Kingdom position within it.

Northern European Chiefs of Mission Conference, London, 19–21 September 1957. Summary of Proceedings. *Foreign Relations of the United States, 1955-1957*, Vol. IV, p. 610.

4.5 The Declaration of Common Purpose

One of the most prized objectives of British foreign and defence policy since 1946 was to restore the collaboration on atomic energy between Britain and the United States, severed by the McMahon Act. Late in 1957, shortly after the Soviet Union launched Sputnik and ushered in a new technological intensity to the Cold War, Macmillan and Eisenhower met and the US President agreed to recommend to Congress revision of the Atomic Energy Act to allow collaboration once more.

We have met together as trusted friends of many years who have come to head the Governments of our respective countries. These two countries have close and historic ties, just as each has intimate and unbreakable ties with other free countries.

Recognising that only in the establishment of a just peace can the deepest aspirations of free peoples be realised, the guiding purpose of our deliberations has been the determination of how best to utilise the moral, intellectual and material strength of our two nations in the performance of our full share of those tasks that will more surely and promptly bring about conditions in which peace can prosper. One of these tasks is to provide adequate security for the free world.

The free nations possess vast assets, both material and moral. These in the aggregate are far greater than those of the Communist world. We do not ignore the fact that the Soviet rulers can achieve formidable material accomplishments by concentrating upon selected developments and scientific applications, and by yoking their people to this effort. Despotisms have often been able to produce spectacular monuments. But the price has been heavy.

For all peoples yearn for intellectual and economic freedom, the more so if from their bondage they see others manifest the glory of freedom. Even despots are forced to permit freedom to grow by an evolutionary process, or in time there will be violent revolution. This principle is inexorable in its operation.

Already it has begun to be noticeable even within the Soviet orbit. If the free nations are steadfast, and if they utilise their resources in harmonious co-operation, the totalitarian menace that now confronts them will in good time recede.

In order, however, that freedom may be secure and show its good fruits, it is necessary first that the collective military strength of the free nations should be adequate to meet the threat against them. At the same time, the aggregate of the free world's military expenditure must be kept within limits compatible with individual freedom. Otherwise we risk losing the very liberties which we seek to defend.

These ideas have been the central theme of our conversations which, in part, were participated in by M. Spaak, the Secretary-General of NATO.

In application of these ideas, and as an example which we believe can and should spread among the nations of the free world, we reached the following understanding:

1. The arrangements which the nations of the free world have made for collective defence and mutual help are based on the recognition that the concept of national self-sufficiency is now out of date. The countries of the free world are interdependent, and only in genuine partnership, by combining their resources and sharing tasks in many fields, can progress and safety be found. For our part, we have agreed that our two countries will henceforth act in accordance with this principle.

2. Our representatives to the North Atlantic Council will urge an enlarged Atlantic effort in scientific research and development in support of greater collective security and the expansion of current

activities of the task force working in this field under the Council's decision of last December.

3. The President of the United States will request the Congress to amend the Atomic Energy Act as may be necessary and desirable to permit of close and fruitful collaboration of scientists and engineers of Great Britain, the United States, and other friendly countries.

4. The disarmament proposals made by the western representatives on the disarmament sub-committee in London and approved by all members of NATO are a sound and fair basis for an agreement which would reduce the threat of war and the burden of armaments. The indefinite accumulation of nuclear weapons and the indiscriminate spreading of the capacity to produce them should be prevented. Effective and reliable inspection must be an integral part of initial steps in the control and reduction of armaments.

5. In the absence of such disarmament as we are seeking, international security now depends not merely upon local defensive shields but upon reinforcing them with the deterrent and retaliatory power of nuclear weapons. So long as the threat of international Communism persists, the free nations must be prepared to provide for their own security. Because the free world measures are purely defensive and for security against outside threat, the period for which they must be maintained cannot be foreseen.

It is not within the capacity of each nation acting alone to make itself fully secure. Only collective measures will suffice. These should preferably be found by implementing the provisions of the United Nations Charter for forces at the disposal of the Security Council.

But if the Soviet Union persists in nullifying these provisions by veto, there must otherwise be developed a greater sense of community security. The framework for this exists in collective defence arrangements now participated in by nearly 50 free nations, as authorised by the Charter. All members of this community, and other free nations which so desire, should possess more knowledge of the total capabilities of security that are in being and in prospect.

There should also be provided greater opportunity to assure that this power will in fact be available in case of need for their common security, and that it will not be misused by any nation for purposes other than individual and collective self-defence, as authorised by the Charter of the United Nations.

For our part we regard our possession of nuclear weapons power as in trust for the defence of the free world.

6. Our two countries plan to discuss these ideas with all of their security partners. So far as the North Atlantic Alliance is concerned, the December meeting may, perhaps, be given a special character in this respect. This has been discussed with the Secretary-general of NATO, M. Spaak.

7. In addition to the North Atlantic Treaty, the South-East Asia Collective Defence Treaty, the Bagdad Pact and other security arrangements constitute a strong bulwark against aggression in the various treaty areas.

There are also vitally important relationships of a somewhat different character. There is the Commonwealth; and in the western hemisphere, the Organisation of American States. There are individual mutual defence agreements and arrangements to which the United States is a party.

8. We recognise that our collective security efforts must be supported and reinforced by co-operative economic action. The present offers a challenging opportunity for improvement of trading conditions and the expansion of trade throughout the free world. It is encouraging that plans are developing for a European free trade area in association with the European common market. We recognise that especially in the less developed countries there should be a steady and significant increase in standards of living and economic development.

9. We took note of specific factors in the ideological struggle in which we are engaged. In particular, we were in full agreement that:

Soviet threats directed against Turkey give solemn significance to the obligation, under Article 5 of the North Atlantic Treaty, to consider an armed attack against any member of the alliance as an attack against all;

The reunification of Germany by free elections is essential. At the Geneva conference of 1955, Mr Khrushchev and Mr Bulganin agreed to this with us and our French allies. Continued repudiation of that agreement and continued suppression of freedom in eastern Europe undermine international confidence and perpetuate an injustice, a folly, and a danger.

The President and the Prime Minister believe that the understandings they have reached will be increasingly effective as they become more widespread between the free nations. By coordinating the strength of all free peoples, safety can be assured, the danger of Communist despotism will in due course be dissipated, and a just and lasting peace will be achieved.

President Eisenhower and Harold Macmillan, Declaration of Common Purpose, 25 October 1957. *Commonwealth Survey*, 29 October 1957, pp. 943–4. Quoted in Ian S. McDonald, *Anglo-American Relations since the Second World War* (London: David & Charles, 1974), pp. 138–42.

4.6 'The implications of interdependence'

In this paper British planners debate the implications of interdependence in security terms with the United States. A balanced attempt is made to assess the benefits and drawbacks of a situation where each country has to rely on the other for important aspects of its defence.

The effects of Anglo-American interdependence on the long-term interests of the United Kingdom

A. *Definition*
Interdependence is both a fact and a policy. It is a fact not only in Anglo-American relations but in the mutual relations of all non-Communist countries. There are two sides to this. The first is that all sovereign states have always been to some extent interdependent, e.g. in trade, and that the growing complexity of international life is rapidly diminishing the extent to which they can act without affecting and being affected by the actions of other powers. The second is that the present communist threat is such that all non-communist countries are dependent upon each other's military, political and economic strength in order to resist it. The extent to which the second point is recognised varies from country to country, and, with it, the willingness of each Government to adopt interdependence as a policy.

2. To adopt interdependence as a policy is to recognise interdependence as a fact and to decide to promote it as the only means of progress and safety. It involves taking a process which is happening anyway and turning it to advantage by extending, accelerating and

proclaiming it. It was this decision that the United States and the United Kingdom Government took at the Washington talks in October, 1957. . . .

C. *The results of the Washington talks*

4. In the present world situation, the United States and the United Kingdom have . . . been dependent upon each other for some time. To some extent this dependence has been one-sided, for at bottom we have needed the United States more than they us, but the balance has been at least partially restored by Russian technological advances which have made American bases in Britain (and elsewhere) essential to the home defence of the United States. Since interdependence was already so far advanced, what changes have the Washington talks in fact brought about?

5. The answer is, at least superficially, a greater recognition by the Americans of the fact of interdependence and a greater willingness to adopt it as a policy. The practical results have been:

(a) The establishment of the Working Groups, covering defence, political, economic and information problems. There now exists, for the first time since the Second World War, machinery for the continuous joint examination of certain international problems, which can be extended to deal with new problems as they arise (as has already been done in the case of Indonesia). Through it we should be able to ensure:

(i) That we always know what American policy on any major problem is (with the possible exception of the Far East and military strategy in general);

(ii) that our views are known to them;

(iii) that we have a chance of influencing American policy at its formative stages.

(b) The drawing up of plans for the pooling of brains and resources in the field of defence and for the allocation of research and production tasks.

(c) The United States undertaking to seek certain amendments to the Atomic Energy Act.

(d) The engagement of United States interest in the defence of Hong Kong. . . .

D. *The implications of interdependence*

(a)   THE ADVANTAGES

7. There is no doubt that in the main the United Kingdom stands to gain greatly from this process.

(i) The United States is so much the most powerful nation in the Western camp that our ability to have our way in the world depends more than anything else upon our influence upon her to act in conformity with our interests. Against her opposition we can do very little (e.g. Suez) and our need for American support is a fact which we cannot ignore. It follows that our policy should certainly be to put ourselves in the position in which we can elicit from her the greatest possible support. The policy of Anglo-American interdependence is well designed to achieve this aim.

(ii) The fact that we are seen to be in close collaboration with the United States enhances our influence and capabilities. Provided that we appear to be playing the part of an influential friend and not that of a subservient minion, governments, which might on the basis of our material power alone be inclined to discount our importance, will be more anxious to gain our good opinion and more willing to listen to what we say.

(iii) It is only to the good that there should be a joint Anglo-American policy in, e.g. the Middle East, instead of two policies pulling in different directions. This is true even if coordination means subordinating our own interests at least in non-essential matters; the force for stability and security which a joint policy will provide is well worth *minor* sacrifices.

(iv) On the defence side, we stand to gain considerably from American technical information and resources.

(v) Interdependence in many cases means that the money we spend and the effort we make produce very much more valuable results. If we act alone our efforts and resources may not bring commensurate benefits. Acting with the United States we far more often get full value or even more for our effort.

(b)   POSSIBLE DISADVANTAGES

8. There are however a number of possible and actual difficulties to be overcome. They may be divided into two classes:

The difficulties of keeping up the momentum of interdependence and the dangers of its abandonment by either side;

The dangers of becoming or seeming to become an American satellite.

(i) KEEPING UP THE MOMENTUM

9. The policy of Anglo-American interdependence to some extent goes against the grain for both sides. Consultation is irksome and cooperation often inconvenient. The administrative machine in Washington is unused and ill-adapted in many respects to cooperation of any kind. The natural tendency of all new initiatives, which involve extra work, to flag and then die, will therefore be aggravated. It will be of the greatest importance to prevent this happening, because if it does we shall continue to incur the unpopularity which is bound to result in some quarters from the belief that we are in a special relationship with the United States, while ceasing to enjoy the benefits. We shall thus get the worst of both worlds.

10. How is this tendency to be overcome? The first way is to keep the machinery of consultation continuously fed with a constant flow of subjects for discussion and to ensure as far as possible that the most important subjects are properly dealt with by the Working Groups. For many reasons there is a strong tendency, when a crisis arises, to deal with it *ad hoc* and at the highest level and to neglect the permanent machinery (which is at a lower level and relatively slow in performance). This is often necessary. But, since the continued existence of this particular machinery is for us an important end in itself, it will be desirable to let it deal with as many of the real crises as possible, and, where other treatment is necessary, to return the handling of the problem to it at the earliest possible moment. This involves foresight and planning.

11. The second way is to extend the machinery so as to make consultation a habitual reaction to any problem in the widest possible circle within both governmental machines. In particular it would be useful to do this in the case of Far Eastern questions. It will therefore be valuable to introduce new subjects for discussion, not only in order to coordinate policy upon them but also to introduce new people to consultation. In addition to civil consultation between the Embassy and the State Department, it might be possible and would surely be desirable to introduce military consultation and joint planning. This is one of the subjects where we remain ignorant of United States thinking, although military planning in the nuclear age cannot be divorced from political planning.

12. It will also be desirable to wind up Working Groups as soon as they stop being useful. We should ensure that the pattern of our consultation changes with the world situation.

(ii) THE DANGERS OF ABANDONMENT

13. However firmly the present administrations of the United States of America and the United Kingdom are committed to the policy of interdependence, there is always a risk that their successors may wish to abandon it. It is not necessary here to consider the position of the United Kingdom if such a decision came from this side, for it would presumably only be taken if it were compatible with the national interest in the circumstances of the time. But it is possible that a United States administration hostile or indifferent to this country might at some time come to power, or the development of inter-continental missiles might conceivably lead the United States to adopt a policy of 'Fortress America'. A United States withdrawal from Anglo-American cooperation would have serious consequences for this country.

14. Their seriousness would depend upon the extent to which the process of interlocking had gone. It must be recognised that in a partnership between two Powers of very unequal resources, it is far more serious for the weaker than for the stronger if the partnership comes to an end. The United States can, so to speak, underwrite the commitment which cooperation with us represents for them, while the United Kingdom cannot. To take an extreme and imaginary example: if it were decided that the United States should provide all the nuclear and the United Kingdom all the conventional forces of the partnership, and the partnership were later dissolved, the United States would be able to turn back and recreate their own conventional forces, but it is doubtful whether the United Kingdom could then similarly recreate her nuclear capacity. Further, it appears at present that the United States will not in fact, to any significant degree, carry through the joint allotment of tasks to a point at which any important task is our responsibility; they are likely to maintain the full apparatus required by an independent country. The United Kingdom in all probability cannot afford to do this – indeed one of the principal advantages of interdependence from our point of view is that we shall not have to. This consideration has a wide application; it could, for example, apply also to overseas commitments. If we hand

over any of them, e.g. the defence of Hong Kong, to the United States, it is highly doubtful whether we could ever take them over again.

15. Two conclusions may be drawn from this. In the first place, it should be our constant effort to increase the degree of Anglo-American interlocking in those fields where American withdrawal would not be highly damaging, in order to make it as difficult as possible for any future American administration to go into reverse. These fields would seem to be those of policy planning and co-ordination. In the second place, we should be careful not to carry interlocking too far in those fields essential to our interests in which American withdrawal would leave us helpless. These fields would include our essential interests overseas, and our basic capacity to defend the United Kingdom.

(iii) THE DANGERS OF BECOMING AN AMERICAN SATELLITE

16. The United Kingdom, in its relatively weak position, is already greatly dependent upon United States support. It would be surprising if the United States did not exact a price for this support, and to some extent she does so. The policy of interdependence will necessarily increase the extent to which the United States can make us pay for this support, for the more we rely upon them, the more we shall be hurt if they withhold it.

17. Too much need not be made of this since it does not seem at present that there are many important fields in which American and British policies conflict and in which we might be forced to give way. Indeed, if there had been many such cases, the Declaration of Common Purpose could hardly have been issued, but the question may arise e.g. over Buraimi. Unfortunately it is improbable that we shall be able to bring similar pressure to bear on the United States although to some extent as interdependence grows the Americans will find themselves in positions where a withdrawal on our side could cause them serious inconvenience and embarrassment, if no more.

18. This aspect of Anglo-American relations will require careful watching. But there is no reason to doubt that we shall be able to hold our own when Anglo-American interests diverge, provided that:

(a) we place no hostages in their hands which in the last resort are vital to us;

(b) we make clear to the United States, whenever necessary, that interdependence is not so much our prime interest that we are prepared to sacrifice all the rest to it.

(iv) THE DANGER OF EXCLUSIVE ANGLO-AMERICAN INTERDEPENDENCE

19. Since our interests and those of the United States do not in fact much diverge, there is relatively little danger of a situation arising in which we have to choose between breaking away and becoming an American satellite. But the danger of seeming to become one is greater. If we give this impression we shall suffer on two counts:

(a) we shall damage our relations with our other friends, particularly the Europeans;

(b) we shall lose influence with the Americans themselves, because this depends upon the extent of our influence elsewhere. . . .

25. . . . our influence with the Americans will, among other things, depend upon the extent of our influence elsewhere and . . . we shall escape appearing to become a satellite only by putting ourselves in a position to lead and represent our other friends. Such a position on our part, moreover, would surely be welcome to the United States of America. Indeed the Americans have always welcomed moves designed to draw the United Kingdom closer to Europe, and would have liked them to have been more numerous and far-reaching than has been possible hitherto. The dangers of Anglo-American exclusiveness indeed do not derive from the American attitude to interdependence at all. Provided they are convinced that our desire is genuinely to bring the free world together along agreed Anglo-American lines, and not to improve our own position by playing off our various friends against each other, they are likely to welcome any moves which will improve our own general prestige and influence and thus enable us to make our *distinctive* contribution to the unity of the free world.

(c) *Conclusion*

26. If the above analysis is broadly accepted, it appears that one of the United Kingdom's principal problems in the context of interdependence, both in the long and in the short term, is to avoid too much the appearance of becoming an American satellite and to strengthen rather than weaken our ties with our other friends – i.e.

to play an active part in the widening of interdependence. How is this to be done?

27. The immediate and perhaps the main problem is in Europe. We have to convince the Europeans, and particularly the French, that we are not tiptoeing out of Europe, and that we are not proposing to desert their interests in order to consolidate our position as America's junior partner. The two principal bones of contention at present are the withdrawal of forces from Germany and the Free Trade Area. It is difficult to assess their comparative importance in European eyes, but it seems clear that it is necessary to examine what concessions the United Kingdom can afford to make in order to strengthen a position in Europe which has deteriorated badly over the last few months. It is fair to say that the maintenance of British forces on the Continent and a firm attitude towards Russian proposals for the neutralisation of Europe, together with our willingness to meet the interests of the Six in the Free Trade Area negotiations are the touchstone by which our attitude to Europe will be tested in European eyes during the next few months. . . .

30. In conclusion, it must be stated that the policy of interdependence probably cannot, if the United Kingdom's essential interests are to be preserved, be a way of saving money. In the first place it is improbable that the division between the United States and the United Kingdom of different tasks in defence research and production will result in the final balance in savings for the United Kingdom. It may enable us to do what would otherwise have been impossible, but ambitious joint programmes are bound to be increasingly expensive for both sides. On the other hand, interdependence should mean that often our money is well spent and that the total harvest from the joint effort is a good one and may be greater than would have been the case if we and the Americans devoted money and effort separately and without agreement or coordination.

31. Secondly, we cannot expect the United States to finance (as opposed to take over) British commitments overseas or to shoulder the entire burden e.g. of 'containment plus'; it will continue to be necessary to prime the pump of American expenditure. Thirdly, even if it were possible to hand over our commitments, it would in many cases be undesirable to do so . . . . Last, and most important, interdependence, so far from reducing our expenditure, is likely to

103

force us to increase it in order to maintain our own status, though this again is subject to the possibility that interdependence, well operated, should bring for both results in return for our expenditure of money and effort. If we are to avoid sinking into insignificance as a seeming instrument of United States policy, we must keep our closer relationship with the Americans in step with a closer relationship with our other friends. The establishment of this closer relationship will in many cases depend upon the expenditure of money and effort (e.g. in making concessions over support costs in Germany), and there will be a resulting strain upon our economy.

32. This is not to say that the United Kingdom cannot afford interdependence. On the contrary, it is perhaps the only policy to hold out hopes of the stability and security without which we cannot prosper. It is a necessary investment and though it will not be cheap or easy to make, it could if we play it right bring us great benefits.

SC (58) 8, Steering Committee, 'Planning paper on interdependence', 27 January 1958. Public Record Office, FO 371/132330.

4.7 Exchanging atomic information: the repeal of the McMahon Act

After the amendment of the American legislation which forbade the sharing of nuclear secrets with other countries, Britain was able once more to receive atomic energy information from the United States. The two states were therefore free to conclude the following major agreement which made nuclear co-operation a core element of the 'special relationship'.

The Government of the United Kingdom of Great Britain and Northern Ireland on its own behalf and on behalf of the United Kingdom Atomic Energy Authority and the Government of the United States of America,

Considering that their mutual security and defense require that they be prepared to meet the contingencies of atomic warfare;

Considering that both countries have made substantial progress in the development of atomic weapons;

104

Rebuilding the alliance

Considering that they are participating together in international arrangements pursuant to which they are making substantial and material contributions to their mutual defense and security;

Recognizing that their common defense and security will be advanced by the exchange of information concerning atomic energy and by the transfer of equipment and materials for use therein;

Believing that such exchange and transfer can be undertaken without risk to the defense and security of either country; and

Taking into consideration the United States Atomic Energy Act of 1954, as amended, which was enacted with these purposes in mind, Have agreed as follows:

Article I
General provision

While the United States and the United Kingdom are participating in an international arrangement for their mutual defense and security and making substantial and material contributions thereto, each Party will communicate to and exchange with the other Party information, and transfer materials and equipment to the other Party, in accordance with the provisions of this Agreement provided that the communicating or transferring Party determines that such cooperation will promote and will not constitute an unreasonable risk to its defense and security.

Article II
Exchange of information

A. Each Party will communicate to or exchange with the other Party such classified information as is jointly determined to be necessary to:

1. the development of defense plans;

2. the training of personnel in the employment of and defense against atomic weapons and other military applications of atomic energy;

3. the evaluation of the capabilities of potential enemies in the employment of atomic weapons and other military applications of atomic energy;

4. the development of delivery systems compatible with the atomic weapons which they carry; and

105

5. research, development and design of military reactors to the extent and by such means as may be agreed.

B. In addition to the cooperation provided for in paragraph A of this Article each Party will exchange with the other Party other classified information concerning atomic weapons when, after consultation with the other Party, the communicating Party determines that the communication of such information is necessary to improve the recipient's atomic weapon design, development and fabrication capability.

Article III
Transfer of submarine nuclear propulsion plant and materials

A. The government of the United States will authorize, subject to terms and conditions acceptable to the Government of the United States, a person to transfer by sale to the Government of the United Kingdom or its agent one complete submarine nuclear propulsion plant with such spare parts therefor as may be agreed by the Parties and to communicate to the Government of the United Kingdom or its agent (or to both) such classified information as relates to safety features and such classified information as is necessary for the design, manufacture and operation of such propulsion plant. A person or persons will also be authorized, for a period of ten years following the date of entry into force of this Agreement and subject to terms and conditions acceptable to the Government of the United States, to transfer replacement cores or fuel elements for such plant.

B. The Government of the United States will transfer by sale agreed amounts of U-235 contained in uranium enriched in the isotope U-235 as needed for use in the submarine nuclear propulsion plant transferred pursuant to paragraph A of this Article, during the ten years following the date of entry into force of this Agreement on such terms and conditions as may be agreed. If the Government of the United Kingdom so requests, the Government of the United States will during such period reprocess any material sold under the present paragraph in facilities of the Government of the United States, on terms and conditions to be agreed, or authorize such reprocessing in private facilities in the United States. Enriched uranium recovered in reprocessing such materials by either Party may be purchased by the Government of the United States under terms and conditions to be agreed. Special nuclear material recovered in reprocessing such materials and not purchased by the Government of the United States may be returned to or retained by the Government of the United Kingdom and any U-235 not purchased by the Government of the United States will be credited to the amounts of U-235 to be transferred by the Government of the United States under this Agreement.

C. The Government of the United States shall be compensated for enriched uranium sold by it pursuant to this Article at the United States Atomic Energy Commission's published charges applicable to the domestic distribution of such material in effect at the time of the sale. Any purchase of enriched uranium by the Government of the United States pursuant to this Article shall be at the applicable price of the United States Atomic Energy Commission for the purchase of enriched uranium in effect at the time of purchase of such enriched uranium.

D. The Parties will exchange classified information on methods of reprocessing fuel elements of the type utilized in the propulsion plant to be transferred under this Article, including classified information on the design, construction and operation of facilities for the reprocessing of such fuel elements.

E. The Government of the United Kingdom shall indemnify and hold harmless the Government of the United States against any and all liabilities whatsoever (including third-party liability) for any damage or injury occurring after the propulsion plant or parts thereof, including spare parts, replacement cores or fuel elements are taken outside the United States, for any cause arising out of or connected with the design, manufacture, assembly, transfer or utilization of the propulsion plant, spare parts, replacement cores or fuel elements transferred pursuant to paragraph A of this Article.

Article IV
Responsibility for use of information, material equipment and devices
The application or use of any information (including design drawings and specifications), material or equipment communicated, exchanged or transferred under this Agreement shall be the responsibility of the Party receiving it, and the other Party does not provide any indemnity, and does not warrant the accuracy or completeness of such information and does not warrant the suit-

ability or completeness of such information, material or equipment for any particular use or application.

Article V
Conditions

A. Cooperation under this Agreement will be carried out by each of the Parties in accordance with its applicable laws.

B. Under this Agreement there will be no transfer by either Party of atomic weapons.

C. Except as may be otherwise agreed for civil uses, the information communicated or exchanged, or the materials or equipment transferred, by either Party pursuant to this Agreement shall be used by the recipient Party exclusively for the preparation or implementation of defense plans in the mutual interests of the two countries.

D. Nothing in this Agreement shall preclude the communication or exchange of classified information which is transmissible under other arrangements between the Parties.

Article VI
Guaranties

A. Classified information, materials and equipment communicated or transferred pursuant to this Agreement shall be accorded full security protection under applicable security arrangements between the Parties and applicable national legislation and regulations of the Parties. In no case shall either Party maintain security standards for safeguarding classified information, materials or equipment made available pursuant to this Agreement less restrictive than those set forth in the applicable security arrangements in effect on the date this Agreement comes into force.

B. Classified information, communicated or exchanged pursuant to this Agreement will be made available through channels existing or hereafter agreed for the communication or exchange of such information between the Parties.

C. Classified information, communicated or exchanged, and any materials or equipment transferred, pursuant to this Agreement shall not be communicated, exchanged or transferred by the recipient Party or persons under its jurisdiction to any unauthorized persons, or, except as provided in Article VII of this Agreement, beyond the jurisdiction of that Party. Each Party may stipulate the degree to which any of the information, materials or equipment communicated, exchanged or transferred by it or persons under its jurisdiction pursuant to this Agreement may be disseminated or distributed; may specify the categories of persons who may have access to such information, materials or equipment; and may impose such other restrictions on the dissemination or distribution of such information, materials or equipment as it deems necessary.

Article VII
Dissemination

Nothing in this Agreement shall be interpreted or operate as a bar or restriction to consultation or cooperation in any field of defense by either Party with other nations or international organizations. Neither Party, however, shall communicate classified information or transfer or permit access to or use of materials, or equipment, made available by the other Party pursuant to this Agreement to any nation or international organization unless authorized to do so by such other Party, or unless such other Party has informed the recipient Party that the same information has been made available to that nation or international organization.

Article VIII
Classification policies

Agreed classification policies shall be maintained with respect to all classified information, materials or equipment communicated, exchanged or transferred under this Agreement. The Parties intend to continue the present practice of consultation with each other on the classification of these matters.

Article IX
Patents

A. With respect to any invention or discovery employing classified information which has been communicated or exchanged pursuant to Article II or derived from the submarine propulsion plant, material or equipment transferred pursuant to Article III, and made or conceived by the recipient Party, or any agency or corporation owned or controlled thereby, or any of their agents or contractors, or any employee of any of the foregoing, after the date of such communication, exchange or transfer but during the period of this Agreement:

1. in the case of any such invention or discovery in which rights are owned by the recipient Party, or any agency or corporation owned or controlled thereby, and not included in subparagraph 2 of this paragraph, the recipient Party shall, to the extent owned by any of them:

(a) transfer and assign to the other Party all right, title and interest in and to the invention or discovery, or patent application or patent thereon, in the country of that other Party, subject to the retention of a royalty-free, non-exclusive, irrevocable license for the governmental purposes of the recipient Party and for the purposes of mutual defense; and

(b) grant to the other Party a royalty-free, non-exclusive, irrevocable license for the governmental purposes of that other Party and for purposes of mutual defense in the country of the recipient Party and third countries, including use in the production of material in such countries for sale to the recipient Party by a contractor of that other Party;

2. in the case of any such invention or discovery which is primarily useful in the production or utilisation of special nuclear material or atomic energy and made or conceived prior to the time that the information it employs is made available for civil uses, the recipient Party shall:

(a) obtain, by appropriate means, sufficient right, title and interest in and to the invention or discovery, or patent application or patent thereon, as may be necessary to fulfill its obligations under the following two subparagraphs;

(b) transfer and assign to the other Party all right, title and interest in and to the invention or discovery, or patent application or patent thereon, in the country of that other Party, subject to the retention of a royalty-free, non-exclusive, irrevocable license, with the right to grant sublicenses, for all purposes; and

(c) grant to the other Party a royalty-free, non-exclusive, irrevocable license, with the right to grant sublicenses, for all purposes in the country of the recipient Party and in third countries.

B.1. Each Party shall, to the extent owned by it, or any agency or corporation owned or controlled thereby, grant to the other Party a royalty-free, non-exclusive, irrevocable license to manufacture and use the subject matter covered by any patent and incorporated in the submarine propulsion plant and spare parts transferred pursuant to paragraph A of Article III for use by the licensed Party for the purposes set forth in paragraph C of Article V.

2. The transferring Party neither warrants nor represents that the submarine propulsion plant or any material or equipment transferred under Article III does not infringe any patent owned or controlled by other persons and assumes no liability or obligation with respect thereto, and the recipient Party agrees to indemnify and hold harmless the transferring Party from any and all liability arising out of any infringement of any such patent.

C. With respect to any invention or discovery, or patent application or patent thereon, or license or sublicense therein, covered by paragraph A of this Article, each Party:

1. may, to the extent of its right, title and interest therein, deal with the same in its own and third counties as it may desire, but shall in no event discriminate against citizens of the other Party in respect of granting any license or sublicense under the patents owned by it in its own or any other country;

2. hereby waives any and all claims against the other Party for compensation, royalty or award, and hereby releases the other Party with respect to any and all such claims.

D.1. No patent application with respect to any classified invention or discovery employing classified information which has been communicated or exchanged pursuant to Article II, or derived from the submarine propulsion plant, material or equipment transferred pursuant to Article III, may be filed:

(a) by either Party or any person in the country of the other Party except in accordance with agreed conditions and procedures; or

(b) in any country not a party to this Agreement except as may be agreed and subject to Articles VI and VII.

2. Appropriate secrecy or prohibition orders shall be issued for the purpose of giving effect to this paragraph.

Article X
Previous agreements for cooperation

Effective from the date on which the present Agreement enters into force, the cooperation between the Parties being carried out under or envisaged by the Agreement for Cooperation Regarding Atomic Information for Mutual Defense Purposes, which was signed at Washington on June 15, 1955, and by paragraph B of Article I *bis*

111

of the Agreement for Cooperation on Civil Uses of Atomic Energy, which was signed at Washington on June 15, 1955, as amended by the Amendment signed at Washington on June 13, 1956, shall be carried out in accordance with the provisions of the present Agreement.

Article XI
Definitions

For the purposes of this Agreement:

A. 'Atomic weapon' means any device utilizing atomic energy, exclusive of the means for transporting or propelling the device (where such means is a separable and divisible part of the device), the principal purpose of which is for use as, or for development of, a weapon, a weapon prototype, or a weapon test device.

B. 'Classified information' means information, data, materials, services or any other matter with the security designation of 'Confidential' or higher applied under the legislation or regulations of either the United Kingdom or the United States, including that designated by the Government of the United States as 'Restricted Data' or 'Formerly Restricted Data' and that designated by the Government of the United Kingdom as 'Atomic.'

C. 'Equipment' means any instrument, apparatus or facility and includes any facility, except an atomic weapon, capable of making use of or producing special nuclear material, and component parts thereof, and includes submarine nuclear propulsion plant, reactor and military reactor.

D. 'Military reactor' means a reactor for the propulsion of naval vessels, aircraft or land vehicles and military package power reactors.

E. 'Person' means

1. any individual, corporation, partnership, firm, association, trust, estate, public or private institution, group, government agency or government corporation other than the United Kingdom Atomic Energy Authority and the United States Atomic Energy Commission; and

2. Any legal successor, representative, agent or agency of the foregoing.

F. 'Reactor' means an apparatus, other than an atomic weapon, in which a self-supporting fission chain reaction is maintained and controlled by utilizing uranium, plutonium or thorium, or any combination of uranium, plutonium or thorium.

G. 'Submarine nuclear propulsion plant' means a propulsion plant and includes the reactor, and such control, primary, auxiliary, steam and electric systems as may be necessary for propulsion of submarines.

H. References in this Agreement to the Government of the United Kingdom include the United Kingdom Atomic Energy Authority.

Article XII
Duration
This Agreement shall enter into force on the date on which each Government shall have received from the other Government written notification that it has complied with all statutory and constitutional requirements for the entry into force of this Agreement, and shall remain in force until terminated by agreement of both Parties, except that, if not so terminated, Article II may be terminated by agreement of both Parties, or by either Party on one year's notice to the other to take effect at the end of a term of ten years, or thereafter on one year's notice to take effect at the end of any succeeding term of five years.

Agreement between the Government of the United Kingdom of Great Britain and Northern Ireland and the Government of the United States of America for cooperation on the uses of atomic energy for mutual defense purposes. Signed at Washington, on 3 July 1958, the agreement came into force on 4 August 1958, the date on which each government received from the other government written notification that it had complied with all statutory and constitutional requirements for the entry into force of the agreement, in accordance with article XII. *United Nations Treaty Series*, 1959, Vol. 326, No. 4707, pp. 4–20.

4.8 Nuclear sufficiency and American reliability

The US nuclear guarantee to Europe was seen by the British government as central to the Western alliance. When the United States enjoyed a monopoly of nuclear weapons, or overwhelming superiority in weapons and delivery systems, the guarantee appeared firm. But once the Soviet Union had launched Sputnik in October 1957 the question arose whether the United States would risk New York to save Paris or Lon-

113

don. The minutes of the meeting below show the Americans
attempting to reassure their allies.

Resuming the discussion on nuclear sufficiency that had taken
place at an earlier meeting, *Mr Sandys* said that he had no personal
doubts that the United States would continue to play their full part
in NATO. However, it must be recognised that there were some
people in Britain, as well as in Europe, who took the view that it
was, to say the least, doubtful whether, when the stage of nuclear
parity had been reached between the free world and the Soviet *bloc*,
the United States would be willing to use her nuclear power in
defence of her European allies. There was a feeling that she might be
more inclined to think that, unless her own territory was directly
threatened, she should not herself intervene in helping to resist some
peripheral attack against the NATO area. He felt that it was most
important that both countries should make it clear beyond doubt to
the rest of NATO, as well as to the Russians, that they would resist
any attack upon any NATO country with all available means,
including if necessary nuclear retaliation, even if it meant that they
would bring down the full weight of Russian nuclear power upon
themselves.

Mr McElroy said that he entirely agreed with what Mr Sandys
had said. The American Government were determined to carry out
their pledges to NATO and would not hesitate, if necessary, to use
to the full their nuclear power in defence of the free world. Happily,
there was no real difference of opinion about this between the
major political parties in the United States and, in general, public
opinion fully supported this policy. However, he recognised that
there was a feeling in certain NATO countries of the kind described
by Mr Sandys, and he thought every opportunity should be taken
of making clear precisely where the United States stood on this. He
did not think that the best way to do this would be by making
any major pronouncement of Government policy at this time.
He thought that the United States' position might appropriately
be made clear by a series of inspired articles in reputable journals,
and he would also invite Mr Dulles to consider the desirability
of making a statement at the Ministerial Meeting of the North
Atlantic Council in December. At the same time, he hoped that
the British Government would see their way to backing up any

pronouncements official or unofficial – that the United States might make on this.

'General Review of Policy – Procurement of Thor IRBMs; Future Deployment of British Forces and Nuclear Sufficiency', meeting between the Hon. Neil McElroy, US Secretary of Defense, and advisers, and the Right Hon. Duncan Sandys, British Minister of Defence, and advisers, Wednesday 24 September 1958. Public Record Office, DEFE 13/394.

4.9   The deployment of Thor commences

In this memorandum Minister of Defence Duncan Sandys updates Prime Minister Harold Macmillan on the progress of the deployment of US Thor missiles to the United Kingdom. The memorandum was in response to a critical article which had appeared in The *Sunday Times* and a request for information from the Prime Minister. At the end of the original copy Harold Macmillan noted, 'This is reassuring.'

Prime Minister

1. Thank you for your minute W.421/58 of 1st December about deliveries of Thor.

2. The report in the *Sunday Times* has no foundation of fact.

3. Under the Agreement we are due to receive 60 missiles, to be deployed in 4 squadrons of 15; each squadron will be deployed on 5 separate sites.

4. The arrangement we have made with the Americans is that we will for the time being accept only 15 missiles, which are required for training purposes. The decision whether we should accept the rest will depend on agreement on operational acceptability and reliability. We shall have to take a decision in the fairly near future whether to accept for the time being deliveries beyond the first 15.

5. Up to the present 10 missiles have been delivered. Three of these have been installed on their launching pads at Feltwell, and one has been installed at Shepherds Grove. The rest are still in hangars at Feltwell.

6. All the missiles which have been delivered are still in the hands of the contractors, and have not been transferred either to the US Air Force or to the Royal Air Force. It is not yet possible to say when the missiles will be transferred. The Air Ministry are negoti-

ating with the US Air Force detailed arrangements for taking over the missiles and all the equipment that goes with them.

7. A further 5 missiles are due for delivery to this country by the end of this month.

8. The Americans are continuing their tests of Thor, which will go on until July 1959. So far there have been 25 test firings at Cape Canaveral of which 10 have been completely successful, 4 partially successful and 11 failures. On the evidence of the trials so far, our own experts consider that there is no doubt that the weapon will be operationally satisfactory. The Americans have agreed that any modifications that are required as a result of the continued trials at Cape Canaveral will be incorporated in the missiles previously supplied to us.

9. No warheads have yet arrived in this country. The design of the warheads requires that the warhead will be permanently in position on the missile, but the arming system is very elaborate and is not completed until the later stages of the rocket's flight. There is therefore no risk of an accidental nuclear explosion on the ground. This was fully explained to the Press when the agreement was announced.

Minister of Defence Duncan Sandys, memorandum to the Prime Minister, 2 December 1958. Public Record Office, DEFE 13/394.

4.10 Setting an example: Dulles on interdependence

In this interview US Secretary of State John Foster Dulles spells out his view of interdependence, stressing that the close mutual reliance of the United States and the United Kingdom should be an example to other nations to encourage them to cooperate rather than an exclusive arrangement.

I think that we are developing into a world where there must be far greater interdependence between all nations, and 'interdependence' is a phrase which was particularly emphasized when your very great Prime Minister, Harold Macmillan, was here talking with President Eisenhower a year or so ago, and it is a key word – interdependence.

You cannot preserve independence nowadays without interdependence. Now who are the people who should set the first example in interdependence? Shouldn't it be our peoples who derive from the same traditions, speak the same language, have the same religion, have the same common-law principles, and so forth? If we can't do it, who can you expect to do it? And I look upon the extremely close cooperation which now exists happily between our countries as setting an example of interdependence. It is not anything which is exclusive to us. It is not an attempt on our part to set ourselves up over the rest of the world. It is setting an example which needs to be set and carried out so that all of us are cooperating more and more. But we, with certain common heritage, have certainly an example to set, and I think we are setting that example.

I think I can say without fear of challenge that never since this nation became independent has there been the close cooperation that exists at the present time. And indeed I doubt whether history shows ever that two countries have been cooperating so closely as we are cooperating at the present time. And let me emphasize again that is not an effort to set up a family of two over the rest of the world. It is setting an example of the kind of thing which we are prepared to do and want to do with other countries, but, because of certain elements in common, we perhaps can set the stage for doing this thing. But we want to have it – I know your country and our country want to develop this theme of interdependence everywhere. But surely we are setting a good example ourselves.

Anglo-American Cooperation in Developing the Concept of Interdependence in International Relations: replies made by the Secretary of State, John Foster Dulles, to questions asked by a representative of the Independent Television Network of the United Kingdom, recorded in Washington, 17 October 1958. *Department of State Bulletin*, 10 November 1958, pp. 738–9.

5

Challenges to the nuclear partnership, 1960–63

Despite the growing defence interdependence which characterised the late 1950s, problems emerged in the early 1960s which once again created serious friction in Anglo-American relations. As with Suez, however, the outcome of the disagreements was a renewal and deepening of the close defence partnership between the two countries.

In February 1960 the Macmillan government took the decision to cancel the largely indigenous Blue Streak intermediate-range ballistic missile. The decision was made on grounds of cost and strategic vulnerability. In its place agreement was reached that the United States would provide an air-launched missile, Skybolt, to supplement Britain's V-bomber force. The problems associated with Britain's growing dependence in the nuclear field were revealed in late 1962 when the Kennedy administration took the decision to cancel Skybolt, thus depriving Britain of the delivery vehicle on which it depended to maintain the viability of its nuclear deterrent. The crisis was resolved in December 1962 at the Nassau conference when the American administration agreed to supply Britain with its most advanced weapon system, Polaris, as a replacement for Skybolt.

The Nassau conference provides a good illustration of the way the British were able to manipulate the concept of the 'special relationship' to achieve their objectives. After the cancellation of Skybolt there were those in the State Department who saw an opportunity to get Britain out of the nuclear business. US support for the British nuclear deterrent was seen as an impediment to the pursuit of a non-proliferation policy and of US interests in a more united Europe. At the beginning of the conference Kennedy appeared reluctant to provide Britain with Polaris missiles, which the British government regarded as the only suitable substitute for Skybolt. Faced with the possibility of a major diplomatic defeat, Macmillan, as he later admitted, had to pull 'out all the stops'. In a highly emotional speech he referred back to the halcyon days of the Second World War and the foundation of the 'special relationship' between the two countries. If agreement could not be reached now, after all these years, he argued, he would prefer not to patch up a compromise. 'Let us part as friends . . . if there is to be a parting, let it be done with honour and dignity.' Britain would not welch on her agreements (by implication: as the Americans had done). Changing tack, he went on to ask the US President whether he wished to be responsible for the fall of his government. He warned that if that happened there would be a wave of anti-American feeling in Britain and even the possibility that an anti-American faction might assume the leadership of the Tory party in an attempt to cling on to power. The result would be the end of the close and harmonious relationship between the two countries. In response to this eloquent and evocative appeal, Kennedy gave in and Britain got the Polaris missiles the government wanted.

George Ball, one of the State Department officials advising Kennedy, later argued that the President had been seduced at Nassau by 'the emotional baggage of the special relationship', which in his view had got in the way of cooler judgement. Nassau, he believed, was an illustration of how the United States 'had yielded to the temptations' of a myth. He argued that 'US interests in both a strong and united Europe and the prevention of nuclear proliferation have been harmed by the over-zealous support for the partnership with Britain, especially in the defence field'. He also suggested, however, that the British themselves had become a victim of their own rhetoric. Because they had come to believe in the 'special relationship', they had failed to adjust their foreign and defence policies to the reality of their reduced status in the world. The close ties with the United States had encouraged successive governments, Ball argued, 'in the belief that she could by her own efforts' play an 'independent great power role and thus it deflected her from coming to terms with her European destiny'.

5.1 Integration and multilateralism: the US view

Preparing for a visit by Harold Macmillan in April 1962, State Department officials discuss the nature of British relations with the United States. Of particular interest are their thoughts on Britain's involvement with the Common Market, NATO and the United States. The continuing US interest in the concept of the 'special relationship' is also worthy of note.

The fact of the meeting itself reaffirms the special friendship that characterizes the US–UK relationship. The United Kingdom is involved in adjustments of great complexity concerned with its shift from major to lesser power status and its move toward the continent, toward European integration. If our hopes regarding European integration are realized, there will be a challenging opportunity for Britain to exert a position of leadership. Although changes will undoubtedly ensue in the precise nature of the US–UK relationship, as well as in the Commonwealth system, it is too early to attempt to define them in detail. What can be said with assurance is that the ties of language, culture and common ideas will endure and continue to be the firm basis for the intimate friendship of our two countries, just as these elements of English history and tradition ensure the continuance of the Commonwealth.

History has pushed Macmillan to very decisive steps. Fundamentally, Macmillan and his group have made the decision about moving toward the continent, but they keep looking back at the US–UK relationship. Any indication at this critical moment that the United Kingdom might be left alone in Europe could provoke a reaction so adverse as to jeopardize British pursuit of the present negotiations with the Common Market. We believe it is inevitable – if not now, then later – that Britain enter the Common Market. Any redefinition of American–British relations should await the larger clarification of the relations between the US and an integrated Western Europe. As this larger pattern develops, US–UK relations, with due cognizance of their special character, will in turn fall into place within the expanded concept. Therefore, we should approach the whole subject matter of US–UK relations in a positive spirit, i.e. focusing on the new US–Europe ties, emphasizing that the US and the UK are both moving into new, changed and closer relations with Europe.

A key part of this positive approach to US–UK relations might well occur in the President painting the kind of integrated Western Europe that we hope will emerge. The leading role of the United Kingdom in such a Western Europe as the President might describe should catch the imagination of the British – for instance, that special political genius of England to which the theory and practice of democracy owes so much.

It is important that the President make no commitments which bind us to perpetuate the present forms of the US–UK relationship. He can understandably respond that we are in a time of great change and look forward to closer US–UK ties with Europe as a whole. The similarity of the US–UK outlook will help us work closely together in Europe and across the Atlantic. . . .

The Prime Minister may attempt to throw the responsibility for resolving his nuclear deterrent dilemma on us. He may attempt to elicit an implied commitment that at least in the 'holy realm' of military nuclear arrangements the special US–UK relationship will be perpetuated. Nuclear weapons have become a status symbol of international power, and the UK will not give up this symbol easily. The French, however, resent the US–UK nuclear monopoly in NATO and a special nuclear status for the UK within the Community would not be tolerated by the Continental powers. In the long run it may become important to the goal of an integrated Western Europe for Britain to contribute its national nuclear deterrent to the Community as a function of developing a multilateral NATO nuclear deterrent. We might at this juncture concentrate on seeking British support for a NATO multilateral MRBM force and in the process point out the dangers of German and French national nuclear cooperation. We see no reason why the President need conceal his lack of enthusiasm for the Defense White Paper with its failure to support the strengthening of NATO's non-nuclear arm . . .

While the discussions with the Prime Minister may convince us that we have reinfused the British with the need to stand firm against the Soviet Union, and we know that in a show-down they would be with us, it is in the gray areas of compromise that might occur at any summit meeting that we have need for concern. It may well be that the purpose of these discussions will be an exchange of briefings for a summit meeting. Against that possibility we want to be sure that the vaunted British spine is stiffened across the board in the day-to-day aspects of East–West confrontation.

In the careful consideration of diplomatic parry and riposte for these talks, it is important that the desirability of acknowledging the special friendship that characterizes the US–UK relationship not be overlooked. Nor should it be labored. Furthermore, a certain amount of reassurance for Macmillan personally is indicated. He has been having a hard time of it. His critics – and even some of his own Tory compatriots – claim he has lost his political magic.

Macmillan and his Conservative Party have had recent political rebuffs. Liberal Party gains in a by-election at Orpington dramatized a decline in the Conservative vote in other recent by-elections. However, the Conservative Party retains its parliamentary majority of over a hundred. The Labor Party has not as yet succeeded in projecting a convincing image of itself as a desirable alternative. On the other hand, the Conservatives have discovered that the UK move toward Europe may be the key to a positive image for the Tories. But there can be no denying that a certain ferment has disturbed the British domestic political calm. No general election is now expected until next year. While Macmillan undoubtedly intends to guide his party through this next contest, he is again rumored to be stepping down after the elections. This is no new rumor, but there are increasing indications that his tired appearance is less studied pose and more a reflection of reality.

Scope paper prepared in the Department of State, Washington, 20 April 1962, for Prime Minister Macmillan's visit to Washington, 27–9 April 1962. *Foreign Relations of the United States, 1961–63*, Vol. XIII, pp. 1064–8.

5.2 'A dandy question': Britain, Europe and America

This memorandum by the President's Special Assistant gives expression to the view that the United States preferred to see Britain playing its part in Europe and contributing conventional rather than nuclear forces to Western defence. It also reflects the lack of enthusiasm in the United States at the time for the British nuclear deterrent.

Taz Shepard relayed your question as to why the President of the United States cannot make commitments which bind the United States to perpetuate the present forms of the US–UK relationship. This is a dandy question.

I hope that what the Department means here is what I was trying to say in a memorandum yesterday: that our close cooperation with the British does not depend on British aloofness from Europe or on the existing preferential treatment of the British on nuclear matters. We want the British in Europe, and we do not really see much point in the separate British nuclear deterrent, beyond our existing Skybolt commitment; we would much rather have British efforts go into conventional weapons and have the British join with the rest of NATO in accepting a single US-dominated nuclear force.

Memorandum from the President's Special Assistant for National Security Affairs, McGeorge Bundy, to President Kennedy, Washington, 24 April 1962. *Foreign Relations of the United States, 1961–63*, Vol. XIII, pp. 1068–9.

Challenges to the nuclear partnership

5.3 Multilateralism versus bilateralism

This letter, written by US Secretary of State Dean Rusk, again articulates the US desire to ensure that Britain's 'special relationship' with the United States does not hinder the development of either state's relations with the EEC. In particular, Rusk reinforces the point that it would be beneficial if Britain were to lose its nuclear deterrent. The United States should certainly not assist it in prolonging the life of the deterrent force.

Dear Bob: You will recall the April 21, 1961 NSC Policy Directive, which states that 'over the long run it would be desirable if the British decided to phase out of the nuclear deterrent business'. It also states that the US should not prolong the life of the British deterrent, except to the extent of continuing development of Skybolt if this is warranted for US purposes alone.

The present situation in Europe underscores the importance of this policy. After the UK–EEC negotiations, the special US–UK relationship may have to be closely re-examined in connection with the evolving relationship of the UK to the continent, our own relationship with the new European Community, and our desire to ensure that future European nuclear efforts are based on genuinely multilateral rather than national programs. Pending such a re-examination of the US–UK special relationship, which will only be feasible when we can get a clearer picture of the future shape of Europe, I believe it is of the utmost importance to avoid any actions to expand the relationship. Such actions could seriously prejudice future decisions and developments and make more difficult the working out of sound multilateral arrangements.

I know we are agreed, in line with the NSC policy referred to above, that any commitment to aid the British in extending their nuclear delivery capability beyond the present V-bomber force, e.g. through their acquisition of Polaris or other missile-bearing submarines, should be avoided at this time and that US decisions relative to Skybolt should be made on the basis solely of US interest in this missile for our own forces.

Maintenance of this US posture is particularly important at this juncture, since the British are probably now beginning to try to develop some tentative views concerning the nuclear arrangements

123

that they may favor after joining the EEC. They probably feel that the V-bomber force, even with Skybolt, is a wasting asset and that any effective Europe-based deterrence must be based, in the long run, primarily on missiles rather than aircraft. They have shown past interest in the long-term possibility of Polaris missile-bearing submarines. They may be considering whether to try, in this way, to continue a UK national force into the missile era – possibly combined with a French national force under some type of 'joint' arrangement. Such an arrangement might be termed a European multilateral force, although it would in fact be neither European (since it would discriminate against the Germans) nor multilateral (since it would involve nationally manned and owned forces). By reason of these facts, such an arrangement would be politically divisive and vastly complicate our efforts to hold pressures for a German national program in check.

British decisions in this field will be a long time in the making and I do not think that we should take remarks which suggest that they are now leaning to such an arrangement – rather than, for example, to participation in a genuinely multilateral force – as necessarily foreshadowing the ultimate outcome. An important factor will be their assessment of possible eventual US willingness to provide aid – by facilitating procurement of MRBM's and Polaris submarines – for an extension of the US–UK special relationship into the missile era.

I hope, therefore, that both our staffs can hold to existing policies in discussions with Defense Minister Thorneycroft – avoiding any indication of future expansion in the US–UK special relationship and making clear, if he asks, that we hold to the view which we have already expressed that we would only facilitate allied procurement of MRBM's for a program involving genuinely multilateral control, manning and ownership.

I do not believe that we should, however, foreshadow any curtailment of the special relationship. This would be counterproductive, in view of the state of political developments in the UK and of the UK–EEC negotiations. I suspect that we can rely on the long-term trends in Europe to bring genuine multilateral courses increasingly to the fore, if we do not indicate a willingness to provide increased aid for less satisfactory alternatives in the meantime.

Thus, if the British raise the question of aid for a hunter-killer (rather than missile-bearing) nuclear powered submarine, such aid would not be precluded by the policy indicated above, in view of our previous sale of a nuclear power plant for a hunter-killer submarine to the UK. In the unlikely event the British raise this question, we might indicate that we would take the matter under consideration and our two Departments could then review timing and other relevant considerations, in the light of pending developments in this field *vis-à-vis* the French.

In connection with the policy of avoiding any extension of the present US–UK special relationship it might also be useful if our staffs could undertake a review of the present extensive collaboration with the British under the Tripartite (US, UK, Canada) Technical Cooperation Program so as to define its scope with greater precision. I understand that this program of cooperation stems from the Eisenhower–Macmillan agreement of December 20, 1957 . . . I have asked that Bill Tyler's people be in touch with your staff about such a review.

I am sending copies of this letter to Mac Bundy and Glenn Seaborg in view of their interest in the subject.

Letter from Secretary of State Rusk to Secretary of Defense McNamara, Washington, 8 September 1962. *Foreign Relations of the United States, 1961–63*, Vol. XIII, pp. 1078–80.

5.4 'A matter of joint decision': the Cuban missile crisis

Ever since the deployment of US bomber aircraft in Britain during the Berlin crisis in 1948, the question of what say Britain had in the use of American nuclear weapons had exercised minds in the British government. The Cuban missile crisis raised this issue again in stark form. In this memorandum by a Foreign Office official the history of the issue in the context of the Cuban missile crisis are traced.

The Lord Privy Seal has asked for further consideration to be given to the question of consultation within the Western Alliance in the light of Cuba. This has already been raised in the House of Commons: on October 31 Mr Harold Wilson alleged that 'the United States failed to consult Britain' and Mr. Grimond alleged that, despite the British H Bomb, 'we were not in any normal sense consulted'. There are questions to the Prime Minister for answer today about consultation over the use of nuclear weapons.

2. In particular the Lord Privy Seal has suggested that it may be necessary to seek confirmation from the United States Government of their undertaking to consult over the use of nuclear weapons in any part of the world.

3. Two different forms of consultation are involved here:

(a) the United States undertakings about the use of nuclear weapons;

(b) consultation between allies on major political decisions.

Consultation on the Use of Nuclear Weapons

4. The United States undertakings to this country are twofold:

(a) The arrangement under which bases in this country are made available to the United States forces provide that the use of the bases in any emergency 'would be a matter for joint decision by the two Governments in the light of circumstances prevailing at the time'. The original agreement on the use of the air bases was made by Mr Attlee with President Truman in October 1951. It was confirmed by Sir W. Churchill with President Truman in January 1952 and was again confirmed in 1958 by President Eisenhower's Administration. It was reaffirmed by President Kennedy in 1961. (The terms of President Kennedy's reaffirmation are confidential and have not been made public.) As the Prime Minister told the House on November 1, 1960, the arrangements for the Polaris base in Holy Loch provide that 'the deployment and use of the submarine depot ship and associated facilities in the United Kingdom will be a matter of joint consultation between the two Governments'. In fact the President's undertaking provides that 'with reference to the launching of missiles from United States Polaris submarines, . . . The United States will take every possible step to consult with Britain and other Allies.'

(b) With regard to the use of nuclear weapons anywhere in the world, President Kennedy wrote to the Prime Minister on February 6, 1961, setting out understandings which as he said 'reflect the agreements in force between our two Governments'. He enclosed a memorandum from which the following extract is relevant:

'There is a second, more general, understanding with the British that we will consult with them before using nuclear weapons anywhere, if possible. The basic understanding on this point is contained in a memorandum of conversation of a meeting between the President [Eisenhower] and Eden on March 9, 1953. Eden had asked for an assurance of consultation by the President with the Prime Minister prior to use of any nuclear weapon. "He (the President) said that the United States would, of course, in the event of increased tension or the threat of war, take every possible step to consult with Britain and our other allies".'

This understanding cannot be revealed in detail. But the Prime Minister told the House on June 26, 1962: 'There is an understanding which I had with President Eisenhower and now have with President Kennedy that neither of us in any part of the world would think of using Power of this kind without consultation with the other.'

(c) Similarly, assurances were given by the United States and the United Kingdom to the North Atlantic Council in April and May 1962 'to consult with the North Atlantic Council, if time permits, concerning the use of nuclear weapons, anywhere in the world.' (Special Report by the Secretary-General of April 17, 1962 – C-M(62)48.) The US undertaking to NATO has been mentioned publicly by the Secretary-General of NATO; the British undertaking has not been made public. . . .

6. . . . [I]t is clear that there is a general undertaking to consult under the North Atlantic Treaty. This is reinforced, in the case of the UK, by the fact that we are concerned with the US in defence agreements covering various parts of the world and therefore have a right to expect consultation on world defence questions generally.

7. But this political consultation can take two forms:

(a) The Power contemplating action may say to its ally, 'I am faced with the following alternatives. What do you advise?'

(b) The first Power may say to its ally, 'I am proposing to do such and such. You must tell me if you see any objection.'

In the case of Cuba, President Kennedy consulted the Prime Minister in the second sense. The Prime Minister had 24 hours (although publicly we can only admit to 12 hours) in which he could have said that he disapproved of the action contemplated, and advised against it, or that if it were taken he would reserve HMG's position, or even that HMG would publicly oppose the action. The Prime Minister did not say any of these things. As a matter of fact he approved of the action which President Kennedy intended to take, although he was not asked by the President to assume any formal responsibility for it.

127

Conclusions

8. It seems to follow that:

(a) If there is further criticism in the House of Commons, related to the Cuba episode, the answer should be that HMG were consulted in the sense that we were given time to express an opinion on the action which the President had decided he must take in a matter vitally affecting the security of the US and the Western hemisphere. (This was not a NATO matter except in the very technical sense that an incident might conceivably have occurred in the NATO area.) Since we thought the decision right we were content that the President should go ahead. If we had thought it wrong, we should have said so and the President would have had to decide whether to go ahead regardless of our opinion. HMG have never claimed, and could not claim, the right of veto over the actions of our principal ally in a vital decision affecting US security. We should similarly expect to make an independent judgment on our own vital interests, although we should naturally consult our allies if we could. (Our possession of the H Bomb has no particular relevance to this question; we were consulted, not for any technical reason, but as part of the general relations existing between HMG and the US Government as allies.)

(b) Political action in matters directly and immediately affecting the NATO Alliance, and especially in respect of Berlin, is somewhat different. On this the line in the House of Commons might be as follows. The North Atlantic Council has a collective responsibility for matters affecting the Alliance. There is joint Three Power responsibility for Berlin, apart from the close German interest. Consultation in NATO and between the Powers concerned with Berlin is continuous and perfectly satisfactory to us. [The North Atlantic Council was informed of the US decision to impose the blockade on Cuba a few hours before it was publicly announced.]

9. With regard to the separate question of the assurances about the use of nuclear weapons, the President's reaffirmation of these is quite recent. The Prime Minister is referring to it in the House today and the draft reply and notes for supplementaries have been cleared with the State Department [and the White House – *handwritten addition*] (which in itself constitutes a form of further reaffirnation [*sic*]). There is no reason to suppose that the President does not intend to live up to these assurances. To ask for a renewal of these

now would suggest a lack of confidence. If it became known to the US press that such a request had been made, it could only lead to adverse criticism of this country (particularly in view of the 'soft' line taken by the British press during the crisis). The Cuba situation did not reach a point, as far as we know, at which the early use of nuclear weapons might have been contemplated or the President required to fulfil his undertaking to consult HMG on their use.

'Cuba and Anglo-American Consultation', report by Evelyn Shuckburgh, who in 1962 went from being Deputy Under-Secretary at the Foreign Office to become Britain's Permanent Representative on the North Atlantic Council, 6 November 1962. Public Record Office, FO 371/166970.

5.5 'Great Britain has lost an empire': Dean Acheson's view

> In this famous and controversial speech Dean Acheson, Secretary of State in the Truman administration, depicts Britain as unsure of its place in world politics, struggling to define its post-imperial role. The speech struck a very sensitive chord in Britain at the time.

. . . Great Britain has lost an Empire and has not yet found a role. The attempt to play a separate power role – that is, a role apart from Europe, a role based on a 'special relationship' with the United States, a role based on being the head of a 'Commonwealth' which has no political structure, or unity, or strength and enjoys a fragile and precarious economic relationship by means of the sterling area and preferences in the British market – this role is about to be played out.

Great Britain, attempting to work alone and be a broker between the United States and Russia, has seemed to conduct a policy as weak as its military power. Her Majesty's Government is now attempting, wisely in my opinion, to re-enter Europe, from which it was banished at the time of the Plantagenets, and the battle seems about as hard fought as those of an earlier day.

Dean Acheson, extract from a speech at West Point, 5 December 1962. *New York Times*, 6 December 1962. Quoted in Ian S. McDonald, *Anglo-American Relations since the Second World War* (London: David & Charles, 1974), pp. 181–2.

5.6 Crisis point: the cancellation of Skybolt

With the abandonment of Britain's own Blue Streak missile in February 1960 the future of the deterrent had come to rest on the provision of the US Skybolt missile, which could prolong the operational life of the V-bomber force. The American decision to halt work on the missile precipitated a crisis in Anglo-American relations. Here Minister of Defence Peter Thorneycroft explains the position to the House of Commons, referring to his recent talks with US Defense Secretary Robert McNamara.

With permission, I should like to make a statement on my recent talks with Mr McNamara in London on 11th December.

The principal subject discussed was, as the House knows, the future of the Skybolt missile. We have, of course, known from the outset of our association with the United States Government on this weapon that it constituted a formidable development problem. We knew of various difficulties that had arisen, and of the steps that were being taken to surmount them. Such difficulties, of course, were not unexpected, nor are they unusual even in simpler missiles.

However, when I visited the United States in September of this year, the situation was that while the increase in costs was causing concern, I was assured that American plans assumed delivery of Skybolt. It was not until the beginning of November that Mr McNamara, while assuring me that no decision would be taken without the fullest consultation, informed me that the future of the weapon was under review. This consultation was carried a further stage last week, and will be continued between the Prime Minister and the President in the Bahamas.

From the point of view of the United States, the weapon is proving more expensive than originally estimated; secondly it looks as though it will be late and possibly not as efficient and reliable as had at first been hoped; and, thirdly, alternative weapon systems available to the United States Government have proved relatively more successful.

I have stressed throughout my talks with Mr McNamara the serious consequences for the United Kingdom of a cancellation of this project, and I can assure the House that the United States Government can be in no doubt on that aspect of the matter. The discussions have, naturally, included the possibility that the United States Government might provide us with alternatives to Skybolt of which the most important is Polaris, but I would stress that no decisions either on Skybolt or on possible alternatives to it have been taken.

Since discussions between our two Governments have not been completed, I am sure that the House will accept that I cannot say any more at the present time. Indeed, as the Prime Minister said last week, it would not be in the interests of the country to do so.

Apart from Skybolt, my meeting with Mr McNamara gave us an opportunity for informal and confidential discussion of a number of matters of joint concern to the two Governments.

Peter Thorneycroft, statement to the House of Commons, 17 December 1962. *Hansard* (*Commons*), Vol. 669, cols. 893–4. Quoted in Ian S. McDonald, *Anglo-American Relations since the Second World War* (London: David & Charles, 1974), pp. 184–5.

5.7   The Nassau conference: Macmillan appeals for Polaris

In the aftermath of the US decision to halt development of Skybolt, Harold Macmillan met President John F. Kennedy at Nassau in the Bahamas. The Prime Minister's challenge was to persuade Kennedy to equip the British with Polaris missiles which would maintain the British deterrent, even though American suspicion of national deterrents was well known. Here Macmillan puts his case.

Mr Macmillan said that he was sorry that the present talks which he had hoped would range over the great world issues had now been overshadowed by the question of the Skybolt missile. However, this question had blown up and must be resolved. He would like to set out the position as he saw it. His memory of government perhaps went back further than that of anyone else in the room and he could recall the time during the war when Tube Alloys were being developed. He fully appreciated the feelings which President Kennedy and his Government had about the dangers of doing anything which might be obnoxious to European countries. He also understood the feeling that nothing should be done which would prevent movement towards larger groupings in the world. The British Government had no desire to hinder such developments of whose necessity they were quite convinced. At the same time Mr Macmillan was sure that the allied countries in Europe, and especially President de Gaulle, were quite aware of the historical background to this question. In the early days all the attention had been focused upon the problem of actually making a bomb. This had originally been largely developed by British scientists and then, when France was occupied, Churchill and Roosevelt had agreed to transfer the work to the United States where the Hiroshima bomb had finally been produced. At that stage Britain and America had in a sense owned an equal share in the equity. After the war this Anglo-American co-operation which had not been covered by any very precise legal agreement was threatened by difficulties such as the spy cases in England which had led to the passing of the McMahon Act. President Eisenhower had felt that this Act had treated Britain too harshly and under his Administration changes had been introduced which, although applicable to all nations were in fact primarily intended to assist Britain as they had done. Since then there had been close co-operation again between the two countries in which Britain had been able to contribute something, certainly all that she had, and had scrupulously maintained the rules about not passing information to third countries. Towards the end of the 1950s attention had begun to shift from the bomb to the means of delivery. At that time Britain was developing the Blue Streak rocket on which she had spent some $200 million. This was a powerful weapon which could have been developed but of course it had disadvantages for a small island like the United Kingdom. The British Government reached the view that they should abandon it if they could get anything better. At Camp David in 1960 President Eisenhower had discussed Skybolt and Polaris and had given the Prime Minister a model of the Polaris submarine. Finally, Mr Macmillan had gratefully accepted President Eisenhower's offer of Skybolt. Although later enshrined in a formal agreement this arrangement had been based upon a broad honourable understanding. At the same time President Eisenhower had mentioned his desire to station some Polaris submarines in Scotland so that fewer ships could do more work. The first British suggestion had been Gair Loch but in the end they had agreed to the American preference for Holy Loch. When since then doubts had been cast on the possibility of successfully completing the Skybolt project British Ministers had accepted American assurances that the development programme was going ahead and had stoutly maintained that the weapon would work. Now the United Kingdom had been told that the United States Administration were to discontinue the programme.

Mr Macmillan thought that it was worth considering what the effect would have been on the French, Germans and Italians if the Skybolt project had been successfully developed. He did not think that they would have been upset. They were all fully aware of the history and of the co-operative arrangements which had made Britain with America a founder member of the nuclear club. They knew about the special arrangements under the McMahon Act and the tradition, which had been renewed – but not started – at Camp David. There would, therefore, have been no problem. Now that Skybolt had failed the question arose of the effect of an American decision to continue to help the United Kingdom in some other way on the possibility of larger groupings in Europe on which so much depended. As regards the Common Market negotiations he could frankly see no objection. The truth of the matter was that the French felt that they had made a very good deal with the Germans about agriculture and the real problem was whether they would be ready to abandon this. There was of course a division between the French concept of the Six building up a somewhat autarchic agricultural structure and reducing imports almost to nothing and the British view that it was the duty of the Europeans, not just to the Commonwealth but to the whole outside world, to accept a reasonable degree of imports, thereby promoting economic stability, preventing political upheavals and fulfilling their moral duty. But the outcome of the Common Market negotiations would not be affected by decisions about nuclear delivery systems.

There had been much talk about a multilateral nuclear force but he was not quite clear what that meant. Was it the same, for example, as what was called a European force? Would it be manufactured in Europe and would it belong to those who had manufactured it? Would it be put into some sort of pool? Personally he could not see any necessary contradiction between the concepts of independence and interdependence. Of course, it was possible to put national forces into alliances and in planning to work inside that framework. But this did not mean that the national forces passed completely under the authority of the commanding General. The United Kingdom had been used to working within this concept

133

from the days of Marlborough onwards. The national forces were independent as regards ultimate political authority and interdependent for the joint campaign. It would, therefore, be possible to put many British forces into some such an interdependent arrangement on this basis. But until there was a Supranational political authority which would exercise juridical control there would have to be interdependence with an ultimate national authority. Interdependence and independence were the two sides of a coin. It was quite possible that when the French got to the point of achieving their own deterrent they might see matters in the same way; and the Prime Minister had made, he thought, some progress in explaining this to General de Gaulle at Rambouillet. The General had, of course, been quite clear that Governments could not lose ultimate control of their own forces. For obvious reasons the Prime Minister had not illustrated his argument to General de Gaulle by using the example which sprang most quickly to his mind; namely that of General Gort, who was under the command of General Gamelin, but when it was clear that General Gamelin had lost control of the battle, obeyed the orders of the British Government to save his own troops and any French troops who wished to join him at Dunkirk. The truth was that until a single supranational State was formed there would have to be a combination of independence and interdependence.

Mr Macmillan did not therefore believe that a switch from the lame horse, Skybolt, to what was now the favourite, Polaris, would upset France and Germany because they accepted the different backgrounds of their national history. If, however, it would help the Prime Minister would consider making some arrangement which might in practice be little more than a gesture but which would have a moral effect. At the moment the British bomber force in conjunction with the United States Strategic Air Command provided a high proportion of the first wave attack on strategic targets. It was possible that in time bombers generally would pass more into a tactical rather than a strategic role or might be used as a second wave after a missile attack. So the United Kingdom would be ready, if it would help, to make available to SACEUR for planning and tactics say one squadron of V-bombers. He believed that the United States had done something similar and the French could be asked to do the same. This would enable the philosophy that nuclear forces were not entirely independent to be developed in a controlled fashion. First moves on these lines might be helpful and a gesture could be made straight away. Countries without a nuclear capacity could be informed of SACEUR's planning and made to feel that they were brought in to the general pattern.

He would like to make one point about the alleged difference between Polaris and Skybolt. It seemed to him that these weapons were not fundamentally different but merely varying ways of delivering ballistic rockets. Whether these were fired from the air or from the sea was just a difference in method.

Lastly, the difficulties which had been mentioned about the allies would be as nothing to the difficulties which would follow if the United States seemed to be using the Skybolt decision as a means of forcing Britain out of an independent nuclear capacity. This would be resented not only by those who were in favour of the British independent deterrent but even by those who opposed it and yet felt that abandonment of this United Kingdom force should come about because of a decision made by Britain and not by others.

President Kennedy agreed on the last point. The United States could not, however, take a decision in this purely on the basis of technical considerations. It was true that it was generally known that the United States did not favour national deterrents. But they were compelled to take account of the fact that Polaris and Minuteman existed. Recognising the British feeling on the question of nuclear capacity they did not wish to appear to have decided for political reasons to abandon Skybolt. That was why he was ready to propose that the United States Government should pay half the further development costs to completion of Skybolt which were estimated at $200 million with Britain paying the other half and having the right to buy missiles. The United States Government could not at this time undertake themselves to buy any Skybolt missiles but if they could develop an aircraft which would stay aloft for several days, they might eventually wish to place an order for Skybolt. With this arrangement Skybolt would be completed as arranged and the United Kingdom would be able to buy what she had wanted to buy. For $100 million plus $1½ million per missile the United Kingdom could obtain the full advantage of all the United States development work. This should certainly be an adequate deterrent for Mr Khrushchev who would probably not know of Skybolt's disadvantages. After all 20 missiles in Cuba had been a deterrent to the United States. How much more would a missile

135

system based on Skybolt deter the Russians even if they thought that the weapon might have the accuracy to fall only in the suburbs and not on the centre of Moscow. He therefore thought it possible to maintain the British deterrent on the basis of the Skybolt offer he had just made. This would be a good answer to those in Britain who thought that the United States was taking a decision on Skybolt because they were against a British independent deterrent.

He was, of course, aware in a general way of the history of Anglo-American cooperation in the nuclear field. He knew that the two countries had cooperated very intimately. The United States however had not supported the French in the nuclear field and the result of this policy had been to sour American relations with France. Rightly or wrongly they had taken this attitude because of Germany. The United States had paid more attention to Germany than had the United Kingdom and had spent a lot of money and effort there. The United States were concerned at what would happen in Germany after Dr Adenauer left the scene. This was one reason why the United States had supported Britain's entry into Europe even though this must pose an economic and political threat to the United States at a time when they could ill afford this. They regarded Germany as potentially the most powerful country in Europe and one whose future was in some doubt. They had not helped President de Gaulle in his nuclear ambitions because they did not believe that the French would really abandon their hostile attitude to NATO because of such help. And if the United States did help France then pressure in Germany for similar help would rise. That was why the United States had moved towards the idea of a multilateral nuclear force; it was precisely for the reason that they wished to avoid dangerous national pressures.

Record of a meeting held at Bali-Hai, the Bahamas, at 9.50 a.m. on Wednesday 19 December 1962. Public Record Office, PREM 11/4229.

5.8 'Supreme national interests at stake': the Nassau agreement

After offering various alternatives President Kennedy agreed at Nassau to supply Britain with Polaris missiles. America's desire for interdependence was satisfied by the assignment of the missile to NATO, Britain's requirement of independence was achieved through the proviso that, where 'supreme national interests' were at stake, Britain could use the missiles itself.

1. The President and the Prime Minister reviewed the development program for the Skybolt missile. The President explained that it was no longer expected that this very complex weapons system would be completed within the cost estimate or the time scale which were projected when the program was begun.

2. The President informed the Prime Minister that for this reason and because of the availability to the United States of alternative weapons systems, he had decided to cancel plans for the production of Skybolt for use by the United States. Nevertheless, recognizing the importance of the Skybolt program for the United Kingdom, and recalling that the purpose of the offer of Skybolt to the United Kingdom in 1960 had been to assist in improving and extending the effective life of the British V-bombers, the President expressed his readiness to continue the development of the missile as a joint enterprise between the United States and the United Kingdom, with each country bearing equal shares of the future cost of completing development, after which the United Kingdom would be able to place a production order to meet its requirements.

3. While recognizing the value of this offer, the Prime Minister decided, after full consideration, not to avail himself of it because of doubts that had been expressed about the prospects of success for this weapons system and because of uncertainty regarding date of completion and final cost of the program.

4. As a possible alternative the President suggested that the Royal Air Force might use the Hound Dog missile. The Prime Minister responded that in the light of the technical difficulties he was unable to accept this suggestion.

5. The Prime Minister then turned to the possibility of provision of the Polaris missile to the United Kingdom by the United States. After careful review, the President and the Prime Minister agreed that a decision on Polaris must be considered in the widest context both of the future defense of the Atlantic Alliance and of the safety of the whole Free World. They reached the conclusion that this issue created an opportunity for the development of new and closer arrangements for the organization and control of strategic Western defense and that such arrangements in turn could make a major contribution to political cohesion among the nations of the Alliance.

6. The Prime Minister suggested, and the President agreed, that for the immediate future a start could be made by subscribing to NATO some part of the forces already in existence. This could include allocations from United States Strategic Forces, from United Kingdom Bomber Command, and from tactical nuclear forces now held in Europe. Such forces would be assigned as part of a NATO nuclear force and targeted in accordance with NATO plans.

7. Returning to Polaris the President and the Prime Minister agreed that the purpose of their two governments with respect to the provision of the Polaris missiles must be the development of a multilateral NATO nuclear force in the closest consultation with other NATO allies. They will use their best endeavours to this end.

8. Accordingly, the President and the Prime Minister agreed that the US will make available on a continuing basis Polaris missiles (less warheads) for British submarines. The US will also study the feasibility of making available certain support facilities for such submarines. The UK Government will construct the submarines in which these weapons will be placed and they will also provide the nuclear warheads for the Polaris missiles. British forces developed under this plan will be assigned and targeted in the same way as the forces described in paragraph 6.

These forces, and at least equal US forces, would be made available for inclusion in a NATO multilateral nuclear force. The Prime Minister made it clear that except where HMG may decide that supreme national interests are at stake, these British forces will be used for the purposes of international defense of the Western Alliance in all circumstances.

9. The President and the Prime Minister are convinced that this new plan will strengthen the nuclear defense of the Western Alliance. In strategic terms this defense is indivisible, and it is their conviction that in all ordinary circumstances of crisis or danger, it is this very unity which is the best protection of the West.

10. The President and the Prime Minister agreed that in addition to having a nuclear shield it is important to have a non-nuclear sword. For this purpose they agreed on the importance of increasing the effectiveness of their conventional forces on a worldwide basis.

President Kennedy and Prime Minister Macmillan, 'Statement on Nuclear Defense Systems' from their joint statement at Nassau, 21 December 1962. *Public Papers of the President*, 1962, pp. 908–10. Quoted in Ian S.

Challenges to the nuclear partnership

McDonald, *Anglo-American Relations since the Second World War* (London: David & Charles, 1974), pp. 187–9.

5.9 The Polaris sales agreement

Following the discussions at the Nassau summit, the governments of the United Kingdom and the United States signed a formal agreement on the supply of Polaris missiles to Britain. The terms of the agreement are widely recognised as enormously generous to the British.

The Government of the United States of America and the Government of the United Kingdom of Great Britain and Northern Ireland, recalling and affirming the 'Statement on Nuclear Defense Systems' included in the joint communiqué issued on December 21, 1962 by the President of the United States of America and the Prime Minister of Her Majesty's Government in the United Kingdom of Great Britain and Northern Ireland;
Have agreed as follows:

Article I

1. The Government of the United States shall provide and the Government of the United Kingdom shall purchase from the Government of the United States Polaris missiles (less warheads), equipment, and supporting services in accordance with the terms and conditions of this Agreement.

2. This Agreement shall be subject to the understandings concerning British submarines equipped with Polaris missiles (referred to in paragraphs 8 and 9 of the Nassau 'Statement on Nuclear Defense systems') agreed by the President of the United States and the Prime Minister of the United Kingdom at their meeting held in the Bahamas between December 18 and December 21, 1962.

Article II

1. In recognition of the complexity of the effort provided for in this agreement and the need for close coordination between the contracting Governments in giving effect to its terms, the two Governments shall promptly establish the organizational machinery provided for in the following paragraphs of this Article.

139

2. The Department of Defense, acting through the Department of the Navy, and the Admiralty, or such other agency as the Government of the United Kingdom shall designate, will be the Executive Agencies of their respective Governments in carrying out the terms of this Agreement. Appropriate representatives of the Executive Agencies are authorized to enter into such technical arrangements, consistent with this Agreement, as may be necessary.

3. A Project Officer will be designated by each Government's Executive Agency with direct responsibility and authority for the management of the activities of that Government under this Agreement. Each Project Officer will designate liaison representatives, in such numbers as may be agreed, who will be authorized to act on his behalf in capacities specified in technical arrangements and who will be attached to the Office of the other Project Officer.

4. A Joint Steering Task Group will be established by the Project Officers to advise them, *inter alia*, concerning the development of new or modified equipment to meet specific requirements of the Government of the United Kingdom, and concerning interfaces between the equipment provided by the two Governments respectively. The Joint Steering Task Group will comprise the Project Officers (or their representatives), and principal liaison representatives, and may include selected leaders from among the scientists, industrialists and government executives of the United States and of the United Kingdom. The Joint Steering Task Group will meet approximately every three months alternatively in the United Kingdom and in the United States under the chairmanship of the resident Project Officer.

Article III

1. The Government of the United States (acting through its Executive Agency) shall provide, pursuant to Article I of this Agreement: Polaris missiles (less warheads), equipment, and supporting services of such types and marks and in such quantities as the Government of the United Kingdom may from time to time require, and in configurations and in accordance with delivery programs or timetables to be agreed between the Project Officers. In the first instance the missiles, equipment, and supporting services provided by the Government of the United States shall be sufficient to meet the requirements of a program drawn up by the Government of the United Kingdom and communicated to the

Government of the United States prior to the entry into force of this Agreement. . . .

Governments of the United States and the United Kingdom, Polaris sales agreement, 6 April 1963. *Department of State Bulletin*, 14 January 1963. Quoted in Ian S. McDonald, *Anglo-American Relations since the Second World War* (London: David & Charles, 1974), pp. 193–5.

5.10   US–European relations: Kennedy's view

One of the reasons for the initial US reluctance to provide Britain with Polaris was concern, especially in the State Department, that such an agreement would complicate US relations with the United States' other European allies. Here President Kennedy sets out his views on the relationship between the United States and Europe, stressing the importance of a strong and united Europe, including Britain, acting as an equal partner with the United States.

Q. Mr President, in the event that Great Britain is shut out of the Common Market, how would that be likely to influence the United States' plan to associate itself with the economic community and how will it, in general, affect American interests?

A. We don't plan to associate ourselves with the community. . . .

We have strongly supported Britain's admission to the Common Market, however, because we think it helps build a United Europe, which, working in equal partnership with the United States, will provide security for Europe, for the United States, and together Europe and the United States – we can concern ourselves with the very pressing problems which affect so much of the world and Latin America, Africa and Asia.

The United States concerns itself particularly, as distinguished Europeans, Dr Adenauer, Mr [Robert] Schuman and others, in building a strong and vital – Mr [Alcide De] Gasperi and others - a strong, vital and vigorous Europe.

Now that is coming about. I would be reluctant to see Europe and the United States, now that Europe is a strong and vital force, to go in separate directions because this battle is not yet won. In Latin America alone, we face critical problems in this decade. If Latin America is unable to trade with Europe and with the Common Market, we face very, very great economic problems which we

141

cannot solve alone in Latin America. So our invitation to Europe is to unite, to be strong, and to join with us as an equal partner in meeting the problems of other parts of the world in the same way that some years ago the United States helped Europe build its strength.

Now, that is our hope. That has been the object of American policy for 15 years. That has been the object of the policy of great Europeans who helped bring about a reconciliation some years ago between France and Germany. We have seen the recent manifestation of the reconciliation.

There are problems throughout the globe that should occupy our attention, and the United States does not have the resources to meet them alone, and we hope Europe and the United States together can do it on the basis of equity. That is why we have supported the admission of Britain to the Common Market.

In the final analysis this must be a judgment of the countries in Europe, the Six. What kind of a Europe do they want? Do they want one looking out or looking in? What do they see as the balance of forces in the world today?

Now Europe is relatively secure. The day may come when Europe will not need the United States and its guarantees. I don't think that day has come yet, but it may come, and we would welcome that. We have no desire to stay in Europe except to participate in the defense of Europe. Once Europe is secure and feels itself secure – the United States has 400,000 troops there and we would, of course, want to bring them home.

We do not desire to influence or dominate. What we desire to do is to see Europe and the United States together engaged in the struggle in other parts of the world. We cannot possibly survive if Europe and the United States are rich and prosperous and isolated. We are asking that Europe together, united, join in this great effort, and I am hopeful they will, because after all that has been the object of the policy, of, as I say, a great many Europeans for a great many years. Now, when success is in sight, we don't want to see this great partnership dissolve.

Statement by President Kennedy, 24 January 1963. *Documents on American Foreign Relations, 1963* (New York: Harper & Row, 1964), pp. 181–3.

5.11 The Neustadt report: the lessons of Skybolt

Asked to report to President Kennedy on what could be
learned from the Skybolt affair and the Nassau meeting,
Richard E. Neustadt stresses the need to institutionalize inter-
state relations so that officials on each side come to view
cooperation with those on the other as natural in achieving its
policy goals, rather than relying on individuals at the head of
government.

My study does suggest a high priority for thought and work
on institution-building *with the British*. Bilateral relationships
are frowned on in some quarters lest they become 'exclusive'.
I do not see why they should. If we now need institutionalized
substitutes for Macmillan, the Germans still appear to need such
substitutes for Dulles. We ought to work on both. While we
are waiting for our own election, and for theirs, and for Paris,
and for Rome to clarify the 'Europe' we shall deal with in a
second term, this sort of work appears to me decidedly worth
doing.

Where might we put our thoughts? Not in overarching mech-
anisms, shadow enterprises, or another set of staffs at NATO (a
place with all the verve of our Department of Commerce). Already
we have more than enough of these. Rather, I suggest, we ought to
think about unpublicized joint ventures, government to government, which actually put bureaucrats to work on matters relevant
for them *and for their Ministers* in the internal conduct of each
government – and so affect the stakes a Ministry will weigh as it
participates in shaping national policy.

Our money and our weaponry have ceased to be decisive; if we
wish a steady influence upon 'alliance policy', which is but a reflection of *national* decisions, we must get down to the boiler room
where such decisions start. We need to help each fireman do what
matters to *him*, until at last he cannot think of shovelling without
us. Of course he will not think it if he has not been inside *our* boiler
room and found it useful in *his* business to be there. I see no point
in starting a 'joint venture' which we are not ready to pursue in
common at decision-making levels. Anything else is 'joint' *à la*
Skybolt, which was not joint at all and surely is a model *not* to
follow.

Assuming we can contemplate some genuine joint ventures, two spheres suggest themselves for careful exploration: research-and-development and defense budgeting.

If a Labour Government takes office in Great Britain, the uniform impression I have gained from shadow-ministers is that they look to us for psychic satisfaction in the form of 'consultation'. They think of their inheritance, Polaris, as their trading-stock. But I doubt that it can buy them what they want. What they talk of wanting seems to me a lot less satisfying in office than out: Ministers of State attendant on the President, staff officers attendant on the JCS, and so forth. These evidently mean more to a shadow-government than a real Government is likely to find in them. The more one knows about *our* crisis operations and 'war plans', the less there is to dignify the shadow-concepts of those shadow-ministers.

Disillusion, I suspect, will follow the enlightenment obtainable in office. Before that time arrives it would be helpful if there were a wide variety of ventures under way between our governments, which civil servants knew to be, and Ministers would find to be, of *use* in their own work and also ours. Budgeting and 'R and D' are a far cry from Great Decisions; this is to their advantage. Down in the depths of governmental processes where incremental choices year by year shape later options day by day, joint ventures offer something *real* to buttress 'consultation'. Ministers and their machines might gain a lot from this, and we as well: their stakes become our ties on their Prime Minister.

With Britain we have numerous connections even now, many of them relics of the War, some new, some in the talk-stage. These span more spheres than defense and include intelligence. In some spheres, notably defense, the talk of new departures both at Whitehall and the Pentagon is well advanced. But so far as I have found, on casual inquiry, present connections and proposed ones are *uneven*. Some may engage real interests, create stakes, for key officials in both governments. Most apparently do not. Many seem to wander in a vacuum, disconnected from decisions by the national establishments. Some are invisible at a first glance.

As a guide to institution-building with the British, it may be well to survey what is now in place or planned, and why it grew, and how it works, *to whose advantage* in both governments. A survey of that sort might show some fatal flaws in trying to make any such bureaucratized joint ventures serve the political purpose sketched above. If so, I would be sorry but inclined to try again. We then should look for *other* means to 'institutionalize Macmillan'. The need remains.

'Skybolt and Nassau: American Policy-making and Anglo-American Relations', report to the President, by Richard E. Neustadt, Professor of Government at Columbia University and consultant to President Kennedy, 15 November 1963. John F. Kennedy Library, NSF 322, Staff Memoranda.

6

The 'close relationship', 1964–70

A gradual cooling of Anglo-American relations in general was evident during the middle and the late 1960s. Despite the wide spectrum of cooperation which continued, in the defence field and other areas of the relationship, difficulties occurred with increasing frequency. Problems arose over such issues as the Multilateral Nuclear Force (MLF) and the Atlantic Nuclear Force (ANF), the war in Vietnam and the decision by the Wilson government to withdraw most British military forces from east of Suez. In contrast to the warm personal relationship between Kennedy and Macmillan, antagonism and animosity often characterised the relationship between Johnson and Wilson.

Despite these difficulties, however, the residual relationship with the United States continued to cause problems for the reorientation of British foreign policy. Like his predecessor, Wilson found that attempts to join the European Common Market in 1967 were dashed by the perception, especially in France, that Britain was not fully committed to Europe. Whether he believed it or not, the French President, Charles de Gaulle, rejected British membership on the grounds that Britain remained wedded to the 'special relationship' with the United States and was not a truly European power. When things went wrong, either economically or militarily, he argued, Britain would always revert to the Anglo-Saxon partnership. Faced with de Gaulle's opposition, Wilson responded by playing down the concept of the 'special relationship'. In symbolic fashion the Prime Minister deliberately talked of a 'close' rather than a 'special' relationship between the two countries.

6.1 Abandoning the deterrent? The Atlantic Nuclear Force

Shortly after the election of the new Labour government, in October 1964, Prime Minister Wilson was to visit the United States. Preparations for the visit included discussions at the

146

Prime Minister's country residence, Chequers. On the agenda was the proposed Atlantic Nuclear Force, which would bring non-nuclear NATO members into the formulation of nuclear policy but had implications for Britain's own independent deterrent, as indicated in this briefing document. The force was designed to counter US pressure for a Multilateral Nuclear Force, which it was feared would undermine Britain's independent nuclear deterrent.

How far will our Atlantic Nuclear Force project measure up to our objectives? It might be best to consider separately:

(a) *Its probable impact on France and the Soviet Union.* It seems probable that, even if we leave the door open for France to join the project subsequently, if she so wishes, she will take no advantage of the offer in the foreseeable future. On the contrary, she will regard it as one more illustration of the 'Atlantic' – as distinct from the 'European' – bias of NATO; and she *may* seek to retaliate by some form of disruptive action aimed at NATO or the EEC. Are we prepared to take this risk?

As regards the Soviet Union, we must assume that she will look on the ANF with no less disfavour than on the original MLF, and for the same reason.

In terms of relations with France and the Soviet Union, therefore, the project may not offer much better prospects than the original MLF of simplifying the problems of dissemination and disarmament. And, in so far as it may provoke France to some form of retaliatory action, it may have the same divisive effect within NATO which we have always criticised in the case of the MLF.

(b) *Its impact on Germany.* By contrast, the project may have considerable attractions for the Germans in so far as it offers them the prospect of something approaching equality of status with ourselves within the Alliance. But the German reaction will also be liable to be conditioned by:

(i) The fact that, since our contribution in the case of the ANF would presumably be proportionately greater than in the case of the MLF, our relative status in the new system would also be greater – and the German relative status correspondingly less.

(ii) The extent to which we should be prepared to surrender our independent deterrent – i.e. in whole or only in part. This question is discussed in paragraphs 27–34, which Ministers will wish to examine very closely, particularly as regards the degree of independent action which we may judge it necessary to preserve for the defence of such overseas commitments as we have decided, during the earlier discussion, to retain. They may conclude that, of the possible courses open to us, the third would be the least unsatisfactory compromise – i.e. to commit part of the Polaris force and part of the V-bomber force unconditionally but to retain the rest under national control as an insurance against our commitments elsewhere in the world. If so, we must decide how many Polaris submarines in total we intend to build.

(iii) The extent to which such forces as we may commit to the ANF will be committed irrevocably or only subject to some reservation, whether expressed or implied. Linked with this question is the vital issue of the control over the ANF, both political (i.e. by veto) and technical (i.e. by the permissive action link (PAL) Ministers will wish to consider these problems carefully, in the light of Sir Solly Zuckerman's latest discussion of PAL techniques in Washington.

(iv) The question whether the ANF would incorporate some MLF element and whether we ourselves would be prepared to make a significant contribution to it. The Foreign Secretary's telegram (Bonn No. 1150) shows the importance which the Germans continue to attach to this point. Ministers will need to consider whether a United Kingdom contribution would be politically acceptable and, if so, what form it should take. If the MLF element were an entirely sea-borne force, would it suffice that we should offer to provide bases in this country and, perhaps, warheads for the missiles? If it were partially land-based as well, must we contemplate contributing some TSR2's and, perhaps, some manpower for mixed-manned missiles?

(c) *Its impact on the USA.* The Foreign Secretary's discussions in Washington suggest that, here too, we shall be liable to meet the same continuing pressure for a significant contribution to the MLF, irrespective of any other form of contribution to an ANF that we may be ready to make. There is little sign, as yet, that the United States Government are prepared to abandon the basic MLF concept, even though they may be willing to let the timetable for decision slip by some months.

Moreover, we have to face the fact that, if we abandon our own independent deterrent, we – like the rest of Europe – will then be dependent on the main United States deterrent for our protection. The third of the objectives enumerated in paragraph 7 of Misc.17/

4 implies that it would be one of our purposes to try to broaden out the type of Allied consultation which the ANF would imply until it comprised the use of nuclear weapons anywhere in the world. No doubt we should make an effort on these lines. But is it realistic to suppose that the United States would ever abandon ultimate *control* over the main body of their independent deterrent? But, if not, and if we abandon our own deterrent, shall we not have to try to ensure (how?) that the United States will nevertheless still remain committed to the nuclear defence of Europe in general and of the United Kingdom in particular?

In effect, therefore, Misc.17/4 poses the following questions:

(i) Are we prepared to abandon our own independent deterrent – wholly or only partially?

(ii) To the extent to which we abandon it, do we do so irrevocably or with some reservation? And, if the latter, what is the reservation; and is it expressed or implied?

(iii) Can we be sure that any reservation which we may make will not be defeated by technical control (i.e. the PAL)?

(iv) If we find that we cannot put our project across unless we are also prepared to make a sizeable contribution to an MLF element which is to be considered an integral part of it, shall we be ready to do so? And, if so, on what scale and in what form?

Before answering these questions, Ministers may wish to consider:

2. *The Elements of a Possible Bargain (Misc.17/5)*

This memorandum indicates the extent to which we might try to bargain our contribution to the ANF (particularly the surrender of our independent deterrent and the acceptance of parity of status with Germany within the Alliance) against some reduction of our defence burden in other respects; and the extent to which we might hope to succeed in so doing.

The area of possible *quid pro quo* can be subdivided into two parts:

(i) We might try to persuade the other members of the Alliance to abandon the MLF entirely. The chances are not bright; but we should certainly press hard for its reduction significantly below the level of the project as originally envisaged.

(ii) We must persuade the United States to undertake to retain their veto indefinitely – both over the use of the nuclear weapons entrusted to the ANF and over any subsequent changes in the control arrangements for the Force. We can be reasonably hopeful on this point. But it is essential that the United States should not only give this undertaking but give it publicly and unequivocally – as they have always hitherto refused to do in relation to the original MLF But, if they do so, of course, the whole project becomes proportionately less attractive to the Germans.

(iii) We must also try to persuade the United States to undertake that, if we abandon our own independent deterrent, they will commit themselves unequivocally and indefinitely to the nuclear defence of Europe and the United Kingdom. This, too, we might achieve. But it is not easy to see how it would best be done: by some new form of NATO treaty?

(iv) We must try to ensure that, if we surrender our nuclear capability, other non-nuclear countries will bind themselves not to manufacture or to acquire nuclear weapons. The undertaking might be in the form of the draft appended to Misc.17/5. It would be aimed, of course, principally at Germany; and it would presumably be valueless in relation to France (and China).

(v) We must also try to make the ANF the occasion for some new initiative in the wider field of disarmament and arms control. But the prospects are not very good, given the probable Soviet reaction to the ANF.

(vi) We should try to secure, in return for contributing our nuclear forces to the defence of Europe, some compensating reduction in the conventional forces which we at present deploy on European territory. The chances are not bright, since the NATO Commanders still consider their forces to be below strength and will argue that they should be increased rather than reduced; and, if we press the point, we may collide with SACEUR and SACLANT on basic issues of strategic policy.

'Defence Policy – Chequers Discussions', paper prepared for the Prime Minister prior to Chequers meeting, 19 November 1964. Public Record Office, PREM 13/026.

6.2 A new Fulton: Wilson and the future of the free world

The Chequers weekend reached the conclusions described here, in a briefing paper prepared for Wilson for his talks with President Lyndon Johnson. Among other things, the Prime

Minister is encouraged to produce an updated version of Churchill's Fulton speech (see Chapter 2) to set the tone for the next decade.

I. *The Chequers philosophy*

To my mind the overriding purpose of your visit to Washington is to secure a broad meeting of minds between yourself and the President on what the world is going to look like from 1965 onwards and what the United States and United Kingdom jointly should do about it. Your object, as I see it, should be to sell to the President the basic philosophy of the Chequers weekend, your view of the world scene as a whole, both because it is right and because it is by worldwide collaboration that we shall preserve, unspoken, the 'special relationship'. The shape of the world to come is, roughly speaking:

1. The East–West conflict stalemated in Europe and thus less acute. Berlin and the Corridor are likely to be quiet.

2. The points of danger shifting Eastwards and Southwards: China vocally belligerent but not yet militarily powerful; Russia and China vying for political influence in the third world; Britain and the United States in trouble in Malaysia and Indo-China, Aden and Libya, Cuba and British Guiana.

3. The danger of North–South conflict with poverty tending to divide the world on racial lines.

In these circumstances, it is manifest nonsense to pile up ever more sophisticated arms for a war which can never be fought (not least because the spoils of war are unobtainable in a nuclear age). It is time the West realised that it has in fact won the battle for Europe. That being so, it is time, while holding the battlefield we have won, to devote our military and economic resources from now on to the problems of the late 60s rather than relive the problems of the 50s.

II. *The atlantic nuclear force*

It is in this broad context, and not in the isolated context of German status-seeking or French pretentiousness, that your approach to the nuclear management of the Alliance makes sense.

The fact is that the problems of the Alliance at present are the problems of a military Alliance that hasn't really got a war

151

to fight. Basically France is only able to pursue rogue elephant policies because she knows that it is perfectly safe for her to do so. Basically, Germany's demand for nuclear status is due to the fear that, with the lessening of East–West tension, Germany's special interest of the 50s, that of manning the front line of freedom against the Communist hordes, is being eroded.

Our plan for the Atlantic nuclear force makes sense:

1. Because it offers the Allies equality of status, not by everyone trading up to British levels but by the British trading down to everyone else's level except the Americans.

2. It closes no doors to the possibility of future moves to lessen East–West tension because it avoids creating a new weapons system by setting up a new system of management of the existing, and perfectly adequate, weapons system.

3. It provides a framework within which France could cooperate the moment her policies are animated by anything other than megalomania.

4. It does all this without creating a new weapons system which is military nonsense, economic waste and political folly.

III. *A new Fulton*

This, it seems to me, should be your approach in Washington. It should be the theme of the Foreign Secretary's main speech to the NATO Ministers in Paris. And it might well provide the main subject matter for your own speech in the Foreign Affairs Debate in the House before Christmas.

I cannot help thinking that it is only in the context of a considerable effort of public enlightenment, at home and abroad, that we shall be able to make sensible progress.

What we need, in fact, is a sort of new 'Fulton' speech, in the sense of a speech that charts the course of the free world for the next decade. What matter if it creates a furore to start with; so did Churchill at Fulton. The occasional uproar every ten years or so is a good thing if it makes people take a fresh look at the world, cease holding retrospective exhibitions of past achievements and take a step into the future.

Briefing for Prime Minister, 'Strategy for Washington', 2 December 1964. Public Record Office, PREM 13/103.

6.3   The Washington summit joint statement

During their talks in Washington in December 1964, Prime Minister Wilson and President Johnson released a joint statement. It was an opportunity to sum up publicly how each felt about Anglo-American relations and the state of international politics.

The President of the United States and the Prime Minister of the United Kingdom met in Washington 7th December to 9th December. They were assisted by Secretary of State Rusk, Secretary of Defense McNamara and Under Secretary of State Ball and by the Foreign Secretary, Mr Gordon Walker and the Secretary of State for Defence, Mr Healey.

In the course of a wide ranging exchange of views, the President and the Prime Minister reviewed the current international situation in light of the responsibilities which their countries carry for maintaining, together with their allies and friends, peace and stability throughout the world. They reaffirmed their determination to support the peacekeeping operations of the United Nations and to do all in their power to strengthen the systems of regional alliance in Europe, the Middle East and the Far East to which they both contribute.

They recognized the importance of strengthening the unity of the Atlantic Alliance in its strategic nuclear defense. They discussed existing proposals for this purpose and an outline of some new proposals presented by the British Government. They agreed that the objective in this field is to cooperate in finding the arrangements which best meet the legitimate interests of all members of the Alliance, while maintaining existing safeguards on the use of nuclear weapons, and preventing their further proliferation. A number of elements of this problem were considered during this initial exchange of views as a preliminary to further discussions among interested members of the Alliance.

They also agreed on the urgency of a world-wide effort to promote the non-dissemination and non-acquisition of nuclear weapons, and of continuing Western initiatives towards arms control and disarmament. They recognized the increasing need for initiatives of this kind in light of the recent detonation of a Chinese nuclear device.

The President and the Prime Minister reaffirmed their determination to continue to contribute to the maintenance of peace and stability in the Middle East and the Far East. In this connection they recognized the particular importance of the military effort which both their countries are making in support of legitimate Governments in South East Asia, particularly in Malaysia and South Vietnam, which seek to maintain their independence and to resist subversion.

They recognized also that a nation's defense policy must be based on a sound economy. The President and the Prime Minister, while determined that their countries should continue to play their full parts in the world-wide peacekeeping effort, affirmed their conviction that the burden of defense should be shared more equitably among the countries of the free world.

They agreed also on the need for improvement in the balance of payments and in the productivity and competitive position of both their economies in order to ensure the underlying economic strength which is essential for fulfilling their heavy international responsibilities. In this connection they arranged to explore in detail the possibilities of closer cooperation between their two countries in defense research and development and in weapons production.

The President and the Prime Minister reaffirmed their belief in the importance of close allied cooperation in international affairs. They agreed that this meeting was only the first stage in their consultation in which the matters that they had discussed would need to be examined in greater detail. They looked forward, too, to continuing discussions at all levels both within the Alliance and in wider international negotiations in pursuit of nuclear and conventional disarmament and all measures to reduce world tension.

President Johnson and Harold Wilson, joint statement, 8 December 1964. *White House Documents*, 8 December 1964. Quoted in Ian S. McDonald, *Anglo-American Relations since the Second World War* (London: David & Charles, 1974), pp. 199–201.

6.4 'A natural closeness': the special relationship in the 1960s

In this oral history interview Lord Gore-Booth, British High Commissioner in India, 1960–65, then Permanent Under-Secretary at the Foreign Office, 1965–69, gives his views on what he sees as the natural closeness between Britain and the

United States which prevailed throughout the 1960s. He also identifies a number of the difficulties which occurred.

Q. Did a special relationship exist during the time you were in the Foreign Office, was it close cooperation?

A. Yes, there's a natural closeness of cooperation between people in the American administration and in the machine in the State Department and people doing the same sort of thing in Britain, which just goes on without anybody having really to think about it. It just happens; and because of the community of language and in seeing things in the way of government by consent of the governed, it's a perfectly natural thing. And really you don't have to take any particular steps to see that it happens; it just happens. And this, right up to the time that I left in January '69, was still certainly the case.

Q. One diplomat while I was in America suggested that the closeness of relations inevitably depended on the areas where the two countries would come into cooperation, that the early '60s was a period of cooperation because there were a lot of areas that did in fact require the two countries to get together and so on and he went on to suggest that with the British intention to withdraw East of Suez, the British refusal to help in Vietnam, that relations weren't as close now largely because there weren't the areas where they could be seen to be close. Comment?

A. I certainly do say that closeness does to some extent depend on frequency and on the broadness of the field covered; to take another case, if American attention is very much focused on Latin America obviously we have less to say, but on the other hand given NATO, given Europe, given the Middle East, given the fact that we shan't wholly lose interest in South East Asia, there are plenty of fields where it will simply go on. Then when you're in the third country where neither of us have a particular interest, it still is the normal habit to compare notes.

Q. With relation to South East Asia, the whole policy in your period when you were in the Foreign Office, the '65–'69 period, how much of an impact do you think the decision on the Suez withdrawal or the refusal by the British government to go into Vietnam, and all the rest, how much do you think this had of an impact on Anglo-American relations?

A. Well I think you have to split it up. I think on the Vietnam decision, the American administration of President Johnson entirely

155

understood Mr Wilson's domestic difficulties and was therefore grateful that while we couldn't come in we at least didn't get pushed over emotionally into an officially anti-American attitude. We, as you know, got to the position of issuing certain warnings, that if they did certain things we should be against them, but we didn't go further than that and I think President Johnson was enough of a politician to realise that, and to be grateful for that amount of mercy.

Q. Did you feel that the Americans, when they went into Vietnam, expected the British to join them?

A. No, I don't think so at all. You see it all originated from the Geneva conference in 1954. The only people who didn't subscribe wholly to what was agreed there were the Americans who made a reservation because the South Vietnamese were not going to accept it. So there was again in a literal sense and not in any tactical sense a special relationship between the Americans and the South Vietnamese, of which we were not part, so they didn't expect us to join them. I have no doubt they'd have been delighted if we did.

Q. I was wondering whether one could make a comparison of the refusal, at least the reluctance of the Americans to go into Laos in the early '60s because they didn't want to intervene alone, and the change of policy with the intervention unilateral to begin with in South Vietnam, whether in fact they felt that Congress required, as it required in Laos with the British to be on their side before they gave approval?

A. I think it's difficult to follow all the way through; I think the getting involved in Vietnam was such a gradual process, wasn't it? I mean it really took about five years for them to realise how far they were in. It all happened in little bits and I think it was rather a unique process in that way.

Q. What of East of Suez?

A. Oh, on that I think the Americans were very much upset both by the nature of the decision and more I think by the way in which it was taken. You see they knew in '67, there's been a great sort of myth created that the South East Asia decision was taken in 1968. It wasn't, it was taken in 1967 and this was a mere acceleration of it; but it was all done with such drama and with the expectation that it wouldn't be done at all that the Americans were naturally extremely upset about it. But American diplomacy these days is very adult. People underestimate this and they have now learnt to take things well, that's the sort of thing that happens.

Q. In discussing these two particular policy issues, how far do you think this has influenced relations in the sense that it's led to a closening of relations between America, Australia and New Zealand; that has tended to lessen relations between America and Britain, that America sees its closest allies in foreign policy as being Australasia as opposed to the British?

A. Well, this is true of South East Asia, of course, but it isn't true generally, because the Australians have very little to say in the Middle East, in Europe, and so on. But it is of course absolutely true as far as South East Asia is concerned and indeed it is interesting that one of the people who had most to do with Australia going that way was Prime Minister Sir Robert Menzies. But he saw the future of Australia quite rightly, strategically, in Asia as being linked with America who had the power and the capacity to help, so he naturally turned that way.

Q. Perhaps before we turn to the more specific subject I had in mind of our discussion, you might like to suggest over the decade of the '60s, in the discussion on personalities, whether you feel that relations have become less emotionally charged, less personal, more institutionalized, more of a practical relationship rather than one based on emotion and heritage. It's now a relationship that requires both sides to get something out of it?

A. I think that's always, even behind the sentiment, been the case. But what I think is true is of course that between shall we say Macmillan and Eisenhower, obviously there was an emotion which derived from them being together personally in the middle of the war – there is nothing which replaces that.

Q. But I ask that question bearing in mind the rather unique position of David Harlech in Washington under Kennedy, postponing the inevitable change of personal relationships after the war.

A. Yes, I should think this is right, I think that that was an intelligent profiting by a personal consideration, which after all could arise again. It did serve the purpose you say, which was a very personal relationship.

Oral history interview by David Nunnerly, 13 July 1970. John F. Kennedy Library.

Anglo-American relations

6.5   British initiative on the Vietnam War, 1967

Refusing to be drawn into the Vietnam War in spite of
American pressure, the British attempted to serve as mediators
in resolving the conflict. This was a major irritant in Anglo-
American relations at the time. Here Lyndon Johnson comments on Harold Wilson's efforts early in 1967 to broker a
peace deal.

... [E]arly in February, Soviet Chairman Kosygin was visiting
Prime Minister Wilson in London. Vietnam was one of the many
matters they discussed. Wilson seemed to feel that he and the Soviet
leader could serve as mediators and bring about a settlement of the
war. I doubted this strongly. I believed that if the Soviets thought
they had a peace formula Hanoi would accept, they would deal
directly with us rather than through a fourth party. But I was
willing for our British friends to try.

At the onset of the London talks, it became clear to me why the
Soviets were willing to discuss Vietnam. Kosygin was pressing
Wilson hard to use his influence to persuade us to accept Hanoi's
vague offer of possible talks in exchange for a bombing halt. When
the Prime Minister asked for our reaction to this proposal, I replied:
'If we are asked to take military action on our side, we need to
know what the military consequences will be – that is, what military
action will be taken by the other side.' I concluded my message to
Wilson by saying: 'I would strongly urge that the two co-chairmen
[of the Geneva conference] not suggest a stoppage of the bombing
in exchange merely for talks, but instead appeal to Hanoi to consider seriously the reasonable proposals we are putting before them,
which would take us not merely into negotiation but a long step
towards peace itself.'

We had informed the British that I was going to tell Ho Chi Minh
that if he agreed to 'an assured stoppage of infiltration into South
Vietnam', we would end the bombing and also stop increasing our
troop strength in the South. I told Wilson that he could talk with
Kosygin on the same basis if he wished, in full confidence that this
represented our official position. We thought that the sequence was
clear: Hanoi would first stop infiltration; we would then stop the
bombing and, in addition, we would agree not to increase our troop
strength in Vietnam. This is what I told Ho Chi Minh in my letter.

158

I recognized, of course, that the new proposal altered the Phase A–Phase B plan we had discussed earlier with the British and had offered to Hanoi. Instead of asking the North Vietnamese to promise to take steps to reduce the fighting after the bombing ended, I wanted them to begin cutting down their actions against the South before we stopped the bombing. I felt strongly that this change was justified by the hard fact that during the bombing pause then under way very large southward movements of men and supplies were taking place in the area above the demilitarized zone. I refused to risk the safety of our men in I Corps by stopping air strikes before Ho Chi Minh had acted. On the other hand, I went further than ever before by proposing to freeze US troop levels in the South.

The British read our message differently. They considered it a restatement of the Phase A–Phase B plan, with which they were familiar – that Hanoi would have to agree to halt infiltration but would not actually stop until after the bombing was suspended. When Wilson discussed this with Kosygin, the Soviet leader asked for the proposal in writing. The British gave a document to him without specific approval from Washington, which was an error, though I am confident that they acted in good faith. The result was a diplomatic mix-up for which we shared a certain amount of the responsibility. The British, with some embarrassment, had to go back to Kosygin with the revised, and correct, version of our proposal. That was the evening of February 10.

Meanwhile, the Tet truce period was running out. It ended on February 11, but with Kosygin still in the United Kingdom, we agreed to extend the bombing stand-down until he returned to Moscow on the 13th. At their final meeting with Kosygin on February 12, the British made a new proposal: If the Soviets could obtain North Vietnam's assurance that infiltration into the South would end the next day, the British would get US assurance that the bombing, which then had been stopped for five days, would not be resumed and, further, that the build-up of American forces would end. We had agreed to this British approach before it was put to Kosygin. The Soviets in turn passed the offer on to Hanoi. By the time Kosygin left London the following day, there was still no word from Hanoi. Nor was an answer waiting when Kosygin got back to Moscow.

Prime Minister Wilson felt that we had given him and the Russians too little time to get an answer, but Hanoi had had several months to study and consider the Phase A–Phase B plan – and the proposal Wilson made to Kosygin was but a variation of that idea. It does not take all that long to cable 'yes' or 'no' or 'we are giving it serious study,' even from as far away as Hanoi. As a matter of fact, Hanoi did not have to send a cable at all. We had already carried out Phase A; the bombing had been stopped. If the leaders in Hanoi wanted to move toward peace, they knew that all they had to do was to take some visible step to cut back their half of the war. That step could have taken many forms – stopping infiltration or sharply reducing it, pulling back some of their units from advanced positions, cutting down the number of attacks, almost anything significant that would have reflected an honest desire on their part to reduce hostilities. We would have quickly recognized such an action and would have responded to it – as we had said time and time again. The hard but unfortunate truth was that the leaders in Hanoi had snubbed the two-phase approach before the Wilson–Kosygin sessions, and they turned it down again late in 1967. So I could not share the Prime Minister's feeling, which he expressed in the House of Commons, that 'a solution could now be reached'.

Wilson's sentiment was understandable but far from unique. During the many years we spent searching for a peace formula, I learned that everyone who engaged in such efforts came to think that his own particular approach was the one that would, or should, succeed. Whether they were Poles or Italians, Swedes or Indians, the Secretary General of the United Nations, or journalists, or merely self-appointed peacemakers, they were all convinced that their moves were the only ones that promised success, that their route was the one to take. If only we would follow their plan – and as time passed that usually meant giving Hanoi more and more – peace could be achieved. In many cases, they did not realize that the proposals they advocated so strongly had already been tried and had been rejected by Hanoi.

Memoirs of Lyndon B. Johnson. Lyndon Baines Johnson, *The Vantage Point. Perspectives of the Presidency, 1963–1969* (London: Weidenfeld & Nicolson, 1971), pp. 253–5.

The 'close relationship'

6.6 A Sign of *The Times*: American support for the special relationship

British entry to the Common Market clearly had implications for Anglo-American relations. In this letter to *The Times* newspaper, various influential American political and academic figures express the belief that the special relationship should be maintained despite Britain's European ambitions.

Sir, – Now that Britain is proceeding to canvass the conditions for her entry into the Common Market, we wish her well in her endeavours.

We would also assert, however, that in our opinion the 'special relationship' between Britain and the United States, based on, among other things, our common cause in two world wars, our common traditions of democracy and law, as well as our closely linked cultures, has produced an enduring friendship unique among sovereign states.

Whether Britain enter Europe or not, and whatever cynics may say to the contrary, we believe this friendship should remain a cornerstone of American foreign policy. We hope it will likewise remain a fundamental part of British policy.

To that end, our respective governments should now begin to consider contingent means, including mutually beneficial trade and fiscal reforms, for saving and strengthening the historic relationship between our nations, whatever the outcome of the EEC negotiations.

Yours truly, Philip H. Hoff, Vermont; Otto Kerner, Illinois; Calvin Rampton, Utah; Tom Mccall, Oregon; Charles Terry, Delaware, Governors. [Also signed by thirty-nine other Senators and Congressmen.] New York, Feb. 15.

'Britain and the United States', letter to *The Times*, from the Governor of Vermont and others. Letters to the Editor, *The Times*, 21 February 1967.

6.7 'Irreparable damage': British withdrawal from the Far East

As in the immediate post-war period, British withdrawal from strategically important areas of the world caused consternation in America and impacted negatively upon Anglo-American relations. In his diaries Richard Crossman, Lord President of the Council and Leader of the House of Commons

161

between 1966 and 1968, records Foreign Secretary George
Brown's account of breaking the news about British withdrawal from east of Suez to the Americans.

By now George Brown had bustled into the room and we decided he
should give us a special report on his interview with Dean Rusk and
on the message from L.B.J. which had arrived at the FO this
morning. Now in considering his behaviour one must realize that
he'd travelled round the world in a week and was obviously psycho-
logically and physically upset by this jolting of the passage of time.
So, not unexpectedly, he sat down and gave us in his most dramatic
and most incoherent way a half-hour description of the appalling
onslaught to which he had been submitted, first by Dean Rusk and
then by a State Department official whose theme had been, 'Be
British, George, be British – how can you betray us?' He told us that
he had faithfully reported the decision to leave Singapore by 1970–
71 and to scrap the F-111 as unalterable Cabinet decisions. They
had expressed nothing but horror and consternation. 'I put the
Cabinet case – the case for the new strategy – as well as possible. I
put it as well as the Lord President of the Council himself could put
it and one can't ask more than that,' he remarked at one point
sarcastically. Despite all his rhetoric and confusion one point stood
out from his report. The main American complaint was not about
the withdrawal from the Far East but about the decision to leave the
Persian Gulf. When the Americans made this clear George Brown
had explained that it didn't cost us much more to hold the Gulf if
we were in Singapore and Malaya but that as we had to abandon
Singapore and Malaya we couldn't hold the Gulf without incurring
colossal expense. His contention was that irreparable damage had
been done by his having to make this statement at all and having to
tell the Americans of our decisions.

Memoirs of Richard Crossman, Friday 12 January 1968. Richard
Crossman, *The Diaries of a Cabinet Minister*, Vol. 2, *Lord President of the
Council and Leader of the House of Commons, 1966–68* (London: Hamish
Hamilton and Jonathan Cape, 1976), pp. 646–7.

6.8   The value of intangibles: Kissinger on the special
relationship

Henry Kissinger was President Nixon's special assistant on
national security affairs. In this extract from his memoirs,

shortly after the Nixon administration took office, and prior to
a trip to Europe, he sums up his understanding of the nature
and importance of the 'special relationship', and comments on
those Americans seeking to sever it.

He [Nixon] tackled head-on the so-called special relationship between Britain and the United States that was so contentious within
our government – by referring to it explicitly twice and in most
positive terms.

This gave no little pain to many of the European integrationists
in the Department of State and outside the government. The
advocates – almost fanatics – of European unity were eager to
terminate the 'special relationship' with our oldest ally as an
alleged favor to Britain to smooth its entry into the Common
Market. They felt it essential to deprive Britain of any special status
with us lest it impede Britain's role in the Europe they cherished.
They urged a formal egalitarianism, unaffected by tradition or
conceptions of the national interest, as the best guarantee of their
Grand Design.

Even if desirable, which I doubted, this was impractical. For the
special relationship with Britain was peculiarly impervious to ab-
stract theories. It did not depend on formal arrangements; it derived
in part from the memory of Britain's heroic wartime effort; it
reflected the common language and culture of two sister peoples. It
owed no little to the superb self-discipline by which Britain had
succeeded in maintaining political influence after its physical power
had waned. When Britain emerged from the Second World War too
enfeebled to insist on its views, it wasted no time in mourning an
irretrievable past. British leaders instead tenaciously elaborated the
'special relationship' with us. This was, in effect, a pattern of
consultation so matter-of-factly intimate that it became psychologi-
cally impossible to ignore British views. They evolved a habit of
meetings so regular that autonomous American action somehow
came to seem to violate club rules. Above all, they used effectively
an abundance of wisdom and trustworthiness of conduct so exceptional that successive American leaders saw it in their self-interest to
obtain British advice before taking major decisions. It was an extraordinary relationship because it rested on no legal claim; it was
formalized by no document; it was carried forward by succeeding
British governments as if no alternative were conceivable. Britain's

influence was great precisely because it never insisted on it; the 'special' relationship' demonstrated the value of intangibles.

One feature of the Anglo-American relationship was the degree to which diplomatic subtlety overcame substantive disagreements. In reality, on European integration the views of Britain's leaders were closer to de Gaulle's than to ours; an integrated supranational Europe was as much anathema in Britain as in France. The major difference between the French and the British was that the British leaders generally conceded us the theory – of European integration or Atlantic unity – while seeking to shape its implementation through the closest contacts with us. Where de Gaulle tended to confront us with *faits accomplis* and doctrinal challenges, Britain turned conciliation into a weapon by making it morally inconceivable that its views could be ignored.

I considered the attacks from within our government on the special relationship as petty and formalistic. Severing our special ties – assuming it could be done – would undermine British self-confidence, and gain us nothing. In a background briefing on February 21 before our departure for Europe, I pointed out:

> My own personal view on this issue is that we do not suffer in the world from such an excess of friends that we should discourage those who feel that they have a special friendship for us. I would think that the answer to the special relationship of Britain would be to raise other countries to the same status, rather than to discourage Britain into a less warm relationship with the United States.

Memoirs of Henry Kissinger, February 1969. Henry Kissinger, *White House Years* (Weidenfeld & Nicolson, 1979), pp. 89–91.

6.9 Not an exclusive relationship: Nixon's view

Arriving in London in February 1969, President Nixon offered his thoughts on the 'special relationship'. Like Kissinger, he affirmed the closeness of the relationship and saw its basis in common values. Also like Kissinger, he spoke of the need to extend the same closeness of relations to other states.

Winston Churchill called ours a special relationship. He was not referring to legal obligations but to human intangibles. He was referring to the means of communication to which Woodrow

Wilson had referred to 50 years ago. And no two nations in the world more commonly and more closely share the means of communication than do the United States and the United Kingdom. We share a common language. We share the common law. We share great institutions of the Parliament. We share other institutions.

Because we share those institutions we enjoy a means of communication which gives us a special relationship. It means, too, that we share something else – a common commitment to a peace that transcends national boundaries and because we are partners in the quest for peace we know that our relationship – that special relationship that we have – is not exclusive because that peace that we seek, the two of us, will be secure only when all nations enjoy the relationship of trust and confidence that unites us.

President Nixon, 'Remarks at the airport on arrival in London', 24 February 1969. *Richard Nixon. Public Papers of the Presidents of the United States* (Washington: US Government Printing Office, 1971), pp. 139–40.

6.10 'A close relationship': Harold Wilson on Anglo-American relations

Speaking in the United States in April 1971, Harold Wilson (then in opposition) offered his views on the 'special relationship'. He preferred not to use that term but spoke of a close relationship, and explained how he saw the relationship operating in the future.

Frequently I am asked, 'what about the special relationship?'

I am never quite sure what this means. I am more interested in a close relationship based on a common purpose, common objectives, and as far as can be achieved community of policy, a relationship based not on condescension or on a backward-looking nostalgia for the past, but on the ability of both parties to put forward their strength and their own unique contribution to our common purpose. Charles Lamb said in one of his essays, 'There is nothing so irrelevant as a poor relation,' and if ever our relationship with you were based on that status the sooner it were ended the better: that is why the first priority in British internal policy is to build up our economic strength so that as partners – in the alliance, in Europe, and the Commonwealth – we are relevant and necessary. It is on that, not on any conception of past greatness that our standing in

the world will depend. Our ability to restore the lost dynamic to
Britain's economic society, to restore a sense of economic and social
and moral purpose, will have far more bearing on our value as an
ally than any vain nuclear posturings ...

... Our closest relationship is based to a large extent on an
identity of view and purpose over a wide area of world problems.
We are not seeking in the main so much to decide on Anglo-
American action in particular areas, as to coordinate our influence
in the acceptance of objectives and plans we have formulated in
common, most frequently in consultation with our other partners –
in NATO and SEATO, in various international economic organizations, above all, in the United States.

Very often on many issues our purpose is complementary, rather
than identical. Britain cannot compete with American power,
whether in defence terms, nuclear and conventional, or in military
and industrial terms. But there are areas of the world where we have
influence or a special *entrée*, as in other areas this is true of our very
powerful neighbour.

We have little to bring to common purposes through the military
value of Britain's nuclear capability. Nothing at all to contribute by
the pretence of being a so-called independent nuclear power. But
our nuclear experience and expertise, both in political and technical
matters, means that we can make an important contribution – for
example in inter-allied discussions – on the Nuclear Planning Group
of NATO, on the new and more streamlined strategy for NATO
and in the consultative discussions that the United States Government holds with our NATO allies about the Strategic Arms Limitation Talks (SALT) with the Soviet Union.

The areas of cooperation therefore I would define as follows.
First the NATO allies. It would be unthinkable that any major new
initiative within NATO whether for increasing its strength and
effectiveness, or combining its power to work for a *détente* with the
Eastern world, could be undertaken without close prior consultation between our two countries and between each of us and our
NATO partners.

Second, we have an important role to play in disarmament, where
again our nuclear experience has value. The main breakthrough in
the 18-national Disarmament Conference took place as a result of
bilateral discussions during Mr Johnson's Presidency between
Washington and Moscow; but at one of the most difficult moments,

it was a British initiative which helped to bring the two sides together. We have throughout supported the United States view that the more generalized advances we all seek cannot be regarded as secure without adequate inspection. New and improving techniques for the outside detection of nuclear tests are continuously being developed, and in this context the very close – and largely unpublicised – consultations between the British Cabinet, scientific secretariat and opposite numbers in the United States can be of vital importance. As indeed can be the work of non-official scientists at such meetings as the Pugwash Conferences with similarly unofficial Soviet scientists. At the end of the day – we have perhaps not quite reached it yet – it will be a matter for combined scientific and political judgement where the balance of advantage rests, between disarmament and security, in deciding how low must be the threshold for the outside detection of nuclear tests we should regard as adequate.

Third, our cooperation is vital in economic matters, as fellow members of the International Monetary Fund and the World Bank, but also of more Atlantic groupings such as the Group of Ten, the monthly meeting of central bankers at Basle, and wider-than-Atlantic organisations, such as the OECD . . .

Press release: Harold Wilson, 'Anglo-American relations: a special case', speech to the University of Texas, 30 April 1971. Quoted in Ian S. McDonald, *Anglo-American Relations since the Second World War* (London: David & Charles, 1974), pp. 219–22.

167

7

The 'natural relationship', 1970–79

Just as Harold Wilson chose to talk about the 'close' relationship, his successor as Prime Minister, Edward Heath, also chose to symbolise the changing nature of British policy in the 1970s by referring to the 'natural' relationship with the United States. As a committed European, Heath quite deliberately turned his back on many of the conventions which had characterised the 'special relationship' in the past. The symbolic change of title and a distinct change in the direction of British foreign policy both played their part in the success of Britain's third application to join the European Community in 1973.

Although there were few serious frictions in Anglo-American relations in the early 1970s there was a growing divergence of interests and an increasing inequality of power which helped to slacken the bonds between the two states. As the United States became more and more preoccupied with superpower problems, such as relations with the Soviet Union and China, as well as ending her disastrous war in Vietnam, so the 'special relationship' with Britain became less and less important to American interests. For her part Britain had her own preoccupations, including severe economic problems, industrial tensions and the coordination of her policies with those of other members of the European Community. As a consequence the attention of both countries tended to be deflected away from the traditional post-war priority given to relations with each other.

The stark choice between Europe and America which characterised Heath's policies was not, however, followed by his successors. The Labour governments which followed under Wilson and especially Callaghan sought to maintain Britain's position within the European Community, while at the same time fostering closer links with the Ford and Carter administrations in the United States. As the *détente* in East–West relations of the early 1970s gradually gave way to the growing tensions of the late 1970s Britain and the United States once again began to rediscover a wide range of common interests in the foreign and defence policy fields.

The 'natural relationship'

7.1 No longer cherished: Edward Heath and the 'special relationship'

Here Edward Heath's biographer describes the new Prime Minister's priorities on taking office in 1970. Without seeing himself as anti-American, Heath set out to dismantle the special relationship as part of his strategy for joining the European Community.

Heath's first priority was to negotiate Britain's entry to the EEC as quickly as possible and – within the constraint of political acceptability – at almost any price. His purpose was to realign the country's sense of identity irrevocably towards Europe. The long-cherished 'special relationship' with the United States was to be abruptly ended, and sentimental allegiance to the Commonwealth briskly shelved. This did not mean, however, that Heath saw himself as in any way anti-American, anti-Commonwealth or anti-Third World. On the contrary, he believed strongly that an enlarged Europe, including Britain, should shoulder a larger role within NATO, becoming a true partner of the United States instead of a resentful dependant, to the benefit of both parties. It was in America's interest – indeed it had long been American policy – that Britain should become a part of Europe. There could be nothing anti-American about that.

. . . The most radical aspect of Heath's foreign policy – differentiating his Government sharply from every previous postwar administration, Conservative or Labour, and from all his successors over the next sixteen years as well – was his determination *not* to have a special relationship with the United States. On the contrary, he was determined to assert Britain's European identity. Remembering de Gaulle's reaction to Macmillan's nuclear deal with President Kennedy at Nassau in 1962, he was specifically determined to show Pompidou that Britain wasn't an American Trojan Horse. He therefore quite deliberately made no early visit to Washington and made very little use of the transatlantic telephone. Instead, President Nixon had to come and see him, for a brief stopover at Chequers in October when the Queen's presence ensured that there was no time for serious talking. This was distressing to Nixon, who actively admired Heath, had been elated by his victory against the odds in June and desperately wanted to have a special relationship with him. They were in some respects, as Henry Kissinger noted, similar

169

men – both loners whose struggles to reach the top from similar social backgrounds had left them introverted, self-reliant and suspicious. But this was no reason to expect them to strike up a personal bond: neither was good at social relaxation. In fact, when they got down to hard discussion they did not get on badly – their views of international politics were broadly parallel; but the essential point was that Heath did not intend to have a personal relationship at all. The Americans found his determination to keep his distance bewildering. Used to Wilson fawning on Johnson and before that Macmillan's avuncular relationship with Kennedy, they could not understand a British Prime Minister deliberately wanting to keep relations cool, especially at a time when Pompidou and Willy Brandt were trying to get closer to Washington. Kissinger wrote in 1982:

> Paradoxically, while the other European leaders strove to improve their relations with us . . . Heath went in the opposite direction. His relations with us were always correct, but they rarely rose above a basic reserve that prevented – in the name of Europe – the close co-operation with us that was his for the taking.

The intimate access to the President which previous prime ministers had enjoyed was reduced to formal diplomatic exchanges. Kissinger found Heath 'incisive, decisive and astute' in discussion of world affairs; yet 'of all British political leaders, Heath was the most indifferent to the American connection and perhaps even to Americans individually'. He 'dealt with us with an unsentimentality totally at variance with the "special relationship"'. As a result, Nixon's relationship with Heath 'was like that of a jilted lover'.

The first formal meeting between the two leaders – discounting Nixon's brief visit to Chequers in October – took place in Washington in December 1970. Heath 'left no doubt about the new priorities in British policy'. Kissinger immediately sensed 'a revolution in Britain's post-war foreign policy', and wrote in his memoirs of a 'painful' transformation. Nevertheless there was no rift. Heath was as supportive of Nixon's gradual disengagement from Vietnam as he had been of the vigorous prosecution of the war when in opposition: 'he argued vigorously that an American withdrawal . . . under conditions interpreted as a collapse of American will might unleash a new round of Soviet aggression in Europe'. Nixon for his part welcomed Heath's Five-Power Defence Pact in the Far East, though the Americans remained sceptical of his apprehension of a Soviet threat in the Indian Ocean and privately critical of the policy of selling arms to South Africa.

Differences multiplied in 1971, however, initially on the economic front. The United States had long supported British membership of the EEC on political grounds, but now that it was about to become reality the Americans suddenly felt themselves threatened by the enlarged Community. For some years the dollar had been coming under mounting pressure, and there were growing demands in Congress for protection against what was perceived as unfair European competition. On 15 August Nixon's combative Treasury Secretary, John Connally, abruptly imposed a 10 per cent import surcharge and suspended the convertibility of the dollar, thus ending the dollar-centred international financial system which had prevailed since the Bretton Woods agreement in 1944. His unilateral action evoked shock and outrage in Europe and Japan, where it was seen almost as an act of economic war. Heath, despite his deliberate refusal of a special relationship, was furious at what he regarded as an act of international irresponsibility on the part of Washington. The world economy was thrown into a period of uncertainty which was not resolved for several years. A temporary realignment of currencies was achieved by the Smithsonian Agreement negotiated by the leading industrial nations in Washington in December. Heath met Nixon a few days later in Bermuda – a summit widely reported as marking the formal end of the 'special relationship': the contrast was drawn with the Kennedy–Macmillan meeting on the same island ten years earlier. The atmosphere was eased by Nixon's announcement of the lifting of the American import surcharge; but the suspension of convertibility remained. Six months later Britain was obliged, despite Heath's past assurances, to allow the pound to 'float'. The devaluation of the dollar continued to have serious repercussions for the British economy right through 1972–3.

Further tension between London and Washington arose over the war between India and Pakistan which resulted in the creation of Bangladesh. Heath had established a good relationship with Mrs Gandhi, sympathised with India's support for Bengal and hoped to play a mediating role. To his annoyance Nixon and Kissinger –

regarding India as a Soviet puppet and just at that moment preparing to reopen relations with Pakistan's protector, China – branded India the aggressor and vigorously supported Pakistan. Nixon regarded the war simplistically as another episode in the Soviet Union's continual testing of Western resolve. Twenty years later, in an unbuttoned interview, Heath asserted that Kissinger tried to involve Britain in the conflict, as Kennedy and Johnson had earlier tried to involve Britain in Vietnam. Whatever the accuracy of his recollections, the contemptuous tone of his remarks vividly expressed his hostility to the 'special relationship':

> What they wanted from the special relationship was to land Britain in it as well. There was the question of the Indo-Pakistan war and what Henry wanted was to land us in that and I was determined not to be landed. We discussed this in Bermuda [in December 1971] . . . President Nixon . . . opened up the discussion and said, 'There seems to be some misunderstanding about this, Henry, try to explain why this was what you wanted,' and so then we had a lecture about the conceptual nature of Kissinger policy. Well, we easily despatched that and Nixon said, 'Well, that's the end of that one, Henry, isn't it?' . . . Did we lose anything by it? No, of course not. We gained an enormous amount. I can quite see that it's rather difficult for some Americans, including Henry, to adjust themselves to this, but it's necessary for them to do it. Now, there are some people who always want to nestle on the shoulder of an American president. That's no future for Britain.

In late 1972, following Nixon's historic opening to China and the conclusion of the first SALT agreement for nuclear parity with the Soviet Union, Kissinger tried to reassure the Europeans by declaring 1973 the 'Year of Europe'. Willy Brandt believed that 'the President had only a superficial knowledge of what Kissinger has set in motion'. Heath, looking back, was equally scornful of this stillborn initiative:

> [Kissinger] created the Year of Europe, which never of course came about, without any discussions with us . . . or with anybody else. He just declared he was going to have a Year of Europe. I said to him, 'Now you've done this, we must have a year of the United States. Who are you to propose that there should be a Year of Europe? You're not part of Europe.'

The 'natural relationship'

Remarks by John Campbell, biographer of Edward Heath. John Campbell, *Edward Heath. A Biography* (London: Cape, 1993), pp. 336–45.

7.2 The Bermuda joint statement

The meeting between the Prime Minister and the President towards the end of 1971 in Bermuda was seen at the time as marking the end of the 'special relationship'. Edward Heath and Richard Nixon issued the following joint statement on their talks.

The President of the United States, the Honorable Richard M. Nixon, and the Prime Minister of the United Kingdom, the Right Honorable Edward Heath, meeting in Government House, Bermuda, on 20 and 21 December 1971, discussed the world situation in all its aspects. They agreed that the period which lies ahead is likely to be one of rapid change, which will offer the free world both opportunity and challenge on an unprecedented scale. This will call for the maintenance of the closest possible degree of understanding and unity of purpose not only between their two countries but also between themselves and their allies and partners. In view of the significance of the natural relationship between the United Kingdom and the United States they resolved to maintain their close and continuing consultation at all levels in their approach to world problems.

They recognized that the fulfillment of their objectives will be promoted by the United Kingdom's forthcoming accession to the European Economic Communities, which will reinforce the strength of the Atlantic Alliance. This Alliance is, and must remain, the cornerstone of the defence of the free world. The President and the Prime Minister agreed that there is no inconsistency between a resolute and determined adherence to the principles which inspire the Alliance and the pursuit of that relaxation of international tension which is necessary to satisfy the natural aspirations of mankind to live in peace and prosperity.

Not the least of the problems confronting the free world is the need to promote conditions for more liberal commercial exchanges. The President and the Prime Minister welcomed the realignment of exchange rates and accompanying measures agreed in Washington on 17 and 18 December and agreed upon the necessity for their two countries, in consultation with their international partners, to intensify their efforts to promote a reformed international monetary system. They noted the importance of reviewing international commercial relations in order to reduce barriers to trade between the major trading countries of the world.

In the same spirit they agreed that one of the most essential tasks of statesmanship today is to lift the sights beyond the problems of immediate urgency to those major political and economic issues, which in the long term will determine the shape of the world in which we all live. They agreed that they would direct all their consultations to this end.

Meeting with Prime Minister Edward Heath of the United Kingdom in Bermuda, 20–1 December 1971: joint statement. *Richard Nixon. Public Papers of the Presidents of the United States, 1971* (Washington: US Government Printing Office, 1972), pp. 1201–2.

7.3 'A grumbling alliance': European–American relations

The Anglo-American relationship operated within the wider context of the relationship between the United States and Europe. That relationship was not without its own stresses and strains, especially as American relative economic strength declined and European strength increased. This article by a leading journalist and academic sets out some of the difficulties facing the relationship in the early 1970s.

In this and the next lecture I am going to talk about the European Community's relations with the rest of the world – starting with the United States. In the early days of the European Common Market, the Six managed to achieve a kind of illusion of privacy within the international system: what I mean is that they treated the often quite profound effects which the arrangements that they made with one another had on the rest of the world as if they were subsidiary matters, certainly of no particular concern to them. They behaved for much of the time rather as though they were living inside a charmed circle, bounded entirely by their own problems and preoccupations. The special circumstances of the later post-war period, when Europe finally withdrew from empire and experienced the longest uninterrupted run of prosperity ever, based on cultivating its own garden, certainly helped.

The forward march of American world power, which accompanied the European withdrawal, was another major factor. The Europeans were provided with a sure military defence through the American nuclear umbrella; and American power, abetted to a diminishing extent by the British, supplied sufficient security for the movement of world trade to guarantee Europe's requirements of vital raw materials like oil. At the same time the American dollar provided an extremely effective international medium of exchange and a common reserve currency for the Europeans. Why should the countries forming the European Community have cared very much about what happened in the world beyond Western Europe?

Meanwhile the politics of the European charmed circle led to the building-up of a network of special agreements between the Community and a number of favoured states on its southerly periphery. Many of these were Mediterranean countries; others were in Black Africa, former colonies of France and Belgium. What has now been established as a result of this is a fairly well-defined zone of client states – more or less dependent commercial partners of the Community. To American eyes, this systematic build-up of privileged trading arrangements by the Europeans, with its corollary of discrimination against the outsider, must look altogether too much like a variation of their own early federal history – a kind of commercial Monroe Doctrine for Eurafrica.

That does not make the Americans of today like it any better. On the contrary, as the design of the European construction which they helped to foster has become clearer, they have grown more indignant about it. They feel cheated on two counts. First of all, there is much less of a unified political power in the Community than they had hoped to see established. The aim of the American supporters of a United Europe was always to bring into being an effective political partner on the other side of the Atlantic who would be able to share with the United States the responsibility for major international decisions. Secondly, the United States was looking for an ally in sustaining a universal system of international trade and payments, based on a uniform set of rules accepted by all and according equal treatment to all comers. The Americans can argue fairly that they made a number of sacrifices during the early post-war period in setting up a system of this kind, which derived from the agreements reached at Bretton Woods in 1944. This was America's grand design for the post-war world. They now find that they

175

face an invigorated Western Europe, owing its success partly to that grand design, which seems to be bent on a policy of discrimination against outsiders.

There is a certain irony in the historic reversal of roles between the two sides of the Atlantic. In the past, from the late nineteenth century right up to the Great Depression of the 1930s, the cult of the universal trading and financial system, with free access on equal terms to all markets, guided the international policies of Britain and a group of smaller European countries which are heavily dependent on foreign commerce. The United States for most of this time was living very much in an enclosed world of its own. It only began to break out of this in the Thirties. The habit of treating foreign trade and finance as if they were essentially matters of domestic politics took the Americans quite a long time to live down. But now, as the chief guardians of the universal order which they have helped to establish since the last war, they are faced with a Europe which is in its turn trying to use international trade to consolidate its own regional arrangements.

Recently there has been an observable sharpening of the American tone towards Europe. Behind this tone there seems to be a considered switch of policy which was spelt out in a special report for the President in 1971 by Mr Peterson, now the Secretary of Commerce, on United States international economic policy. There he makes the point that not only the content of American policies but also 'the methods of diplomacy will have to be changed'. He goes on: 'Our international negotiating stance will have to meet its trading partners with a clearer, more assertive version of new national interest. This will make us more predicable in the eyes of our trading partners.'

There are two questions that I want to explore. First, how far is the United States likely to push its new aggressive and demanding policy towards Europe? And secondly, how is the European posture towards the United States likely to develop during the 1970s in the face of this American pressure?

To make the first question concrete, is it conceivable that if the Americans continue to feel very frustrated about European behaviour, they will withdraw their military forces altogether from Western Europe? From a European point of view, the main purpose served by the American presence is to provide a visible guarantee of the military involvement of the United States in the defence of this territory. It is important that American troops should not only be about in Europe, but should also be in some clear sense in the front line – so that any attempt by the other side to invade a piece of territory or, say, to conduct a raid across the frontier in Berlin would immediately risk engaging American military forces in battle. Thus to remove American soldiers altogether from Europe would be likely to be interpreted as meaning a significant weakening of the American nuclear guarantee against the Soviet Union and its allies. It would be an extreme step to take. It is also hard to envisage the circumstances in which the United States would not wish to have some of its forces stationed on the territories of its closest military allies, who happen also to be extremely rich and economically powerful. Unless the United States ceases to be a world power, it will need to maintain substantial armed forces somewhere, and West Europe is a convenient place in which to keep some of them. The truth is that the European military establishment of the United States is a not very expensive way of maintaining the posture of a great power. Of course, the establishment need not be as big as it is now. But then a cut in this force seems likely whether the Europeans co-operate with the Americans in their economic policies or not.

There seem, therefore, to be strong reasons for thinking that the American response even to extreme friction with the European Community would fall well short of a complete military withdrawal. A more likely outcome would be some less precise but nevertheless marked change in American behaviour towards the European Community on matters on which the Europeans are themselves divided. Hitherto the American interest in furthering European integration has meant that when the member states have had deep differences, the United States has not exploited them. On the contrary, its desire to have them speak with a common voice has been the dominant motive. But there were signs during the 1971 dollar crisis that the Americans were at least contemplating the possibility of bargaining with the member countries individually, giving the favoured ones special concessions on trade. It is perhaps this kind of tactical manoeuvre which we should expect to see pursued rather more vigorously if friction grows in the future. It could, in certain circumstances, prove to be very damaging.

The answer to the second question depends on how far the differences of approach to the major issues of economic and

177

financial policy which at present divide the United States and Europe are of a fundamental character. If, in spite of the close American military connection with Europe and the reasonable prospects of continuing European integration, I foresee a more difficult relationship between the United States and Western Europe during the period ahead, it is because of certain essential features of contemporary international economic relations. These do suggest that there are profound forces at work which are likely to make the European Community an awkward partner for the US in economic and financial affairs, which is precisely where the strength of the European Community is greatest. The United States still produces somewhat more than the combined output of the enlarged Community of nine countries, but the Nine are much more important as world traders – they are together responsible for some 40 per cent of all international trade – and they own over half of all the world's currency reserves. There is a historical tendency for the United States to see the relatively low proportion of its national income that is derived from international trade as a powerful source of bargaining strength. In a crisis where the United States is in disagreement with the rest of the world on some aspect of economic policy there is a standard reflex action on the part of a substantial section of American public opinion. It crows: 'In the last resort we can opt out; you can't.'

It is the visceral American reaction, recalling with satisfaction that it is, after all, only dealing with the bad Old World from which it escaped long ago. One noticed the reaction once again during the dollar crisis in 1971. In effect, the line taken by the United States Treasury was that the essential strength of the dollar reflected the overwhelming productive power of the nation, which was responsible for about one-third of the total measured output of the world; and if the Europeans didn't like the way the Americans were handling the dollar, they could either lump it or take their business elsewhere. The choice was a matter of indifference to the United States.

Now I believe this line of thought to be based on an American delusion. The Americans, in fact, lost their secluded playground some time ago. They are still playing the same sports, and the immediate landscape may look the same, but it happened to be set in the middle of a busy and populous city. The people outside are all within shouting distance all of the time. I shall not attempt to list the factors that have so greatly increased America's interdependence with the rest of the world. The most important are in any case political and psychological. The United States is a world power, exercising authority and influence on a scale that is probably larger than has ever been done before. It cannot both be and do that, and opt out . . .

Back in the Twenties President Coolidge said: 'The business of the United States is business.' He summed up an important strand in American thinking – which is that governments do best when they simply provide the opportunity for the forces of private commerce to assert themselves. By the same token one might say today: 'The business of the European Community is politics and social welfare.' Again, the Americans, who tend to see this European venture as an exercise in classic New World federalism, designed to liberate the forces of private enterprise from the interference of national states, are going to be disappointed. For the fact is this is a very interventionist Community, most active in regulating the domestic affairs of its member countries and at the same time annoyingly deficient in clear-cut authority when it comes to conducting its relations with outsiders. From an American point of view this looks like a nasty combination of busybodying at home and sloth abroad.

The new American political tactics, as they have emerged in the 1970s, appear to be an attempt to blackmail the Europeans into creating the collective authority which they lack by presenting them with the threat of massive inaction by the United States. The theory is that once the Europeans realise that the leadership and initiative are no longer coming from the United States, they will produce some leadership of their own. This approach was much in evidence, as I have said, during the dollar crisis of the latter part of 1971 and afterwards. The Europeans are now being told, in effect, that they must either put up their own substitute for the dollar system – or shut up, and accept the monetary arrangements that are designed to meet American convenience. I suspect that this ploy may have long-term consequences that the Americans may find by no means convenient. It is always risky to invite a number of people to look for a means of agreeing among themselves by ganging up against you. They may, after all, find one! The Europeans are genuinely irked by certain aspects of the American dominance of the world monetary system, and I believe that they can make their own financial arrangements much less dependent on the dollar, while stopping far short of the creation of a fully-fledged European monetary union.

The point is a little technical, but what I am arguing is that the countries of the European Community could arrive at an agreed set of restrictive rules designed to control certain transactions in dollars and to limit the use of dollars as part of their currency reserves. In that case they would in effect reduce the freedom of manoeuvre of all dollar-holders – and most of these are, after all, still Americans. They could also put the American Treasury in a very awkward position if they decided that henceforth the dollar was no longer an acceptable asset to go into their currency reserves. There are already vast quantities of spare dollars in the hands of European central banks, and it is to be expected that they will try to reduce the amount and to agree on common rules restricting the future acquisition of dollars.

Once again, there is here a built-in formula for feeding the fires of mutual resentment. For the Americans undoubtedly believe that offering the world the opportunity of converting itself to a dollar currency system was a great service performed at considerable sacrifice to themselves. They point to the fact that in the course of it they lost control over their own currency, because too many other people outside the United States were using it. The Europeans do not deny this fact, but they emphasise the very large financial advantages which the Americans have had in the process. The question, however, is not who is right, but how to find some means of mitigating the quarrel. What is clear is that the recent American tactic of treating it as if it was someone else's problem is not very promising from this point of view.

One can, I think, understand the American aim better if one sees it as part of a more general realignment of policies in the context of what may now be called the Nixon–Kissinger doctrine. This is the view that by the late Sixties the American posture in world affairs was both excessively exposed and excessively rigid. The most spectacular moves designed to reduce both exposure and rigidity have concentrated on the United States' enemies, China and Russia. But the allies have also been subjected to an effort to reformulate the terms of their bargain with the United States in such a way as to limit the degree of American involvement. The Americans tend to argue that their own bargaining position has been significantly weakened, because their allies have been able to exploit the fact that America has such a large stake in the maintenance of the international system itself. It is almost as if the United States Government felt that it, too, had to demonstrate every now and then that it could play hookey!

My point is that in practice the United States can't. It has too much at stake in the world economic and financial system to opt out. But equally, it is not inclined towards the alternative approach, which I have called the 'Community method', because that involves too great a departure from old established habits of conducting international relations. It is the complete opposite of opting out: indeed, it commits you to opt *into* a bargaining process with a lot of foreigners on almost every subject of domestic interest. One would have to be very sanguine to envisage anything more than a highly tentative approach to arrangements of this kind for some time yet. In the meanwhile, the likelihood is that the United States will grow increasingly impatient with the lack of European leadership, and that the logic of the slow and laborious process of European integration will produce a rich crop of European bargains which in one way or another hurt United States interests.

At the back of all this is the awkward but inescapable fact that the two regions facing each other now across the Atlantic are not only the most developed economically and the most practised in the sophisticated techniques of representative democracy: they are also the most pluralistic societies in the world. To make a significant decision in either of them requires an extensive and complicated process of internal bargaining with powerful interest groups, as well as widespread skills in achieving workable compromises. The upshot tends to be that when the domestic compromises have been made and either group has to move on to a further stage of negotiating with an outsider, its position has already acquired a high degree of rigidity. No doubt this is considerably worse for the European Community, whose member states are only now gradually getting to understand each other and to learn the techniques of effective compromise. But it would be wrong to underestimate the profound difficulty which a pluralistic society like the United States, with lots of pressure groups and an open democratic process, experiences in bargaining abroad about matters involving domestic interests. And this suggests the conclusion that if the Europeans were ever to appoint a President and an executive branch of govern-

181

ment, like the Americans, they would still be an awkward lot to bargain with.

Article by Andrew Shonfield, 'A grumbling alliance'. Among other posts Shonfield was Foreign Editor of the *Financial Times* and later Director of Studies at the Royal Institute of International Affairs. *The Listener,* 23 November 1972. Quoted in Ian S. McDonald, *Anglo-American Relations since the Second World War* (London: David & Charles, 1974, pp. 238–47.

7.4 American–European relations: Edward Heath's view

Seeking to establish Britain within the European Community, Edward Heath deliberately played down the 'special relationship'. Here, speaking in the United States, he gives his views on relations between Europe and the United States, with little reference to Britain itself.

Last October the Leaders of the nine Community countries met in Paris. We were not concerned to exchange smiles and platitudes. We were aiming to draw up an ambitious and imaginative programme for the future of the Community. That is what we aimed at, and that is what we achieved. The significance of that programme has not yet been fully realised.

We were not content with general principles. We set deadlines for work, decisions and action in many fields. We will encourage the development of industry on a European scale. We will work out European policies to protect our energy resources, to spread prosperity through the various regions, and promote improved conditions of work and employment. We aim to transform the whole complex of relations between European countries into a European union before the end of the present decade.

This will be a new type of union. That is why I myself have never used the phrase 'United States of Europe'. That phrase gives the impression that we shall simply be following in the footsteps of your own remarkable achievement in creating a nation. We are dealing with an entirely different situation. We are dealing with ancient European nations, each with its own traditions and background, each determined to retain its identity. Our intention is not to destroy that identity but to build on to it a new European dimension which will enable us to secure, by common action, benefits which would be beyond our reach as separate nations. That is what we mean by a European Community.

I am confident that the will exists to carry through the whole of this existing programme. In my own country we have come to the end of 20 years of discussion about our relationship with Europe. As you may know this discussion has cut right across Party lines. Now that the decision is taken and we are a member of the Community I find that forward-looking people of all political persuasions are moving in to take advantage of the opportunities open to them in the Community.

In the foreign field we are also moving towards unity. At the Summit we agreed that the aim should be to work out common medium and long-term positions on foreign policy matters. We already have a common commercial policy and speak with one voice in international trade negotiations. More and more I hope that the European countries will act as one. This is essential now that the Community is the largest unit in world trade.

So once again Europe is on the move. Successive United States Administrations can take a big share of the credit for this. Over the years you have accepted the creation of a friendly, stable and prosperous Western Europe as a major interest of the United States. You have accepted that this will mean greater competition for your industries. It will mean an independent European voice in the world which will not always share exactly the same views which you hold. But you have thought, rightly I am sure, that this was a price well worth paying in return for the larger goal. I would like to pay tribute to the farsightedness and consistency with which the United States has helped Europe forward along this path.

The effect of these changes in Europe will be far-reaching. Just as the growth of the population and the increased industrial prosperity of the United States has led to the consolidation of her world power, so we can expect the new union in Western Europe to alter fundamentally the authority of individual Western European states in world affairs.

This position will not be used irresponsibly by the members of the Community. We made a public statement of our view in the Communiqué issued at the end of the Paris Summit meeting. We said then that the Nine had decided to maintain a 'constructive dialogue' with the United States, Japan, Canada and their other industrialised trade partners. By this we mean that we are ready to talk about the whole field of our relations. There are two areas in which there are serious and urgent problems – monetary reform and questions of international commercial policy. The Community and the United States have agreed to hold negotiations for the further liberalisation of international trade. Discussions on the international monetary system have already begun . . .

. . . Of course, defence is still an essential part of the relationship between the United States and Europe. We are rightly pursuing *détente* in discussions with the Russians and other Eastern Europeans in a number of different contexts. I hope that these discussions can achieve real progress. But until real *détente* has been achieved it would be foolish for the Western powers to weaken the solidarity or military power of our alliance. I think that this is common ground on both sides of the Atlantic. It is perfectly natural that you in the United States should from time to time re-examine the reasons for which you station forces in Europe. I believe that each such examination is bound to lead to the same conclusion. American forces are in Europe, not to do us a favour, but to preserve an essential American interest and to take part in the common defence of the Atlantic partnership.

It is equally natural that the American effort should be compared with the effort of your European partners. We certainly recognise that as the relative economic strength of Europe increases, so too should the share of the common defence burden which Europe bears. Already we have shown that we intend to improve our defence effort. In 1970 we carried through a billion dollar European defence improvement programme. In 1971 and 1972 there have been co-ordinated national force improvements of one billion and 1.5 billion dollars. The European allies now provide 90 per cent of NATO's ground forces in Europe, 75 per cent of her air forces and 80 per cent of her naval forces. There are 10 Western Europeans under arms for every American serviceman in Europe.

I have tried to show you how we in Britain and we in Europe see our own future and our relationship with the United States. We want to fortify the present relationship. We want to make it strong and durable, to take account of the shifts and changes of the past few years, the effect of which should not be overlooked; and to find common solutions which meet your needs and interests as well as our own. I am sure that this is the next major task we have to tackle together, and that is the main reason why I am here.

The 'natural relationship'

Edward Heath, speech at the National Press Club, Washington, 1 February 1973. British embassy, Washington, press release. Quoted in Ian S. McDonald, *Anglo-American Relations since the Second World War* (London: David & Charles, 1974, pp. 247–51.

7.5 A US–European 'special relationship'

By 1973 Kissinger had become Secretary of State. During a speech in Britain in December he once more stresses the importance of Anglo-American relations, but also offers the Europeans a 'special relationship' with the United States.

I am grateful for the opportunity to speak to you this evening because, like most Americans, I am seized by a mixture of pride and terror when invited to appear before a British audience. In my particular case, and without any reflection on this distinguished assemblage, it is probably more terror than pride; for there is no blinking the fact – it is there for all to hear – that my forebears missed the *Mayflower* by some 300 years.

Our two peoples have been more closely associated than any other two nations in modern history – in culture and economics, in peace and in war. We have sometimes disagreed. But the dominant theme of our relationship in this century has been intimate alliance and mighty creations.

In 1950, while the Atlantic alliance was considering a continuing political body, my great predecessor Dean Acheson spoke to this society. Describing the travails of creation, Acheson noted that a 'strange and confusing dissonance has crowded the trans-Atlantic frequencies'. But he added that this 'dissonance flows from the very awareness that difficult decisions must be made and is a part of the process of making them'.

Again today America and Western Europe find themselves at a moment of great promise and evident difficulty, of renewed efforts to unite and old problems which divide. It is a time of both hope and concern for all of us who value the partnership we have built together. Today, as in 1950, we and Europe face the necessity, the opportunity, and the dilemma of fundamental choice.

The Year of Europe

Because we have a historical and intimate relationship, I want to speak tonight frankly of what has been called the 'Year of Europe'

185

– of the difficulties of 1973 and the possibilities of 1974 and beyond.

Last April the President asked me to propose that Europe and the United States strive together to reinvigorate our partnership. He did so because it was obvious that the assumptions on which the alliance was founded have been outstripped by events:

– Europe's economic strength, political cohesion, and new confidence – the monumental achievements of Western unity – have radically altered a relationship that was originally shaped in an era of European weakness and American predominance.

– American nuclear monopoly has given way to nuclear parity, raising wholly new problems of defense and deterrence – problems which demand a broad re-examination of the requirements of our security and the relative contribution to it of the United States and its allies.

– The lessening of confrontation between East and West has offered new hope for a relaxation of tensions and new opportunities for creative diplomacy.

– It has become starkly apparent that the great industrialized democracies of Japan, Europe and North America could pursue divergent paths only at the cost of their prosperity and their partnersip. . . .

We have every reason of duty and self-interest to preserve the most successful partnership in history. The United States is committed to making the Atlantic community a vital positive force for the future as it was in the past. What has recently been taken for granted must now be reviewed. This is not an American challenge to Europe; it is history's challenge to us all.

The United Kingdom, we believe, is in a unique position. We welcome your membership in the European Community – though the loosening of some of our old ties has been painful at times. But you can make another historic contribution in helping develop between the United States and a unifying Europe the same special confidence and intimacy that benefited our two nations for decades. We are prepared to offer a unifying Europe a 'special relationship', for we believe that the unity of the Western world is essential for the well-being of all its parts.

In his memoirs Secretary Acheson described the events of his visit to London in the spring of 1950. He described the need of his time for an 'act of will, a decision to do something' at a crucial juncture.

186

We require another act of will – a determination to surmount tactical squabbles and legalistic preoccupations and to become the master of our destinies. We in this room are heirs to a rich heritage of trust and friendship. If we are true to ourselves, we have it in our power to extend it to a united Europe and to pass it on, further enriched and ennobled, to succeeding generations.

'The United States and a unifying Europe – the necessity for partnership', address by Secretary of State Kissinger before the Pilgrims of Great Britain, London, 12 December 1973. Department of State press release 452; text from *US Department of State Bulletin*, Vol. 69, 31 December 1973, pp. 777–82.

7.6 A view from Labour: James Callaghan on the US and Europe

The future Labour Prime Minister, James Callaghan, here makes a contribution to the debate over US–European relations, seeking a middle path between hostility and obsequiousness to the United States on behalf of the Europeans.

I must emphasise that we repudiate the view that Europe will emerge only out of a process of struggle against America. We do not agree that a Europe which excludes the fullest and most intimate cooperation with the United States is a desirable or attainable objective.

That does not mean that European countries become satellites of the United States. A Labour Government will certainly want a great measure of control over multinational enterprises and companies in this country. We are in favour of maintaining the national identity of key enterprises either by a measure of public ownership or in other ways. Nor should anyone wish to see a community organised in the interests of large-scale industry at the expense of the ordinary worker.

James Callaghan, speaking in a House of Commons debate. *Hansard* (*Commons*), Vol. 870, 19 March 1974, cols. 858–66.

7.7 Hankering for the 'special relationship': the Labour Party

The return to office in 1974 of Harold Wilson brought a new tone to British foreign policy regarding the United States. This review, by an influential journalist, Louis Heren, of a new book on Anglo-American relations takes the opportunity to discuss Wilson's and the Labour Party's approach to the subject.

The Labour Party's hankering for the long-departed special relationship with the United States is difficult to understand in spite of Mr Wilson's professed preference for Bourbon whiskey. Judged by the standards of the party's manifesto the two are, to say the least, incompatible.

By Labour standards, American capitalism has a more unacceptable face than the local visage. If Mr Scanlon and Mr Jones were American Labour leaders they would bring the economy to a standstill in their efforts to repeal the Taft–Hartley Act. Labour contracts of two or three years' duration would surely be anathema.

On the other hand, the American trade union movement believes that the business of America is business. If Mr Meany was general secretary of the TUC, he would call in the Special Branch to purge the movement of those he would regard as commies and comsymps.

For these and other reasons, many Labour MPs really do not like Americans and what is known as the American way of life. Some are offended by the American willingness to recognize and support military juntas, and have been much exercised by the earlier American reluctance to recognize communist regimes.

And what about Holy Loch? Would the nuclear submarines have to sail away if the special relationship was resurrected? That question alone underlines their incompatibility.

Political memories are short of course, but it was war – the Second World War and the Cold War – which created the special relationship. It was perpetuated, long after the unequal status of the two countries became painfully evident, because of British insistence, even in the face of American reluctance and embarrassment.

The Anglo-American special relationship was a long time dying because of official British reluctance to accept the diminished status of the post-imperial era. It was kept alive first by Mr Macmillan, who established an almost avuncular personal relationship with President Kennedy, and then by Mr Wilson when he went to Washington as Prime Minister in 1964.

He kept it alive by insisting that the United States and Britain were the only two world powers capable of maintaining the peace, a fiction which President Johnson happily accepted because it promised to relieve him of a few of his defence commitments. It was finally killed by Mr Wilson when he refused to send a token force to Vietnam and subsequently withdrew from the Persian Gulf.

In political terms all this was a long time ago. Hence the usefulness of Ian McDonald's *Anglo-American Relations since the Second World War*. It is a narrative largely based on official documents which records the achievements and failures of the relationship. Above all, it is a reminder that when the policies of the two countries differed, the interests of the United States invariably prevailed.

The biggest confrontation was of course the 1956 Suez crisis. McDonald, who was a member of *The Times* staff in Washington, recalls that the British government felt, with reason, that the United States had failed to stand by its most loyal ally in a matter vital to that ally's interest. In the long run, the American refusal to support the Anglo-French venture probably saved the two nations from becoming entangled in a far worse situation, but the manner in which the United States abandoned its allies rankled deeply.

The Skybolt incident showed, when British defence policies conflicted with America's changing strategic plans, that the United States was swift to disregard any claims of the 'special relationship'. To many Britons it appeared at times that the relationship was a one-way street in which Britain received very little in return for her loyalty.

This was not strictly true. The mutual contempt that the then British Foreign Secretary and American Secretary of State had for each other did not help, but the United States could not have been expected to support Suez, a venture which also had bitterly divided Britain. The then American Defence Secretary may have cancelled Skybolt without giving a thought to British requirements. He was a man without political sensibility, but the affair dramatically illustrated that Britain just did not have the necessary economic strength to masquerade as a partner to a superpower.

The Americans were impatient with British nuclear pretensions, but charitable enough to make amends by providing Polaris. The offer aroused the wrath of de Gaulle, who blackballed Britain's application for European membership and threw the Atlantic Alliance into a state of disarray from which it never recovered.

No one could forecast what would have happened if this train of events had been avoided, but even before the Skybolt incident President Kennedy, for all his affection for Mr Macmillan, had indicated that Britain was only one of the European allies and that her place was in Europe. Perhaps the Americans did not press hard enough. Perhaps they were too kind or sentimental. Whatever the reason, the special relationship did not serve Britain's interest.

One thing is obvious. Britain's place, as Americans see it, is in Europe. The diplomatic and defence arrangements which were the special relationship belong to the past. McDonald makes the point by quoting what Dr Henry Kissinger said as early as 1964.

After remarking that Anglo-American relations would always be 'special' because of the unique ties of language and culture, Dr Kissinger said: 'As the postwar period progressed, many influential Americans have come to believe that Britain has been claiming influence out of proportion to its power. Consequently they have pressed the British to substitute close association with Europe for special ties across the Atlantic. . . . They believe that Britain should be treated as simply one or other European country.'

Dr Kissinger then spoke in a private capacity, but he has not changed his mind since becoming Secretary of State. Indeed, he seems to regard Britain as so many mist-shrouded islands.

President Gerald Ford is no Anglophobe, but he is certainly not an Anglophile. He is typical of Middle Westerners without strong ethnic ties. They have outlived their xenophobia, but Europe means little or nothing to them except as a place in which to spend a vacation.

Mr Ford does not share the residual contempt, but he is hardly likely to respond enthusiastically to sentimental appeals from London, especially from a leader of a party divided over Europe. It is not at all impossible that Bonn will be regarded as the first European capital.

The lesson is clear. If Mr Wilson wants to retain a normal relationship with Washington, which is all he can hope for, he should read McDonald and make sure that Britain remains a member of the European Economic Community.

The 'natural relationship'

'Mr Wilson must realize the "special relationship" is dead', review by Louis Heren of Ian McDonald, *Anglo-American Relations since the Second World War* (London and Newton Abbot: David & Charles, 1974). *The Times*, 12 August 1974.

7.8   The Guadaloupe 'understanding'

During his period as Prime Minister from 1976 to 1979 James Callaghan was determined to restore close relations with the United States. One of the most difficult issues he had to deal with towards the end of his period in office was the future of the Anglo-American nuclear relationship. It was clear by early 1979 that a decision would have to be made soon on a replacement for Polaris. The difficulty the Prime Minister faced was that the Labour Party conference had voted against a new generation of nuclear weapons. Without committing the government, however, Callaghan raised the issue at the Guadaloupe summit in early 1979 and by so doing laid the foundations of the Trident agreement reached by his successor, Margaret Thatcher.

During the visit to Guadaloupe I took the opportunity of having a discussion with President Carter about Britain's future as a strategic nuclear power, including whether or not we should continue in that role. Polaris was getting older but would remain serviceable until the 1990s and this had prompted the Government military advisers to come to me early in 1978 with the opinion that because of the long building time, a decision would be needed by 1980 if Polaris was to be replaced.

I decided to have a study made by officials of the factors that would affect the future of the United Kingdom deterrent. The terms of reference were strict and limited. The preamble stated that no decision on the future of the deterrent would be needed during the lifetime of the present Parliament, which could conceivably have ended in the autumn of 1978, or at the latest 1979. The study should examine and report on all the factors which the next Government of whatever Party would need to take into account in reaching a decision. It was instructed not to make recommendations, but to put forward the facts and balanced arguments on which Cabinet decisions could be taken. Its sole purpose, said the terms of reference, was to provide the basis on which a fully informed decision could be taken. Officials were given a year in which to complete the study.

I received the report eight months later, in December 1978, and it was clear that the authors had fulfilled my remit exactly. The paper examined the strategic environment in the 1990s and beyond and considered the nuclear programmes of the Soviet Union, the United States, France and China against the background of possible arms control negotiations such as SALT III. It set out a series of options in their international, political and military aspects but, as instructed, it took no account of domestic political considerations. It examined various alternative possibilities if Britain did not continue with its ballistic missile system, but decided to opt for something else.

In the first instance, I decided to circulate the document to those Ministers most immediately concerned, namely the Defence Secretary, the Foreign Secretary and the Chancellor of the Exchequer, suggesting that we have a preliminary discussion at a meeting which had been arranged for 21 December to brief me in advance of Guadaloupe. When we met, I said that there had been little time since the report was received for preparation of views or for consultation with the Cabinet. Moreover, the intention of the Guadaloupe meeting was to focus on other aspects of nuclear weapons policy, but the British strategic deterrent was related in subject matter and the meeting would afford an opportunity to have a preliminary discussion with the President. What were my colleagues' views about such a talk? A long discussion ensued about the essential nature of Britain's future defence strategy and whether it could be sustained without radical change, and the conclusion was reached that our own studies could not go much further without consultation with the United States.

At the second briefing meeting, held on 2 January 1979, just forty-eight hours before I left for Guadaloupe, it was apparent that opinions had crystallised in favour of my having a talk with the President provided it took place without commitment on my part: I should work out with him the best way of exploring Britain's nuclear options more fully. I should ascertain the views of the President on whether and in what form American help could be forthcoming if the Cabinet were to decide upon the replacement of Polaris. We were all aware that a decision would not be necessary for the next twelve months and I suggested that in the intervening period there would be advantage in more public discussion of the issue. The Labour Party Conference had expressed itself very clearly against the replacement of Polaris, and while a decision would not come before the existing Cabinet, if I eventually concluded that it was in the national interest to go ahead there would be a difficult decision for colleagues in the next Labour Cabinet to take and a major argument would ensue in the Labour Party. To prepare for such an eventuality it would be wise to have an informed public opinion, so that the choices as well as the dilemmas were well understood. At that moment, I told my colleagues, if our eventual decision turned out to be that Polaris should be replaced, on the basis of the information we had before us I would favour the C4 Trident submarine.

My opportunity to talk with the President came in a break between the sessions on the afternoon of 5 February. Rosalynn Carter and Audrey had gone with the other ladies to visit a neighbouring island and I knew he would be alone. I walked the few yards across the grass to his hut next door and found him resting. No one else was present during our talk, but when it was over and I had returned to my hut I called for Sir John Hunt, the Secretary to the Cabinet, and repeated the substance of the conversation to him. I told the President the nature of the report I had commissioned and said I was speaking with him at this stage because the Ministers immediately concerned were of the view that we could not proceed further with exploring the options about the future of our nuclear deterrent until we received some indication of America's attitude towards the supply of weapons. I then gave an outline of my view. For Britain, as a nation, the balance of advantage in procuring a successor to Polaris would be no better than marginal. There was a good case for arguing that any available resources could be used to better effect in strengthening our conventional forces and my own approach was that any chosen successor weapon must be shown to be cost-effective. But another factor weighed with me, namely that Britain had a responsibility not only for her own defence, but also shared a responsibility for the defence of Europe.

It was for this reason that I had put a question about Germany's attitude to Britain's nuclear deterrent to Helmut Schmidt during our earlier session and had received a reply similar to others he had given me when I had discussed the matter on earlier occasions. His consistent view was that Germany would prefer that France was not alone as the sole European power possessing strategic nuclear weapons, and that he would feel more comfortable if Britain also were in the field . . .

I could not estimate what decision Britain would arrive at on the future of the deterrent, and my views might not find a ready echo in all my Party, but when the time arrived to reach a conclusion it would be necessary to take into account not only Britain's own security but also the extent to which Germany felt the need for reassurance, and whatever our decision, it must contribute to the total security of Europe.

The President heard me out. He said that like Helmut Schmidt, he also was glad that Britain possessed the nuclear deterrent. He did not take up my comments about Germany directly, but said that he hoped that Britain as well as France would remain a nuclear power. In his view, it was better that there should be a shared responsibility in Europe, rather than that America should go it alone, as he would not wish the United States to be the only country in confrontation. He was disturbed that the four of us had not reached a common position about the modernisation of the intermediate range weapons, as it would make his intended talks with Brezhnev more difficult. But in view of the traditional French attitude, it would be necessary for him and me to talk in the near future about how Britain might be associated with the SALT III talks when they got under way.

The Soviet Union, he added, argued that the more they agreed with the United States on a mutual reduction of nuclear armaments the more significant the smaller numbers of nuclear arms of other countries would become. In saying this, the President probably had in mind Helmut Schmidt's view that if the SALT III talks produced a further limitation in long-range United States/USSR systems without a parallel reduction in Soviet SS20s, this would undermine Germany's confidence in the commitment of the United States and have a destabilising effect. Carter said further that the Soviet Union was concerned about China's developing arsenal and this influenced their attitude to the possession of the SS20s. This led us on to a discussion of nuclear systems and the President enquired what systems we were thinking of. I replied that we were at this stage not committed, even in principle, to a successor to Polaris, but on the technical issue the Ministers most directly concerned were divided about which would be the best weapon. Hitherto the option I thought most likely to meet our requirements, if we decided to go ahead, was the Trident C4 submarine which would carry multiple independent re-entry vehicles.

The President said that he could see no objection to transferring this technology to the United Kingdom and it would assist the United States to meet the unit costs of production. I picked up this point. Cost would be one of several factors in our decision, and I remarked that I had seen a figure of $10 billions mentioned. This would be beyond our means. The President responded that he thought it should be possible to work out satisfactory terms and I suggested that I should send two officials to Washington to discuss technical and financial aspects further. I named Professor Mason and Sir Clive Rose for this purpose. Both of them were very experienced. Mason, a Merthyr-born boy, had risen by sheer ability to become the Chief Scientist in the Ministry of Defence, and Clive Rose was a Deputy Secretary in the Cabinet Office who had previously been head of the British negotiating team on Force Reductions in Central Europe.

The President at once consented to the visit and said that he would nominate Harold Brown, the United States Defence Secretary, to discuss the matter. Before our *tête à tête* ended, I repeated that I hoped he had understood that I had not been stating a final British position. The Cabinet had not begun to consider the matter and it might turn out that as a result of successful SALT III negotiations there could be an advantage to world peace and to the strength of the Alliance if Britain gave up her nuclear capacity. Such a possibility should not be ruled out. The President replied that he understood I had not been putting forward policy positions, but raising matters that we would need to consider together later on, order [sic] to reach decisions. With that, we ended our discussion on nuclear matters and turned to other questions.

On my return to Britain, I found that Professor Mason was to be in the United States in mid-February 1979 in connection with a test-firing at Cape Canaveral by Britain's Polaris submarine HMS *Repulse*, and I authorised him and Clive Rose to go to Washington to begin 'exploratory' talks. By this time other domestic matters had assumed major proportions, and I sensed that the Government's life might come to a sudden end. Accordingly, on my birthday, 27 March 1979, I sat down and wrote a letter to the President.

I told him that the Government was facing a crucial vote of confidence on the following day and I could not tell which way the vote might go. But whether we won or not, a general election could not be far off and I therefore wished to put on record my understanding of what had passed between us at Guadaloupe. I had informed him that I had recently begun to think about the options for the next Government in deciding whether it should develop a successor to Polaris, in view of the fact that a decision would be needed within twelve months. I then repeated that I understood the United States was willing to receive Mason and Clive Rose to discuss the technical and financial aspects of a successor weapon, such as the Trident C4, and concluded: 'I thought it right to put our conversation on record in view of certain eventualities here, although the onus of suggesting a visit would of course still lie with me or my successor. I hope my understanding is the same as yours.'

I had my letter to the President placed on file and there it rests. On 4 May, the day following the general election, before I left Downing Street for the last time I wrote my final minute on the subject. This authorised that my correspondence with the President on the future of the nuclear deterrent, together with the report I had received the previous December, should be made available to the incoming Prime Minister to prevent her from being at a disadvantage in any future exchange she might have with President Carter about the replacement or otherwise of Polaris.

Memoirs of James Callaghan. James Callaghan, *Time and Chance* (London: Collins, 1987), pp. 552–7.

8

The 'extraordinary' alliance restored, 1979–89

Despite the improvements in Anglo-American relations in the late 1970s it was Margaret Thatcher and Ronald Reagan who resurrected the 'special relationship' in the 1980s. The close personal relationship between the British Prime Minister and the American President laid the foundations of what Mrs Thatcher described as the 'extraordinary relationship'. Her abrasive and confrontational approach towards the European Community contrasted with her determination to play the role of the most loyal of America's allies in the new Cold War which had broken out between the United States and the Soviet Union.

The restoration of the 'special relationship' during the Thatcher–Reagan era was symbolised by the Trident agreements of July 1980 and March 1982 and the close military (and intelligence) collaboration during the Falklands War in 1982. Despite her misgivings, the Prime Minister was also prepared to face considerable domestic political costs in supporting the deployment of cruise missiles in Britain and allowing American F-111 aircraft to use British bases to bomb Libya in 1986. In the latter case, Mrs Thatcher points out in her memoirs the benefits which support for the United States brought to Britain. Special weight, she says, was given to British views on arms control negotiations with the Russians and the US administration promised to give extra support to the extradition treaty which the government regarded as vital in bringing IRA terrorists back to Britain. The fact that so few had stuck by America in her time of trial strengthened the 'special relationship', which in Mrs Thatcher's view would always be special because of cultural and historical links between the two countries.

Despite this emphasis on the importance of 'the cultural and historical links', 'interests' rather than 'sentiment' were the crucial basis of the 'special relationship' during this period. This is revealed in Mrs Thatcher's comment: 'I knew that the cost to Britain of not backing American action was unthinkable'. The continuity going back to the Korean War is clear.

There is no doubt that the Prime Minister valued her close personal relationship with the American President, but it is also clear that she deliberately used the 'special relationship' as a tool of diplomacy during her period in office to reassert Britain's place on the world stage and to reinforce what she perceived to be Britain's vital national interests. Britain as a staunch ally was also seen as being a major US interest.

8.1   The British deterrent secured: the Trident II agreement

The future of Britain's deterrent appeared to have been secured in 1980 when Margaret Thatcher and Jimmy Carter agreed that America would provide Britain with Trident I missiles to replace the ageing Polaris force. By 1982, with a new President in office and an improved version of the Trident missile in prospect, the British had to approach the Americans again for guarantees about the future of their independent deterrent.

Text of a letter of 11 March from the Prime Minister to the
President of the United States

I wrote to your predecessor on 10 July 1980 to ask whether the United States Government would be ready to supply Trident I missiles, equipment and supporting services to the United Kingdom on a similar basis to that on which the Polaris missiles were supplied under the Polaris Sales Agreement of 6 April 1963. President Carter replied on 14 July confirming that the United States Government were prepared to do so, subject to and in accordance with applicable United States law and procedures.

2. In the light of decisions taken by the United States Government in 1981 to accelerate their own programme to procure Trident II missiles, and to phase out the Trident I programme earlier than had hitherto been intended, the United Kingdom Government have carried out a review of their nuclear deterrent programme. In the light of this review, I am now writing to ask whether in place of Trident I missiles the United States Government would be ready to supply Trident II missiles, equipment and supporting services on a continuing basis and in a manner generally similar to that in which Polaris was supplied. The United Kingdom Government would wish to purchase these missiles complete with multiple, independently targettable re-entry vehicles but without the warheads themselves. I propose that, as in the past, close coordination should be

maintained between the executive agencies of the two Governments in order to assure compatibility of equipment.

3. Like the Polaris force, and consistently with the agreement reached in 1980 on the supply of Trident I missiles, the United Kingdom Trident II force will be assigned to the North Atlantic Treaty Organisation; and except where the United Kingdom Government may decide that supreme national interests are at stake, this successor force will be used for the purposes of international defence of the Western alliance in all circumstances. It is my understanding that cooperation in the modernisation of the United Kingdom nuclear deterrent in the manner proposed would be consistent with the present and prospective international obligations of both parties.

4. I would like to assure you that the United Kingdom Government remain wholly committed to the strengthening of the Alliance's conventional forces. The United Kingdom Government have in recent years substantially increased their defence spending and further increases are planned for the future in order to sustain the United Kingdom's all-round contribution to allied deterrence and defence. The economies made possible by the United States Government's cooperation with respect to the supply of the Trident II missile system will be used in order to reinforce the United Kingdom Government's continuing efforts to upgrade their conventional forces.

5. If the United States Government are prepared to meet this request, I hope that as the next step you will be prepared to receive technical and financial missions to pursue these matters using the framework of the Polaris Sales Agreement where appropriate.

*Text of President Reagan's reply of 11 March to the Prime
Minister's letter of the same date*

Thank you for your letter of today's date. I am pleased to confirm that the United States Government are prepared to supply to the United Kingdom Trident II missiles, equipment and supporting services as proposed in your letter, subject to and in accordance with applicable United States law and procedures.

2. The United States readiness to provide these systems is a demonstration of the great importance which the United States Government attach to the maintenance by the United Kingdom of an independent nuclear deterrent capability. I can assure you of the

United States' willingness to cooperate closely with the United Kingdom Government in maintaining and modernising that capability.

3. I attach great importance to your assurance that the United Kingdom Trident II force will be assigned to NATO and that the economies realised through cooperation between our two governments will be used to reinforce the United Kingdom's efforts to upgrade its conventional forces. Such nuclear and conventional force improvements are of the highest priority for NATO's security.

4. I agree that, as the next step, our two governments should initiate the technical and financial negotiations which you propose.

Texts of letters exchanged between the Prime Minister and President, and between the Secretary of State for Defence and the US Secretary of Defense, March 1982. Reproduced in John Baylis, *Anglo-American Defence Relations, 1939-1984. The Special Relationship* (London: Macmillan, 1984, second edition), pp. 202-3.

8.2 Britain, America and the Falkland Islands

The Argentinean invasion of the Falkland Islands posed important questions for the 'special relationship', because United States and British interests were by no means identical. This *Times* editorial draws attention to the balancing act which the United States sought to play to maintain its relationship with Britain and Europe while safeguarding its interests in Latin America.

Mr Haig's spectacular intercontinental shuttle makes it clear that the United States administration is giving top priority to the resolution of the Falkland Islands crisis. Britain has welcomed that, since the United States is both our ally and in a better position than any other state to exercise leverage over Argentina. But there have, perhaps inevitably, been some misgivings about the spirit in which the administration approaches the crisis. Some British commentators have even gone so far as to suggest there could have been collusion between the United States and Argentina before the invasion.

That is a wild accusation, unsupported by any evidence. But it is true that there has been an ambivalence in the American response to the crisis that contrasts with the impressive backing that Britain has now received from the other members of the European community. The United States has not been unfriendly to the British case. It supported Britain in the United Nations and it is concentrating on seeking an acceptable settlement. But in doing so it has been trying hard to preserve its friendship with Argentina as well. So its public reaction has been as even-handed as possible. It has refrained from giving the unequivocal support to Britain that would be justified both on the grounds of friendship and on the merits of the case.

The reasons for this are that the United States has interests in this crisis which differ from those of Britain or Argentina; and that it believes it has a distinctive role to play partly because of its power and influence and partly because of those special interests. The American administration is afraid of the dispute over the Falklands further undermining stability in Central America. It had looked upon Argentina as a potential partner in Latin America and would like still to be able to do so. In particular it wants to avoid the Rio Treaty being invoked against the introduction of forces from outside the continent into the American hemisphere.

If it comes to that point, the United States will not agree to the Treaty being applied in this instance. Whenever it is forced to make a critical choice between Britain and Argentina, the administration will not be so even-handed as it appears. But it would be reluctant to do anything that would weaken the authority of the Rio Treaty, which it sees as a valuable instrument against any intrusion of Soviet forces into the American hemisphere. The United States is extremely anxious therefore to prevent the treaty being invoked, which gives added urgency to its activities as a mediator.

It believes that it is more likely to be successful in this role if it has not adopted the public posture of a partisan. There is some force in this argument. The United States is the only country with the authority to act as a mediator, and there is value in having an honest broker if it can bring about a settlement that is consistent with the interests both of Britain and of the Falkland Islanders themselves. In so far as a certain diplomatic blandness is required to enable the United States to play this role it is reasonable enough.

But there are two dangers. The United States must not make the mistake of which it has sometimes with justice accused its European allies of putting local convenience above broader international con-

201

sideration. Just as it was wrong for a number of European countries to respond feebly to the Soviet aggression in Afghanistan, for fear of disturbing *détente* in Europe, so it would be unforgivable now for the United States to allow its conduct over the Falklands to be governed by its preoccupation with Central America. A degree of circumspection is necessary in a mediator. But for the United States to go beyond that simply in order to protect its own local interests would not be consistent with the obligations which it owes to Britain as an ally or with its own broader purposes in the world. In its activities as a mediator it must not be so hungry for a speedy settlement that it fails to take full account of the merits of the issue.

The second danger is that the American administration may fail to think sufficiently of the effect that its conduct in this crisis will have upon the future of the Atlantic Alliance. This is partly a matter of the impression that it creates as a mediator and partly of what it will do if mediation fails. It will be a tragedy if the United States allows itself to become so entwined in diplomatic niceties that it appears to be an unreliable ally.

This is what is disturbing much well-informed opinion in Washington, which is critical of the administration for failing to recognize the broader realities of the crisis. Britain has warmer friends in the United States than might be appreciated from the administration's public pronouncements. But it is inevitably the administration's attitude that is noticed in other countries, and there will be no winners in the Western world if the memory left by this conflict is of the United States keeping its distance while the European community stood together. The Falkland Islands present issues that are important in themselves and the United States is naturally much concerned about Central America. But it will be no cause for congratulations if the price for resolving this dispute is to undermine confidence in the American commitment to its European partners.

'An ally, not an umpire', leading article in *The Times*, 12 April 1982, p. 7.

8.3 'Family friends': the Thatcher–Reagan relationship

The personal relationships between Prime Ministers and Presidents have always been crucial to the 'special relationship'.

The 'extraordinary' alliance restored

That between Margaret Thatcher and Ronald Reagan was characterised by warmth and mutual respect, as the Prime Minister makes clear in this speech.

Much has been said and written over the years, Mr President, about the relations between our two countries. And there's no need for me to add to the generalities on the subject today, because we've had before our eyes in recent weeks the most concrete expression of what, in practice, our friendship means. I refer to your awareness of our readiness to resist aggression in the Falklands even at great sacrifice and to our awareness of your readiness to give support to us even at considerable costs to American interests.

It is this preparedness on both sides for sacrifices in the common interest and, indeed, in the wider interest that characterizes our partnership. And I should like to pay tribute to you, Mr President, and to you, Mr Secretary Haig, whom I also greet here heartily today, and through you to the American people for your predictably generous response.

Believe me, Mr President, we don't take it for granted. We are grateful from the depth of our national being for your tremendous efforts in our support.

Mr President, your mission to London and to other capitals of Europe is a remarkable one, and we are fully conscious both of its symbolism and of its substance.

From the day you took office, you were determined to breathe new life into the Alliance. One of your predecessors, also much loved in this, our country, President Eisenhower, put it so well when he said, 'One truth must rule all we think and all we do. The unity of all who dwell in freedom is their only sure defense.'

You recognized how central your allies were to American interests, and vice versa. But no country, however strong, can remain an island in the modern world. And I want you to know how fully we reciprocate your conviction about the need for a dynamic, two-way alliance.

We here also realize, Mr President, what you have done, both to increase immediate American military strength and to reanimate talks on arms reductions, objectives that must go hand in hand. You've seized the initiative in East–West relations, and as seen by us in Western Europe, that is already a considerable achievement.

May I also stress what you stand for in international economic life, your commitment to an open world trade system, whatever the immediate pressures for restriction. That is our role, too, and we will strive for it alongside you.

Mr President, both before and since you took office, I've come to know you as a personal friend who can be relied on in times of danger, who's not going to compromise on the values of the free world, who seeks the reduction of world tensions and the strengthening of world security, who will do everything possible to encourage creative enterprise and initiative, who wants the individual to flourish in freedom, in justice, and in peace.

But I've found in my three years in office, as I'm sure my predecessors did – and we're delighted to see some of them here today – that there is one further characteristic that is dominant to those concerned with policy. I refer to our ability to discuss with you problems of common interest – which means in today's world practically everything – to discuss them freely and candidly, not necessarily always agreeing, but giving and taking advice as family friends, without exciting anxiety or envy.

You, Mr President, and you, Mr Haig, have always shown this spirit. It's something unique between us and is of priceless value to the cause we both share.

You, Mr President, this morning, quoted our greatest statesman of this century, Winston Churchill. You well know that in Parliament Square, as well as Winston Churchill, there stands the statue of Abraham Lincoln who, in his most famous speech of all at Gettysburg – and I was very worried this morning when the Chancellor, too, quoted Gettysburg. And I thought, 'Has he trumped my ace again!' But you know we all adore the Lord Chancellor who, in his own inimitable way, put everything we felt so much.

But you know that speech at Gettysburg – every sentence is a quote. He gave one of them. May I say another of them which, I believe, fits in with the cause which you and I share. You'll remember that Abraham Lincoln, on that famous occasion, said:

> The world will little note nor long remember what we say here, but it can never forget what they did here. It is for us the living to be dedicated here to the unfinished work that they who fought here have thus far so nobly advanced.

It is in that spirit, and mindful of that unfinished work, that I ask you all to rise and drink a toast to the enduring alliance between the United States and the United Kingdom, coupled with the names of the President and Mrs Reagan. The alliance, the President, and Mrs Reagan: to your health, success, and happiness.

Toast of the British Prime Minister, Margaret Thatcher, at a Luncheon honoring the President in London, 8 June 1982. *Public Papers of the President*, pp. 748–50.

8.4 'Kinship and homecoming': Ronald Reagan in Britain

In this speech, delivered to both Houses of Parliament in June 1982, President Reagan focuses on the joint interests of Britain and the United States in the twentieth century in fostering democracy and standing up to totalitarianism.

My Lord Chancellor, Mr Speaker:

The journey of which this visit forms a part is a long one. Already it has taken me to two great cities of the West, Rome and Paris, and to the economic summit at Versailles. And there, once again, our sister democracies have proved that even in a time of severe economic strain, free peoples can work together freely and voluntarily to address problems as serious as inflation, unemployment, trade, and economic development in a spirit of cooperation and solidarity.

Other milestones lie ahead. Later this week, in Germany, we and our NATO allies will discuss measures for our joint defense and America's latest initiatives for a more peaceful, secure world through arms reductions.

Each stop of this trip is important, but among them all, this moment occupies a special place in my heart and in the hearts of my countrymen – a moment of kinship and homecoming in these hallowed halls.

Speaking for all Americans, I want to say how very much at home we feel in your house. Every American would, because this is, as we have been so eloquently told, one of democracy's shrines. Here the rights of free people and the processes of representation have been debated and refined.

It has been said that an institution is the lengthening shadow of a man. This institution is the lengthening shadow of all the men and women who have sat here and all those who have voted to send representatives here.

This is my second visit to Great Britain as President of the United States. My first opportunity to stand on British soil occurred almost a year and a half ago when your Prime Minister graciously hosted a diplomatic dinner at the British Embassy in Washington. Mrs Thatcher said then that she hoped I was not distressed to find staring down at me from the grand staircase a portrait of His Royal Majesty King George III. She suggested it was best to let bygones be bygones, and in view of our two countries' remarkable friendship in succeeding years, she added that most Englishmen today would agree with Thomas Jefferson that 'a little rebellion now and then is a very good thing'.

The Strength of Democracy

We're approaching the end of a bloody century plagued by a terrible political invention – totalitarianism. Optimism comes less easily today, not because democracy is less vigorous, but because democracy's enemies have refined their instruments of repression. Yet optimism is in order, because day by day democracy is proving itself to be a not-at-all-fragile flower. From Stettin on the Baltic to Varna on the Black Sea, the regimes planted by totalitarianism have had more than 30 years to establish their legitimacy. But none – not one regime – has yet been able to risk free elections. Regimes planted by bayonets do not take root. . . .

America's time as a player on the stage of world history has been brief. I think understanding this fact has always made you patient with your younger cousins – well, not always patient. I do recall that, on one occasion, Sir Winston Churchill said in exasperation about one of our most distinguished diplomats, 'He is the only case I know of a bull who carries his china shop with him.'

But witty as Sir Winston was, he also had that special attribute of great statesmen – the gift of vision, the willingness to see the future based on the experience of the past. It is this sense of history, this understanding of the past that I want to talk with you about today, for it is in remembering what we share of the past that our two nations can make common cause for the future. . . .

If history teaches [that] anything it teaches [that] self-delusion in the face of unpleasant facts is folly. We see around us today the marks of our terrible dilemma – predictions of doomsday, antinuclear demonstrations, an arms race in which the West must, for its own protection, be an unwilling participant. At the same time we see totalitarian forces in the world who seek subversion and conflict around the globe to further their barbarous assault on the human spirit. What, then, is our course? Must civilization perish in a hail of fiery atoms? Must freedom wither in a quiet, deadening accommodation with totalitarian evil?

Sir Winston Churchill refused to accept the inevitability of war or even that it was imminent. He said, 'I do not believe that Soviet Russia desires war. What they desire is the fruits of war and the indefinite expansion of their power and doctrines. But what we have to consider here today while time remains is the permanent prevention of war and the establishment of conditions of freedom and democracy as rapidly as possible in all countries.' . . .

During the dark days of the Second World War, when this island was incandescent with courage, Winston Churchill exclaimed about Britain's adversaries. 'What kind of a people do they think we are?' Well, Britain's adversaries found out what extraordinary people the British are. But all the democracies paid a terrible price for allowing the dictators to underestimate us. We dare not make that mistake again. So, let us ask ourselves, 'What kind of people do we think we are?' And let us answer, 'Free people, worthy of freedom and determined not only to remain so but to help others gain their freedom as well.'

Sir Winston led his people to great victory in war and then lost an election just as the fruits of victory were about to be enjoyed. But he left office honorably, and, as it turned out, temporarily, knowing that the liberty of his people was more important than the fate of any single leader. History recalls his greatness in ways no dictator will ever know. And he left us a message of hope for the future, as timely now as when he first uttered it, as opposition leader in the Commons nearly 27 years ago, when he said 'When we look back on all the perils through which we have passed and at the mighty foes that we have laid low and all the dark and deadly designs that we have frustrated, why should we fear for our future? We have,' he said, 'come safely through the worst.'

Well, the task I've set forth will long outlive our own generation. But together, we too have come through the worst. Let us now begin a major effort to secure the best – a crusade for freedom that will engage the faith and fortitude of the next generation. For the sake of peace and justice, let us move toward a world in which all people are at least free to determine their own destiny.

President Reagan's speech to both Houses of Parliament, 8 June 1982. *Historic Documents of 1982, Congressional Quarterly*, 1983.

8.5 'Dismayed and let down': Thatcher and the US invasion of Grenada

The close personal relationship between Margaret Thatcher and Ronald Reagan did not prevent misunderstandings and clashes of interest. When, against her advice, the Americans intervened in Grenada following a *coup* in 1983, Mrs Thatcher found herself in an embarrassing position, as she recalls in her memoirs.

On Wednesday 19 October 1983 a pro-Soviet military *coup* had overthrown the Government of Grenada. The new regime were certainly a vicious and unstable bunch. With the exception of General Austin, who led the *coup*, they were all in their twenties and a number of them had a record of violence and torture. Maurice Bishop, the overthrown Prime Minister, and five of his close supporters were shot dead. There was outrage at what had happened among most of the other Caribbean countries. Jamaica and Barbados wanted military intervention in which they would have liked the Americans and us to take part. My immediate reaction was that it would be most unwise of the Americans, let alone us, to accede to this suggestion. I was afraid that it would put foreign communities in Grenada at severe risk. There were some 200 British civilians there and many more Americans. The main organization of Caribbean States, CARICOM, was not prepared to agree to military intervention in Grenada. However, the Organization of Eastern Caribbean States, the OECS, decided unanimously to put together a force and called on other governments to help in restoring peace and order in the island. Clearly, the American reaction would be crucial.

It was easy to see why the United States might be tempted to go in and deal with the thugs who had taken over in Grenada. But as I always pointed out to the Americans afterwards, though apparently to little effect, Grenada was not transformed from a democratic island paradise into a Soviet surrogate overnight in October

1983. The Marxist Maurice Bishop had already come to power there through an earlier *coup* in March 1979: he had suspended the Constitution and put many of his opponents in gaol. He was, indeed, a personal friend of Fidel Castro. The Americans had had hostile relations with his Government for years. Bishop was, admittedly, something of a pragmatist and had even made a visit to the United States at the end of May 1983. It seems that it was, in part, a dispute about the Grenada Government's attitude to private enterprise which brought about the clash with his colleagues in the Marxist 'New Jewel Movement' that ultimately led to his fall.

The new 'hemispheric' strategy which President Reagan's Administration was pursuing, combined with experience of living beside the Soviet satellite of Cuba, in our view led the United States to exaggerate the threat which a Marxist Grenada posed. Our intelligence suggested that the Soviets had only a peripheral interest in the island. By contrast, the Government of Cuba certainly was deeply involved. A new airfield was being constructed as an extension to the existing airport. It was due to open in March 1984, though aircraft would be able to land there from about January. The Americans saw this as having a military purpose. It did indeed seem likely that the Cubans, who were providing the workforce for the project – and an uncertain number of Cuban military personnel also – regarded it in this light. For them, it would be a way of managing more easily the traffic of their thousands of troops in Angola and Ethiopia back and forth to Cuba. It would also be useful if the Cubans wished to intervene closer to home. But our view remained that the Grenada Government's main purpose was, as they claimed, a commercial one, planning to cater for the undoubtedly exaggerated projections of their currently minimal tourist industry. So the position on the eve of the overthrow of Maurice Bishop was that Grenada had an unsavoury and undemocratic regime with close and friendly relations with Cuba. On such an analysis, the *coup* of 19 October 1983, morally objectionable as it was, was a change in degree rather than in kind.

On Saturday 22 October – the day before the Beirut bomb outrages – I received a report of the conclusions of the United States National Security Council meeting about Grenada. I was told that it had been decided that the Administration would proceed very cautiously. An American carrier group based on the USS *Independence*, which had been heading for the Mediterranean, had been diverted south to the Caribbean; it was now east of the southern tip of Florida and due north of Puerto Rico. An amphibious group with 1,900 marines and two landing craft was 200 miles further east. The *Independence* would reach the area the following day but would remain well to the east of Dominica and well to the north of Grenada. The amphibious group would reach the same area later on the following day. The existence of this force would give the Americans the option to react if the situation warranted it. It was emphasized, however, that they had made no decision going beyond these contingency deployments. They had received a firm request from the east Caribbean heads of government to help them restore peace and order in Grenada. Jamaica and Barbados were supporting the request. If the Americans took action to evacuate US citizens they promised to evacuate British citizens as well. We were also assured that there would be consultation if they decided to take any further steps. . . .

Suddenly the whole position changed. What precisely happened in Washington I still do not know, but I find it hard to believe that outrage at the Beirut bombing had nothing to do with it. I am sure that this was not a matter of calculation, but rather of frustrated anger – yet that did not make it any easier for me to defend, not least to a British House of Commons in which anti-American feeling on both right and left was increasing. The fact that Grenada was also a Commonwealth member, and that the Queen was Head of State, made it harder still.

At 7.15 in the evening of Monday 24 October I received a message from President Reagan while I was hosting a reception at Downing Street. The President wrote that he was giving serious consideration to the OECS request for military action. He asked for my thoughts and advice. I was strongly against intervention and asked that a draft reply be prepared at once on lines which I laid down. I then had to go to a farewell dinner given by Princess Alexandra and her husband, Angus Ogilvy, for the outgoing American Ambassador, J. J. Louis, Jnr. I said to him: 'Do you know what is happening about Grenada? Something is going on.' He knew nothing about it.

I received a telephone call during the dinner to return immediately to No. 10 and arrived back at 11.30 p.m. By then a second message had arrived from the President. In this he stated that he had decided to respond positively to the request for military action. I immediately called a meeting with Geoffrey Howe, Michael Heseltine and the military and we prepared my reply to the President's two messages, which was sent at 12.30 a.m. There was no difficulty in agreeing a common line. My message concluded:

> This action will be seen as intervention by a Western country in the internal affairs of a small independent nation, however unattractive its regime. I ask you to consider this in the context of our wider East–West relations and of the fact that we will be having in the next few days to present to our Parliament and people the siting of Cruise missiles in this country. I must ask you to think most carefully about these points. I cannot conceal that I am deeply disturbed by your latest communication. You asked for my advice. I have set it out and hope that even at this late stage you will take it into account before events are irrevocable.

I followed this up twenty minutes later by telephoning President Reagan on the hot-line. I told him that I did not wish to speak at any length over the telephone but I did want him to consider very carefully the reply which I had just sent. He undertook to do so but said, 'We are already at zero.'

At 7.45 that morning a further message arrived, in which the President said that he had weighed very carefully the considerations that I had raised but believed them to be outweighed by other factors. In fact, the US military operation to invade Grenada began early that morning. After some fierce fighting the leaders of the regime were taken prisoner.

At the time I felt dismayed and let down by what had happened. At best, the British Government had been made to looked impotent; at worst we looked deceitful. Only the previous afternoon Geoffrey had told the House of Commons that he had no knowledge of any American intention to intervene in Grenada. Now he and I would have to explain how it had happened that a member of the Commonwealth had been invaded by our closest ally, and more than that, whatever our private feelings, we would also have to defend the United States' reputation in the face of widespread condemnation.

Margaret Thatcher recalls the US invasion of Grenada in her memoirs. Margaret Thatcher, *The Downing Street Years* (London: HarperCollins, 1993), pp. 328–32.

8.6 'Regrettably less than we would have wished': US consultation over Grenada

As Margaret Thatcher notes above, her government faced awkward times in defending the US action on Grenada, as this House of Commons debate shows. Moreover, if the Americans would not consult Britain fully over Grenada, would they do so over the use of nuclear weapons based in Britain? Opposition MPs raised this point in the context of the imminent arrival of US cruise missiles in Britain.

Mr Denis Healey (Leeds, East). I beg to move,
That this House do now adjourn.

When I asked your permission yesterday, Mr Speaker, to move this motion, I said that the invasion of Grenada appeared to be a violation of the United Nations charter, that it had split the Commonwealth countries of the Caribbean in two and that it raised the most fundamental questions about relations between Britain and her most important ally. Everything that has happened in the past 24 hours confirms the justice of what I then said.

Let me start by quoting an editorial in *The Times* today – a paper that is not notorious for supporting the sort of views that I put forward. It says: 'There is no getting around the fact that the United States and its Caribbean allies have committed an act of aggression against Grenada. They are in breach of international law and the Charter of the United Nations.' I hope that the Foreign Secretary will confirm that judgement when he speaks this afternoon, because international law is the only thing that stands between the world and anarchy.

If Governments arrogate to themselves the right to change the governments of other sovereign states, there can be no peace in this world in perhaps the most dangerous age which the human race has ever known. It is quite improper for hon. Members to condemn, as we have, the violation of international law by the Soviet Union in its attacks on Czechoslovakia and Afghanistan if we do not apply the same standards to the United States' attack on Grenada two days ago.

The Security Council is meeting at this moment to consider the matter. I want first to ask the Foreign Secretary to assure the House that Her Majesty's Government will put at this meeting a resolution similar in terms to that which was put at the meeting 18 months ago when British territory in an island in another part of the south Atlantic was attacked by another aggressor, and that they will insist on the immediate withdrawal of all foreign troops from Grenada and the immediate cessation of hostilities. . . .

I come now to the impact of the invasion on relations between Britain and her most important ally, the United States. I fear that I must start by saying that information that has come to light in the past 24 hours makes it clear that the statements made by the Foreign Secretary on Monday and Tuesday of this week – I bow to the ruling that you made, Mr Speaker, at the beginning of the debate not to use unparliamentary expressions – were imperfect, disingenuous and lacking in candour.

The Organisation of Eastern Caribbean States issued a communiqué in which it made it clear that its member Governments met last Friday in Barbados and decided then to undertake what was described in the communiqué as 'a pre-emptive defensive strike' against an independent member of the Commonwealth – Grenada – and to seek assistance for this purpose from friendly countries both in the area and outside.

We now know that President Reagan received this request on Friday night last week but we learnt from Prime Minister Adams on the radio at lunchtime today that Her Majesty's Government received this request on Friday night last week. This was stated in the clearest terms by Prime Minister Adams on the radio at 1 o'clock. He also expressed his disappointment that Her Majesty's Government had not acceded to the invitation. The House will want to know how, in the light of this fact, the Foreign Secretary could tell us simply: 'There were reports that some members of the smaller group'– in the Caribbean Commonwealth – 'were seeking military support . . . during the weekend.' [Official Report, 25 October 1983; Vol. 47, c. 147.] Even more, how could the Minister of State, Foreign and Commonwealth Office, say quite specifically in her statement in the House of Lords on Monday that no approach had been received from Commonwealth countries on this matter at the time when she spoke on Monday afternoon?

I can well imagine that the Foreign Secretary himself chose the formulation in his statement yesterday: 'No formal invitation was extended' [Official Report, 25 October 1983; Vol. 47, c. 147] until Monday evening. However, the plain fact is that the Government were approached by the Organisation of Eastern Caribbean States

213

on Friday. I gather that I may not say, Mr Speaker, that the Foreign Secretary was deceiving the House, but he was certainly misleading it in the words that he used; and it is impossible to justify, by any stretch of the meaning of words, the statement of the Minister of State in another place on Monday afternoon.

We now know from what was said in Washington yesterday that the United States began considering military intervention against Grenada as soon as the military *coup* took place on 13 October, a fortnight ago. Reports from Washington on British television yesterday declared that the CIA had been planning such an operation for months before a *coup* took place. Indeed, Mr Bishop – over whose death the President of the United States wept crocodile tears in his statement on Monday – expressed, in an interview on British radio last August, his concern about the imminence of an invasion of Grenada organised by the United States.

Indeed, our Foreign Affairs Select Committee, on examining the situation in the Caribbean 12 months ago, warned the Government of those fears, and the Foreign Office chose not to comment on this part of its report in the answer that it offered to the House last spring.

It is very difficult to resist the suspicion that the United States organised the invitation from the Organisation of Eastern Caribbean States so as to justify its invasion. This suspicion is attributed to British officials – from the Foreign Office, I presume – in a report in today's *Daily Telegraph*, which also attributes to British officials the words that it was seen by the United States as a figleaf for intervention – the same words as were used by the Soviet Government in their statement yesterday. . . .

I should like the Foreign Secretary to tell us whether it is true, as widely reported in the newspapers this morning, that both the Prime Minister and the Palace first heard of the invasion from press reports. Is it also true that a telex from the Government of Grenada announcing the invasion was delivered to an old Foreign Office number which now belongs to a Scandinavian plastics company? [*Interruption.*] It is difficult to believe that incompetence and lack of grip could go any further. How on earth could the Prime Minister possibly imagine that a couple of minutes on the telephone with President Reagan, when the invasion was already under way, would make any difference?

I hope that the Foreign Secretary will tell us this afternoon what the Prime Minister said to the President during that fraught couple of minutes, and what he said to her. I must confess that my imagination leads me rather in the direction of a dialogue between the Glums.

I turn to the wider implication of what has happened for relations between Britain and the United States of America. The Prime Minister has made something of a cult of her special relationship with the American President at the expense of British interests, of her relations with our European partners and of our relations with the Commonwealth. Indeed, in her recent visit to the United States, she tried to outdo the American President in that astonishing outburst that was so rightly castigated by Lord Carrington a few days later as megaphone diplomacy. Nowhere has her servility to the American President been more evident than on the problems of central America and the Caribbean region. Contrary to all her undertakings at the European summit, she supported the use of force for the solution of the problems of central America although she had signed a communiqué, along with the other heads of Community Governments, specifically disavowing the use of force as a useful solution to the problems.

The Prime Minister has been an obedient poodle to the American President. [*Interruption.*] The true state of the relationship was put with brutal clarity by Secretary of State Shultz yesterday when he said: 'We are, of course, always impressed with the views of the British Government and Mrs Thatcher, but that doesn't mean that we always have to agree with them and, of course, we also have to make decisions in the light of the security situation of our citizens as we see it.' So much for the obligation to consult between allies, and so much for the relevance of a joint decision on the use of cruise missiles placed in Britain. To make these points is not to be anti-American, because members of the American Congress make them with as much force as I do.

The fact is that President Reagan has broken the post-war diplomatic tradition of all Governments in the United States since 1945, whether Republican or Democrat. He has abandoned reliance on co-operation and consensus with his allies in favour of what has come to be called a sort of global unilateralism. That tendancy [*sic*] of the United States to go it alone in every aspect of world affairs carries with it immense dangers for world peace, since the American President at the moment sees the world exclusively in terms of red and white. He sees Russia as the foes [*sic*] of all evil in the world – [*Hon. Members*: 'Hear, hear.'] Hon. Members may say 'Hear, hear' but there were wars in the world before October 1917. There were conflicts in the middle east, Latin America and Europe. That inability to see the world except in the terms of the most primitive comic strip is immensely dangerous.

Of course, the experience that the Prime Minister has undergone in the past week or so was undergone not long ago by President Mitterrand over Chad. Some of the propositions attributed to the American President over the Grenada affair almost beggar the imagination. Apparently he asked the Prime Minister to make Grenada a Crown colony. So much for entering Grenada to restore democratic government. He told the world yesterday that he planned to ask the Governor-General to try to sort things out. I hope that the Prime Minister is aware that the Governor-General of Grenada is responsible to Her Majesty the Queen and not to the American President. I am glad to see that she concedes that point.

It really is time that the Prime Minister got off her knees and joined other allies of the United States, who are deeply concerned about the present trend in American policy. I shall put three specific and urgent suggestions to her. First, along, I hope, with her European partners, she must not offer support for a multinational force in the Lebanon unless the United States joins the European governments in pressing President Gemayel to give the Muslim majority in the Lebanon a fair share of power, and concedes the right of Syria to have an interest in the problems [*Interruption*]. Well, the Foreign Secretary apparently conceded that in his answer to a question I put on Monday. I just hope that he sticks to his guns when he meets Mr Shultz tomorrow in Paris

Secondly, the Prime Minister must fulfil the obligations that she accepted with other Community Governments to warn the United States of America against the use of force to solve central American problems. Nobody attacked American action in Grenada more strongly yesterday in the Security Council than the Government of Mexico. That Government certainly cannot be called Communist by any stretch of the imagination. It is about time that the Prime Minister started working with Governments who want conciliation in central America rather than with those who support confrontation.

One of the most worrying things that the President has said in recent days is that we cannot pick and choose where we defend freedom. [*An Hon Member*: 'Hear, hear.'] 'Hear, hear,' says someone. I do not know whether we can really expect the United States to defend freedom in El Salvador and Guatemala by the same means as the President has chosen to defend it in Grenada. However, I do think that there is a grave danger that he may choose the same methods in 'defending freedom' in Nicaragua. It is vital that the influence of all America's allies is brought to bear at this moment to dissuade the American Administration from so dangerous and catastrophic a course.

Thirdly, if events continue as now foreseen, the British Government must, at the very minimum, refuse to accept the deployment of American missiles on British soil unless Britain has the physical power to prevent the use of those missiles against her will. What has happened in Grenada must be a warning to the Secretary of State for Defence, the Prime Minister and the Foreign Secretary in that regard. We on this side of the House – and I believe many on the other side of the House – believe that America's action against Grenada was a catastrophic blunder and that the failure of Her Majesty's Government to prevent it was an unforgivable dereliction of duty.

However, something at least may be gained from the experience of the past few days. This experience should warn America's allies of the danger of servility to a leadership from Washington which could be disastrous to the interests of the Western world. It should remind all of America's allies of the need to unite to shift American policy to the ways of co-operation and common sense.

The Secretary of State for Foreign and Commonwealth Affairs (Sir Geoffrey Howe). . . . The fact that, despite the reservations that we had expressed to them, the Americans decided to intervene in Grenada may be a matter of regret. We do not agree with the Americans on every issue, any more than they always agree with us – nor are we expected to do so. On some issues, our perceptions and those of the Americans are bound to be different. In this case, the United States had Caribbean countries that had called on it to help resolve the crisis. Nevertheless, the extent of the consultation with us was regrettably less than we would have wished.

In the course of that consultation, my right hon. Friend made it plain to the United States Administration the views that we took, as one would expect her to do. For the right hon. Member for Leeds, East (Mr Healey), when there is a difference of view between the two countries plainly expressed [*Hon. Members*: 'You did not express it.'] to take that occasion as one for denouncing my right hon. Friend as anybody's poodle is disgraceful. Moreover, the right hon. Gentleman sought to make light –

Mr Jack Straw (Blackburn). In view of what the Foreign Secretary has now said, which is very different from what he said yesterday, does he now condemn what the Americans have done?

Sir Geoffrey Howe. Not so, Sir. What I have just clearly said to the House is that this was an occasion when the United States, in company with a number of Commonwealth Caribbean countries, has taken one view and the United Kingdom, together with a number of other Caribbean Commonwealth countries, has taken another view. . . .

What has happened in this case does not, and must not be allowed to, weaken the essential fabric of our alliance with the United States. It does not, and must not be allowed to, cast any doubt on the firmness of our joint commitment to the North Atlantic Treaty Organisation and all that that means. . . .

The right hon. Member for Leeds, East suggested that this week's events are relevant to decisions that might have to be taken about the use of nuclear weapons. There is no credible analogy between our exchanges with the Americans on Monday night and the consultations that would take place before any decision could be taken to fire American nuclear missiles from Britain. . . .

As we have made clear to the House, there are quite specific understandings between the British and United States' Governments on the use by the Americans of their nuclear weapons and bases in Britain. Those understandings have been jointly reviewed in the light of the planned deployment here of cruise missiles and we are satisfied that they are effective. As I say, these understandings are specific, as are the arrangements for implementing them. They mean that no nuclear weapon would be fired or launched from British territory without the British Prime Minister's agreement. . . .

Mr J. Enoch Powell (Down, South). Consultation and common decision mean for the United States that it will from time to time

218

take such steps and such decisions as, in its judgement, it considers to be right in the interest of the United States, that it will permit representations to be made to it by its allies, but that in the end it will go its own way regardless.

This has not been the first case from which we can learn that lesson. I disagree with the right hon. Member for Leeds, East (Mr Healey) in thinking that this is at all a recent experience. It has been the pattern of behaviour of the United States over the past 20 or 30 years. During the Yom Kippur war in 1973, when the European members of the NATO Alliance said that they saw no reason for it, the United States put its forces on full nuclear alert. It did not listen to the views, and it did not concert its action with the views, of its European allies. Again, hon. Members who were in the last Parliament will remember the humiliating experience of being driven to place upon the statute book a sanctions Act against Iran. Yet hardly had the House recovered from the fatigue of sitting up all night to do so than it heard that, without consultation or information to those who were endeavouring to support it, the United States had engaged in a wild and unlawful attack on the territory of Iran itself.

This pattern of behaviour of the United States is perfectly consistent throughout; it is a pattern that can be accounted for by the policy and outlook of that country.

At the invitation of Her Majesty's Government, the United States is about to station on the soil of the United Kingdom nuclear weapons which, we are told, will be used only after consultation and by joint decision with Her Majesty's Government. Anyone who, after the experience of the last few days and of recent years, imagines that the United States will defer to the views of the Government of this country if it considers it necessary to use those weapons is living in a dangerous fool's paradise. Anyone in office who entertains that illusion is in no position to serve the security of this country.

The United States is dominated by two mutually supporting delusions. The first is that it is within the power of any nation, let alone the United States, to create what it calls freedom and democracy by external military force – that it is within its power to decide how the inhabitants of other countries should, in its interests, be governed, and to bring that about in the last resort by military interposition.

219

It also believes that the world is involved in a Manichaean struggle between the powers of light and the powers of darkness and that the mantle of leading the powers of light has fallen on the United States. I do not think that the consequences of that delusion, a nationwide delusion held and expressed by Americans of every class and creed, can be better expressed that it was – significantly over 20 years ago – by the Washington correspondent of *The Times* during the Cuba crisis. He wrote: 'The President . . . in effect has assumed the supreme political authority that was always inherent in the American nuclear deterrent. The firm belief is that as the leaders of the Alliance, with control of most of the nuclear power available to the West, the Administration has a right and duty to defend itself and its allies – even to the extent of bringing about a nuclear exchange. It is also firmly believed' – and these last words are the most significant for what will happen unless the Government have wiser thoughts in the coming weeks – 'in the present situation that there will be no time for consultation; that a threat of war cannot be met by committee decisions.'

What we should have learnt, or been reminded of, in the last few days is that the only condition compatible with our national honour and independence for those weapons being stationed on our soil, if indeed they are to be so stationed, is that this country should hold the physical control and ultimate power of decision over their use.

I commend to the Government and the House – and, greatly presuming, if I may, to our American allies – a remarkable and profound statement by, of all people, George Washington. He is reported as having said: 'The nation which indulges towards another a habitual hatred or a habitual fondness is in some degree a slave. It is a slave to its animosity or to its affection, either of which is sufficient to lead it astray from its duty and its interest.' It is an habitual hatred which has diverted the United States from a true perception and appreciation of the real state of the world in which it has to live. It is an habitual fondness which has turned this country into something horribly resembling a satellite of the United States.

I hope that after what we have experienced in recent days we can set aside those prejudices which would divert us from our interest and duty, and that Her Majesty's Government, free of habitual hatred or habitual fondness, will preserve and pursue their sole duty to the interest of the United Kingdom.

The 'extraordinary' alliance restored

House of Commons debate on the invasion of Grenada. *Hansard* (*Commons*), Vol. 47, 26 October 1983, col. 291–309.

8.7 Moss Bros missiles: 'the independent' deterrent

Maintaining an independent nuclear deterrent which depended largely on the United States always left the British government in an awkward position. The claim that Britain would not own the missiles which it acquired from the United States, but would borrow them from a pool, switching them occasionally for others, further brought the independence of the deterrent into question, as Denis Healey argued in the House of Commons.

Mr Denis Healey (*Leeds, East*). . . . Most Ministers, in common with the Minister who opened the debate this afternoon, have been somewhat ambiguous and mealy-mouthed about the reasons why the Government support the Trident programme. They have sought to disguise the Prime Minister's motivation by the kinds of phrases that have been used by the Minister this afternoon. Fortunately, the right hon. Lady has been quite unequivocal about it.

I think that the clearest statement that the Prime Minister gave of her views was the one that she made on Moscow television earlier this year to the people of the Soviet Union, when she justified our acquisition of what she called an independent strategic nuclear force on the grounds that 'Nuclear weapons are the only means allowing a small country to stand up to a big one'. There is no doubt that this is the right hon. Lady's view and, to be fair, many ordinary people in the country feel that that may well be the case. That is one reason why they support her.

Of course, if one took seriously what the Prime Minister said, the implications for nuclear proliferation and for an increase in the danger of a nuclear holocaust would be horrifying. Fortunately, hardly any other small countries – I can think of only one – have taken the route to which the Prime Minister has pointed. She has been inspired by that belief. . . .

Because the Prime Minister has now made Britain totally dependent on the United States for the supply and maintenance of its strategic nuclear missiles and for the testing of its warheads, Britain is totally incapable of standing up to that great power on any major issue of defence or foreign policy. I suggest that that is something that should disturb Conservative Members as much as it disturbs us.

The long period during which this dependence on the United States will last is rarely recognised. According to the Government, the initial supply of Trident missiles will not be completed until the next century. Under the rent-a-rocket arrangement, we have to swap those Moss Bros missiles every seven or eight years for other missiles from the American stockpile. That will be so as long as the Trident force is operational, which I trust will be some 30 years from the launch of the first submarines.

At any time in the next 40 years the United States has the physical ability to cease supplying our Trident forces with missiles or to refuse to replace them. Many Members may say, 'Yes, it may have the ability, but it would never refuse to supply the missiles or to replace them, because it is committed by treaty to continue to supply them.' Such people have short memories. Indeed, the Minister has a shorter memory than most. He cannot even remember what happened in 1982, under his Government's Administration, when the Trident agreement was signed. I should have thought that it was his duty to inform himself on that point as soon as he took office.

The fact is that, under President Truman, the American Administration broke the wartime agreement on nuclear co-operation with Britain as soon as the war ended. In the early 1960s, the Americans broke the agreement to supply Britain with the Skybolt missile because they decided not to go ahead with the production of the Skybolt missile for themselves. I know that that was before the Minster's time, but – . . .

Denis Healey, Shadow Foreign Secretary, speaking in a House of Commons defence debate, October 1987. *Hansard* (*Commons*), Vol. 121, 28 October 1987, cols. 326–7.

9

The post-Cold War era

The end of the Cold War in the 1990s threatened to undermine the whole basis of the 'special relationship' which had been restored in the 1980s. With the break-up of the Soviet Union and the dissolution of the Warsaw Pact the cement which had kept the 'special relationship' together for much of the previous fifty years was beginning to crumble. The absence of a clear and identifiable enemy meant that the close military partnership which had been at the core of the 'special relationship' was no longer regarded as being of such crucial importance.

For some writers, the change in the structure of international politics which occurred when the Cold War ended, signalled the end of the 'special relationship'. John Dickie has argued that 'when there was no longer a communist threat requiring Britain to be the alliance standard bearer in Europe for the Americans, the principal *raison d'être* of that relationship had gone'. With the growing problem of the Bosnian conflict, differences over the Sinn Fein leader, Gerry Adams's, visit to the United States, and personal difficulties reported between Prime Minister John Major and President Bill Clinton, Dickie's assessment seemed to many contemporary observers to be justified. The growing interest of the British government in developing a closer European security and defence identity in the mid-1990s provided further support for this view.

At the same time, however, an alternative view of Anglo-American relations emerged in the post-Cold War era. It was based on the view that the 'special relationship' had become so institutionalised at the working level (through constant visits by officials, joint working groups and personal working relationships) that the close ties of the past were likely to continue despite the end of the Cold War. According to this view, the implementation of the Trident agreement would help to maintain nuclear collaboration well into the next century and intelligence cooperation was also likely to continue in a wide variety of areas where interests continued to coincide. The contemporary need for intervention forces was also likely to lead to close ties between British and US military forces for the foreseeable future. This more optimistic view of the future of Anglo-American relations was based on the argument that a close security community has been established by Britain and the United States which was likely to continue in the uncertain and constantly changing international environment of the post-Cold War world.

By the mid-1990s the arguments about the prospects for Anglo-American relations in future seemed to be evenly balanced. The alliance had been written off prematurely many times in the past but never had the pressures on the relationship been as great as they were at this time.

9.1 Special relations and free riders: the Gulf War

The Iraqi invasion of Kuwait challenged the United States to reassert itself militarily. In doing so the United States discovered a staunch ally in Margaret Thatcher and less enthusiastic support from other Western states, offering Britain the chance to renew the 'special relationship' which had seemed decreasingly important during the Bush presidency, as this newspaper article describes.

Washington. As it moves closer to war with Iraq with the recall of 40,000 reservists to the colours, America has put aside the malaise and self-doubt of past months and is grimly proud still to be the world's policeman. President Bush is enjoying some of the highest poll ratings of any president since Kennedy outfaced the Soviets during the Cuban missile crisis of 1962. The Pentagon boasts of a 7,000 mile movement of troops and equipment bigger than the Berlin airlift, almost 500,000 tons to date, equivalent, it is said, to moving the city of Jefferson, Missouri (population 36,000), down to the last car and hamburger.

'All the talk about Japan or Germany being the new number one has faded quickly. The Iraq crisis shows that the US is the only true superpower,' declares *The Wall Street Journal.* 'The obituaries were premature,' proclaims *The New York Times.* 'There is still one superpower, and it is the US. Washington is not the backwater that it seemed to some when the action was all in the streets of Prague or at the Berlin Wall.'

The strength and value of the Anglo-American special relationship has also been reaffirmed, and not merely because Britain was the first to back the US militarily. Mr Bush, whose attitude to Mrs

Thatcher was noticeably distant compared with Ronald Reagan's, now appears incapable of mentioning her without an effusion of praise. 'Thank God for allies and friends like Margaret Thatcher when the going gets tough,' he declared on Monday.

The New Republic, mouthpiece of liberal Democratic opinion, records that 'Thatcher's influence was critical' in the immediate aftermath of Iraq's invasion of Kuwait. Mr Bush flew to Aspen, Colorado, that day not to fulfil a speaking engagement, but to consult her. 'Thatcher laid out precisely what Bush decided for himself the next day,' the magazine reported. A Bush aide who attended the meeting said: 'She was a big influence on the basic decision he had to make: what are the US and Western interests in the Gulf, are they long-term or short-term, and are they worth defending? She told Bush they were towering, long-term and must be aggressively defended.' The prime minister, he said, 'never flinched'.

In contrast to praise for Britain's support there has been barely-concealed dismay at the weakness of other industrialised nations. 'This crisis really exposed the hollowness of European pretensions,' Bernard Lewis, a Princeton University historian, told *The Washington Post*. There is growing resentment at the 'free ride' of Japan and West Germany, America's principal economic rivals. If the American military effort succeeds, they will enjoy reasonably priced oil having borne only a fraction of the US burden.

Martin Fletcher, *Times* journalist, 'Glory restored, but what of the cost?', newspaper article. *The Times*, 23 August 1990, from *The Times* and *Sunday Times* Compact Disc Edition.

9.2   Transatlantic differences: intervention in Bosnia

British and US views were less harmonious on the subject of intervention in Bosnia than on the Gulf War. In this article Peter Riddell explains how divergences of opinion were handled.

The Western review of policy towards Bosnia is too often glibly depicted as a clash between impetuous American idealism and cautious European realism, like a Henry James novel. There are elements of both strands, but to talk of a transatlantic clash is misleading. Rather, there is an anguished debate on both sides of the Atlantic not just about whether to use force but about the inherent limits on outside intervention. Differences are those of perspective and degree of existing involvement.

To listen to President Clinton in the past few days is not to hear a leader raring to intervene, a modern-day Teddy Roosevelt. His comments in a news conference last Friday and in subsequent interviews reflect caution and doubts. Bosnia is, he said, 'clearly the most difficult foreign policy problem we and our allies face'. America has a special responsibility as 'the world's only super-power. We do have to lead the world.'

His views of the limits on possible actions match those heard in London. 'If the United States takes action, we must have a clearly defined objective that can be met, we must be able to understand it, and its limitations must be clear.' The US should not become involved as a partisan in a war.

There are stronger pressures for intervention from within the Clinton administration than from either the British or French governments. The use of force is favoured by Madeleine Albright, American ambassador at the UN, by key National Security Council staff and by several officials in the State Department. In Britain, the most Thatcherite members of the cabinet are among the strongest opponents of intervention, one of the few issues where they diverge from their mentor. In both countries, defence and intelligence advisers have stressed the risks of military action.

The real transatlantic difference is in the degree of impatience, the extent of the feeling that 'something must be done'. That is why Baroness Thatcher's comments two weeks ago struck such chords in America. In that respect, America has been leading the current policy review, forcing the Europeans to re-examine options which they had previously ruled out, going beyond the tightening of sanctions against Serbia which took effect yesterday.

Viewed from London, the process is the familiar one of trying to influence American policy as it is being formed, operating as a participant in the inter-agency debate in Washington.

In his interview with *The Times* last week, Douglas Hurd offered a good definition of that much abused term the special relationship; 'what it actually means in practice is that we are involved in their thinking at an earlier stage than most people, and that is crucial. It does not mean they always take our advice.'

It means feeding in suggestions and reservations, or, as some officials would say, educating the Americans, and particularly a new administration.

The main British hope now is to ensure that Mr Clinton's decisions take account of all the factors involved, defining the strategic aim, specific targets, numbers of planes, the legal basis and, above all, the impact on the existing humanitarian efforts on the ground.

Britain remains more opposed to any lifting of the arms embargo to aid the Bosnian Muslims than to limited air attacks. The latest comments by Mr Clinton suggest that any military moves will be restricted in their ambitions. They may go further than ministers in London would have liked a week or two ago, and there may be continuing reservations but, in the end, there will be no open breach with Washington.

Peter Riddell, *Times* columnist, 'Bosnia policy puts Britain's special relationship to test', newspaper article. *The Times*, 28 April 1993, from *The Times* and *Sunday Times* Compact Disc Edition.

9.3   Smoothing relations: an ambassador's job

Following remarks by President Bill Clinton on 19 October 1993 critical of John Major's policies towards Bosnia, Sir Robin Renwick, the British ambassador to the United States, had the opportunity at a speech in Washington to comment on the health of the Anglo-American relationship. This article reports his views.

Washington. In order to survive the upheaval and uncertainty of the post-Cold War era, the United States and Great Britain must reject isolationism and preserve close relations with each other, Sir Robin Renwick, the British Ambassador to the US, said Oct. 26 in a speech at American University in Washington DC.

Sir Robin, who prefers the phrase 'especially close relationship' to 'special relationship', recalled the evolving relationship between the two countries from British troops burning the White House in 1814 to US troops defending Britain in World War II. He said the friendship begun in the 1940s should continue.

227

'We (the British) must remember the very great debt we owe the United States,' Sir Robin said. 'If I have anything to do with it, we must maintain the relationship we have had since 1941, trying to act as your closest friend and most valuable ally.'

This relationship is not based on nostalgia or on mere contact between governments, he said. Rather, shared values, a commitment to democratic institutions, cultural similarities and mutual trade sustain the friendship.

'From time to time there are those who suggest that times have changed and we no longer need such a close alliance,' said the career diplomat, who has been in Washington since August 1991. 'When that happens, some crisis always seems to come along to confound the sceptics and remind us of the value of that enduring friendship.'

The turmoil in Bosnia, Russia, Somalia, Haiti and South Africa – which all must be dealt with individually – cannot be ignored in favor of domestic problems, Sir Robin said. He believed that though domestic problems such as violent crime and unemployment affect both countries, they should not take precedence over foreign policy.

'The words "foreign policy" scarcely seemed to figure during the [1992 presidential] election campaign,' he said. '. . . Since the election, there has been a realization that some crises certainly are not going to wait.'

Yet the US should be able to depend on European allies in military operations, he said. 'The world has changed and it is unreasonable to expect the US to go on bearing any burden in defense of its allies,' Sir Robin said. 'The European allies must do more to develop defense cooperation between them.'

With two attempted *coups* in Russia in just two years, the US and Britain must be wary of becoming too comfortable with the Cold War's end. 'Having won the Cold War, it still remains to win the peace,' he said. 'What we are witnessing today is not the end of histroy [*sic*] but the return of history, and with a vengeance – in the Balkans, in what was the Soviet Union and in Somalia.'

Sir Robin defended the US intervention in Somalia, calling it an 'honorable undertaking'. But he warned the public against being manipulated by television news coverage of the situation. He said pictures of starving children once urged the public to support involvement but recent pictures of mistreated American soldiers are now forcing public opinion the other way.

The ambassador also had harsh words for *The New York Times'* criticism of Britain for not taking military action against the Serbs in Bosnia. British troops have been involved in peace-keeping and relief capacities.

'[British] troops have saved tens of thousands of Bosnian lives ... but far from being applauded for this rather courageous and risky effort, we are criticized,' he said.

Sir Robin said because public support does not exist for sending either US or British troops, military action in Bosnia should be restricted to peace-keeping missions and NATO forces enforcing the no-fly zone and the embargo.

Newspaper article by Heather Bruce, reporting a speech by the British ambassador to the United States, Sir Robin Renwick, given on 26 October 1993. *The American*, 5 November 1993, pp. 1 and 8.

9.4 'A shamefaced deceit': Clinton, Major and Adams

Bill Clinton's election as US President brought to power a man who had studied in Britain but who showed no special warmth at least towards the Major government. Clinton's decision to grant a visa to Sinn Fein leader Gerry Adams at an early and delicate stage of the Northern Irish peace process worsened relations between the leaders. Traditional resentment of American intervention in the Irish problem was reawoken in some sectors of British public opinion, as this *Sunday Times* editorial shows.

The disgraceful decision by President Clinton to grant a visa to one of the world's leading terrorists (whose public front is to pose as the IRA's peace-loving political apologist, a propaganda act of Orwellian proportions swallowed enthusiastically by gullible American journalists) is only a blip in the never-ending story of the Ulster troubles. But it speaks volumes for the manner in which Mr Clinton chooses to conduct American foreign policy and the sorry consequences it has had for the Anglo-American relationship.

The president was advised by his secretary of state, his attorney general, his ambassador in London, his consulate in Belfast and even by the director of the FBI that there should be no visa for a man who talks peace but practises terror. Mr Clinton chose to overrule them on the pretext that Mr Adams' visit would help the peace process (though quite how it was to be furthered by allowing the greatest obstacle to peace to grandstand, largely unchallenged, for 48 hours on America's airwaves was never explained). This was a shamefaced deceit: the president already knew from his own intelligence reports that Mr Adams has no intention of signing up to the Anglo-Irish peace accord. But Mr Clinton had the Irish-American lobby to assuage.

Some 40 members of Congress, including two of its most powerful senators from the Irish lobby, Edward Kennedy and Patrick Moynihan, wanted Mr Adams in and Mr Clinton needs their votes for his current political priority, his controversial healthcare reforms (Mr Moynihan has been a critic of the reforms and, as chairman of the Senate finance committee, is in a key position to thwart them). So, for the sake of domestic political advantage, the president opened the gate. Presidential aides even coached Mr Adams on the weasel words of peace he should mouth to give the president cover for his shameful decision. The fact that it meant slighting America's closest ally and plunging the special relationship into its worst crisis since Suez counted for naught.

The harsh fact for Britain is that in Mr Clinton's Washington that relationship does indeed increasingly count for nothing. This is an administration which, when it thinks of foreign policy (and that it does rarely), thinks of Asia. It does so because its foreign policy objectives are almost entirely conditioned by its domestic agenda. Candidate Clinton summed up his domestic priority with these watchwords: 'The economy, stupid.' Today, Japan is the yardstick by which America judges its economic success. The central thrust of Mr Clinton's international economic policy is at the heart of his foreign policy. He wants to open up the burgeoning markets of the Pacific Rim, particularly Japan, to American products, services and investment. Foreign policy is as much about job creation for Mr Clinton as it is about diplomacy. He thinks a lot about the economic opportunities for America in Japan, China, South Korea and Vietnam; he thinks very little about Europe and almost not at all about Britain.

This is bad news for Europe because so many of the foreign policy challenges it faces, such as Bosnia and Russia, cry out for the leadership of an involved, confident American president. But Mr Clinton is not interested. It is particularly bad news for Britain. As the European country closest to the United States we have the most to lose from American disengagement. It is a plight made all the worse by personal rancour between Downing Street and the White House. It still rankles with Mr Clinton that Conservative Central Office worked with the Bush campaign during the 1992 election; and there is no forgiveness from the president or some of his closest advisers that the Home Office, at the behest of the Bush campaign, searched its files for the time Mr Clinton was at Oxford to see if there was anything juicy (there wasn't). 'Bill Clinton does not have a great fondness for John Major,' a senior presidential aide told *The Sunday Times* this week, with evident understatement. A White House foreign policy adviser was more blunt: 'Clinton hates Major.'

It was perhaps inevitable that there would be some cooling of the special relationship after Margaret Thatcher, who was a towering world figure and enjoyed especially close relations with Ronald Reagan and George Bush. It is inconceivable, for example, that Mr Adams would have won his visa during the Thatcher years. 'The departure of Thatcher means that Britain is less on the American mind these days,' says one senior White House official. 'She was consulted on almost everything. Clinton does not really care what Major thinks, and never thinks of asking him. Major had to struggle to get a 10-minute bilateral meeting with the president at the NATO summit.' The White House is also well aware that Mr Major is a prime minister in deep domestic trouble, which only adds to his lack of clout in Washington.

Mr Major's particular problems in Washington, however, only give personal edge to greater forces that are pulling Mr Clinton's America away from Europe. It is, perhaps, inevitable that any American president, with the end of the Cold War, would want to look east, where economic growth is often in double digits and growing affluence has created a gigantic market of several billion new consumers, rather than a sclerotic Europe, self-absorbed with its own problems, such as Maastricht and the European exchange-rate mechanism (unintelligible to most Europeans, never mind Americans), and wallowing in a recession which has only reinforced the American view that, on the brink of a new information age, Europe is in the dark ages.

Of course, longstanding transatlantic ties cannot be undone overnight. America and Europe are not about to cast each other adrift. The Anglo-American relationship may be less than special these days but both countries remain bound by cultural, economic, intelligence and nuclear ties; and events could easily reverse Mr Clinton's eastward-looking strategy. There is at least an even chance within the next few years of a more authoritarian regime in Moscow, which would make the security of Eastern Europe less secure; and there is the probability of serious strife between Russia and the Ukraine. Either would force Washington to look to Europe once more as the frontline of its national security, and breathe new life into the Atlantic alliance. In the meantime, Britain's politicians would be best employed giving some thought to where exactly this country's future lies, in a world in which the special relationship has diminished, but close relations with a Maastricht-style Europe are still suspect.

'Adams and the alliance', *Sunday Times* leading article. *Sunday Times*, 6 February 1994, from *The Times* and *Sunday Times* Compact Disc Edition.

9.5 Mending fences

However irritating, the Gerry Adams affair remained only one aspect of Anglo-American relations. Prior to a visit by John Major to Washington, Anthony Hartley advises in *The Times* that the value of the overall relationship should be reaffirmed.

It is never agreeable to be snubbed by an old friend. Also it is shaming to see one of the founders of the world anti-terrorist club suddenly reserve itself and admit Gerry Adams to the open arms of television interviewers. What would Washington have said if Britain had granted a visa to George Habash on the ground that he had something to contribute to the Middle Eastern peace process – something other than bombs, that is?

But there are more important, though not less irritating, things for Bill Clinton and John Major to talk about than Mr Adams. There is the future of NATO, for example, placed at risk by Bosnian 'decisions and revisions which a minute will reverse'. Democratic administrations have always been peculiarly liable to pressure from the Irish lobbies of Boston and New York. A policy disagreement like that over Suez was a more serious affair altogether, but even that rift was soon mended. Five years later, Harold Macmillan was playing the wise old Greek to John F. Kennedy's energetic young Roman, a role that was rewarded by the Nassau agreement and the salvaging of Britain's nuclear deterrent through Washington's readiness to provide Polaris.

So will Mr Major find the special relationship between Britain and the United States on its deathbed? If so, it is a remarkably sudden demise. To take only one aspect of it, over the last 50 years three Prime Ministers have had close personal relations with their opposite number in the White House. From 1940 onwards, there have been regular meetings between British and American officials and a confidential relationship between intelligence services. Co-operation has been continuous over many decades. That might be thought a little special; at least, it is not to be found in relations between the US and other countries.

If now there is a coolness, partly due to the idiocy of Conservative Central Office, that will hardly sweep away so much history, so much engrained habit. In fact, Anglo-American relations cover much more than contacts between governments.

The political ties were acquired in two world wars, which themselves were part of a process through which the US took over from Britain the difficult responsibility of maintaining the European balance of power. Between 1890 and 1947, attitudes in the US changed from suspicion of an imperialist Britain to a realisation of the need to replace it, first in a struggle against German expansion and, much later, in the defence of Western Europe against a perceived Soviet threat.

In the course of this association, Anglo-American relations took on an intimacy for which it is hard to find a parallel. Like all intimate relationships, it includes the possibility of one or other side feeling aggrieved. When Dean Acheson remarked that Britain had lost an empire and not found a role, he was speaking as a candid friend. He would never have used the same language to Adenauer or de Gaulle.

This intimacy sprang from many kinds of human contact, other than political. A common language is perhaps the major factor. Whatever divergences of usage there may be between the two sides of the Atlantic, Hollywood and television are steering us towards understanding and, incidentally, ensuring that the US should be by far the greatest cultural influence on British life. Not that the traffic is one way. Hollywood's victorious occupation of the British screen finds a counterpart in the infiltration of American newspapers by British journalists.

But is Britain, where an increasingly egalitarian society has become more like that of the US over the past 20 years, merely a sally-port through which American culture makes forays into Europe? Not merely are there many examples of 'feedback' across the Atlantic, but it is easy to observe the emergence of a mid-Atlantic idiom which heralds the onset of a global culture with English for its medium.

The economic ties between Britain and America hardly need pointing out. Britain receives the lion's share of American investment in Europe.

It is also the largest foreign investor in the US, only falling slightly behind Japan in 1992. Germany apart, America still remains Britain's largest trading partner. Wall Street and the City of London, competing but also complementary markets, exist in a symbiosis which can only grow as the North American Free Trade Area offers new opportunities for the construction of a global economy.

Britain's support for free trade within the European Union makes it an important partner for the US in a world from which protectionism has not been banished by the Uruguay Round.

The relationship between Britain and America has deep roots within the societies of both countries, which gives political relations their resilience and enables them to recover from periodic fits of tactlessness and resentment.

But, it is often said, Britain's economic failures and diminished standing in the world make this country a less desirable ally. Germany is now the flavour of the month in Foggy Bottom, and it is the spices of the Asian rim that titillate the palate of American executives. Opponents of Baroness Thatcher, too, are very willing to regard her close relations with the Washington of Ronald Reagan as a delusion that prevents Britain from getting on with its proper business of building the EU. For them, not only is Britain becoming less important to the US, but America should become less important to Britain.

Foreign policy, however, is not a monogamous affair. To allow our relations with the US to languish to demonstrate our newly acquired European sincerity would be a ludicrous act of diplomatic self-mutilation, unpopular with the British electorate and incomprehensible to everyone else.

British foreign policy has always tried to find a balance between its 'continental commitment' and its position as a country that faces the Atlantic. In the past these options have been complementary, not contradictory, and there is no reason why we should abandon such flexibility now. The US is still our major ally. It is natural that British Governments should value relations with Washington.

America's European commitment has not been changed as much as appeared after the collapse of the Soviet Union. Three major objectives of American policy – non-proliferation of nuclear weapons, continuation of the arms control dialogue with the successor states of the Soviet Union, and safeguarding the oil resources of the Gulf – require European bases and reliable allies with efficient armed forces that can be deployed overseas if necessary.

If America is the only credible intervener in the world today, Britain and France are the only European countries with troops available to stand at its side, as they did during the Gulf War. Despite the present honeymoon between Paris and Washington over Bosnia, Britain is more likely to view issues from the same perspective as the US.

As for the future reliance on the European Union, the contradictions and errors of a divided Community from the very start of the Yugoslav civil war show how chimerical were the hopes attached to the Maastricht Treaty. The words in which the new European kid on the block declared he could handle Bosnia make odd reading now. When action is needed, it is back to NATO and leadership from Washington.

When John Major arrives in Washington, he will have to tell President Clinton that Britain and America are too useful to each other for lasting sulks, but also that a familiar relationship does not excuse tactlessness. Our two countries have lived on close terms for a long time. Our views of international problems are usually the same; we are both convinced free-traders and supporters of a market economy; we both have experience of global power.

America still needs a reliable ally in Europe; Britain still needs a protector from across the Atlantic. Does this add up to a special relationship? Yes, if we realise that this does not always mean the ability to influence each other's policies.

Mr Major must understand that American respect is gained by success in areas that count: a well-managed economy, effective armed forces and the visible exercise of political leadership. As *The Wall Street Journal* put it delicately: 'While Mrs Thatcher was

Prime Minister, Britain was not a nation in decline.' Her relationship with the US was 'special' indeed, but she had earned it.

'Special relationship can survive a cold shoulder', newspaper article by Anthony Hartley, author of *America and Britain*, pamphlet for the Centre for Policy Studies. *The Times*, 28 February 1994, from *The Times* and *Sunday Times* Compact Disc Edition.

9.6 Post-Cold War US views of Britain in Europe

Reflecting the consistent post-war policy of encouraging Britain to play a greater role in Europe, in this extract Raymond Seitz argues that Britain's influence in Washington is likely to increase if Britain has more influence in Paris and Bonn. At the same time, however, he argues, there will always be a 'special' Anglo-American relationship.

During my time here as US Ambassador I have often been confronted with the question whether the established nature of the relationship between our two countries can endure. The press here has been especially if spasmodically fixed on the issue. I can count four occasions in the past year and a half when the headlines have read less like a news item about the relationship than an obituary.

When I arrived here three years ago I said I would eschew the phrase 'special relationship', not because I had any particular aversion to it, but because I felt its misty quality clouded what was at stake. The phrase had become too nostalgic and backward-looking. To declare a relationship special does not make it so.

Many believe the end of the Cold War has changed the basic quality of the relationship. There is a lot of truth in this. Much of our relationship over the past half-century has developed around a central strategic fact – that is, the presence in central Europe of a large, hostile, anti-democratic force, first Nazi and then Soviet.

The essentials of our transatlantic relationship for 50 years rested on this fundamental challenge. All of that has changed now. The last Russian soldier leaves eastern Germany this August. Only a fraction of the nuclear force that once bristled on the Continent remains. Whether we like it or not, there are now gradations of security in Europe where the interests of the various allies are bound to differ. To insist otherwise would not be publicly credible or politically sustainable. Quite apart from its own horror, Bosnia has demonstrated that security in Europe is now a far more complex and subtle affair.

What is clear, however, is the continuing recognition that America's security cannot be detached from Europe's, and that for the foreseeable future, there is no genuine security in Europe without a significant American presence.

There is another proposition around these days. It says that Britain's gradual, irreversible, step-by-step involvement in the European Union is bound to erode its independent ties to the United States. When I contrast my time in my current job with my first assignment here, in the mid-1970s, the omnipresence of the European Union is striking.

Ministers are always going back and forth to Brussels. Britain's position on innumerable issues is set in a European context and its choices [are] constrained by a European framework. Douglas Hurd pointed out the other day that a quarter of the British budget flows through the Union, and no complex of issues from Maastricht to 'enlargement' has so confounded British politics over my three years at the Embassy.

What is equally true, however, is that America's transatlantic policy is European in scope. It is not a series of individual or compartmentalised bilateral policies, and never has been. It is the policy of one continent to another. There is a simple observation that if Britain's voice is less influential in Paris or Bonn, it is likely to be less influential in Washington.

So while Britain's role in the Union is indisputably complicating to our relationship it is also indispensible [sic] to the relationship. And this is perhaps truer today than in the past, when economic issues have come to define security as much as defence issues.

There are a couple of other chestnuts around. One suggests that America's interest in Britain and in Europe is bound to diminish as the demographic composition of the United States is transformed. I won't argue too vigorously against this except to say that its logic is superficial.

Of course our foreign policy will in some measure reflect our ethnic profile. It always has. The Irish-American community, for example, has been influential in American politics for 150 years. But it is equally true that the nineteenth century, when our political establishment was almost wholly made up of British stock, was also the period of our greatest alienation from Britain.

I would simply observe that a nation's foreign policy in the first instance is based on its foreign interests, both security and economic, and less on its genetics.

And finally let me mention one other commentary that I have often encountered. This says that America's interests in the Pacific are outstripping America's interests in the Atlantic. That may be so but I am always a little startled at the European discovery of the Pacific. That ocean has been there a long time.

What is remarkable about the Anglo-American relationship is the degree to which our respective interests have historically run in parallel. Much of our official exchange – in defence and intelligence, finance and trade – reinforces this phenomenon, and over the years we have built up a structure of relations which neither of us could replicate with any other nation.

Perhaps most important we share historical concepts given body over generations: human and civil rights, liberty, the common law and the rule of law, tolerance and equity, the manners of property, and the basic freedoms.

I suspect our priorities won't match with quite the same frequency as they once did. Still, whatever the threats and opportunities that lie ahead, our destinies are deeply rooted in a common soil and nurtured by the countless transactions of everyday life.

'Britain belongs to Europe', article by the US ambassador to Britain, Raymond Seitz, on the state of the special relationship. *The Times*, 20 April 1994.

9.7   US support for the Irish peace process

In spite of the controversy over US intervention in the peace process, with the granting of a visa to Gerry Adams, the United States continued to search for a role in bringing the conflict to an end. Here President Clinton states his position.

I welcome today's announcement by Irish Prime Minister Bruton and British Prime Minister Major of the launching of a Joint Framework Document outlining their shared proposals for inclusive talks on the future of Northern Ireland. The publication of this document marks another significant step forward in the peace process. I congratulate both Prime Ministers, former Irish Prime Minister Albert Reynolds, Irish Foreign Minister Dick Spring, and British Secretary of State for Northern Ireland Sir Patrick Mayhew, all of whom have worked hard and risked much in the search for a new path forward to reconciliation and lasting peace.

The Framework Document lays the foundation for all-party talks among the British and Irish governments and the political parties in Northern Ireland. The talks are intended to be all-inclusive, with all issues on the table. As the Irish and British governments have emphasized, the document is designed to assist discussion and negotiation on Northern Ireland and will not be imposed on any party. The clear wish of the people of Northern Ireland is for a lasting peace. We call upon all the parties to examine the document carefully and move forward on the basis of it.

The guns and bombs have been silent in Northern Ireland for almost six months. The benefits of peace are obvious to all, and I urge the parties to seize this opportunity. I will continue to strongly support the peace process in Northern Ireland and to work with the governments of Ireland and the United Kingdom to build on today's courageous step forward toward lasting peace. In [*sic*] addition, I look forward to our Trade and Investment Conference to be held this May as a way to underscore the tangible benefits to peace.

EUR305 02/22/95, 'Clinton welcomes proposals on the future of Northern Ireland', text of the statement released by the Office of the Press Secretary of the White House. USIS Wireless File, 23 February 1995.

9.8   The 'special relationship' in jeopardy once more

> When President Clinton met Gerry Adams in Washington, causing much anguish in Britain, many lamented the death of the 'special relationship'. This *Sunday Times* article exemplifies the argument that Britain should cease to rely upon the 'special relationship'.

Much has been written in recent years about the end of the special relationship between Britain and the United States, but the brutal truth is that for most of its existence it has only been special on one side. Though it was forged in part from shared culture, language and aims, it reached its zenith during Britain's desperate struggle to survive the Second World War. Thereafter, Britain sought to use it to salvage its increasingly precarious global position as the United States forged ahead to become the unquestioned economic and military colossus.

America became a big country cousin to these islands, sometimes giving us a friendly cuff round the ear, stealing our sweets and occasionally taking off with other relations. At times Washington would help out, often when it suited its own interests, and though Britain clearly remained an important ally the phrase 'special relationship' met blank stares from most Americans. It was special to Britain because we needed it more.

The decision last week to allow Gerry Adams to raise funds in the United States, and for the president to invite him to a White House party, is another step on that downward path – yet one that has much significance. It was made despite appeals by No. 10 and Sir Robin Renwick, the British ambassador to Washington, to stop Mr Adams being permitted to raise money or getting the red-carpet treatment. These appeals become all the more significant in the light of this newspaper's report today showing how the IRA has moved into multi-million-pound racketeering. The British were so alarmed at the prospect of a Sinn Fein propaganda triumph that Sir Patrick Mayhew, the Northern Ireland secretary, uncharacteristically admitted in Washington that it would be 'dismaying' to see Mr Adams shake hands with the president. None of this has cut much ice with the White House.

Mr Adams was allowed into the United States three times in 1994 despite being dubbed a 'Goebbels' figure by Sir Robin. Add to that Bill Clinton's decision to stay away from Britain's Victory in Europe celebrations this spring (that he wanted to go to Moscow instead shows just how much he values the relationship with Britain), and the steady retreat of American forces from Europe, and the foundations of British foreign policy for the past 50 years appear to be suffering acute subsidence.

This, of course, is not the first setback in the relationship. London and Washington have had tiffs in the past and still remained friends. At the end of the war Churchill was furious that Roosevelt and Stalin had excluded him from a secret meeting during the Yalta conference. There was real bitterness at the time of Suez. But much has changed since then. The new, sceptical attitude in Washington, the end of the Cold War, the growth in economic power in Germany, Japan and the Pacific rim, the policy vacuum in Bosnia, the deepening of the European Community and newly emerged American isolationism have put what was special about the relationship in jeopardy.

At least confrontation with the Soviet Union tied the two countries together. It was ironic that as the Soviet Union disintegrated, Margaret Thatcher and Ronald Reagan were in power. That meant Britain received invaluable help during the Falklands war and, in turn, allowed the United States to use its British bases to launch bombing raids against Libya. There was also co-operation over nuclear weapons, including Trident, a high level of intelligence sharing and the heady unity of the Gulf war.

Even so, the warning signs were there when George Bush came to power six years ago. Britain was more closely integrated in Europe and a unified Germany was suddenly carrying more clout. It was not, however, until Mr Clinton, the former Rhodes scholar who knew more about Britain than any of his predecessors, took office that the relationship really soured. Already hostile because of perceived Conservative support for Mr Bush, the new administration set about wilfully playing down the role of Britain. Despite its massive diplomatic presence in Washington, Britain became just another player clamouring for the administration's ear.

As the relationship deteriorated with American snubs, so the British began to respond in kind. Kenneth Clarke dismissively described Tony Blair's policies as 'Clinton-esque' while Sir Patrick wondered aloud about how Mr Adams, who 18 months ago was carrying the coffin of the Shankill Road bomber, could now be greeted in the White House.

Ireland is clearly the sharpest point of contact in a prickly relationship, and Mr Adams is outflanking British policy. One of his prime aims has been to dislocate the special relationship so as to promote the nationalist cause. He promised the IRA that if he delivered a ceasefire he would deliver the White House. Mr Clinton gambled last year that by giving Mr Adams a visa against the wishes of the State Department and the British, the Sinn Fein leader would be able to win a ceasefire at home. To their eyes, the gamble paid off. The visa was a clear signal to the IRA that British policy no longer dictated White House behaviour. Now Mr Clinton is gambling that Mr Adams will be able to deliver disarmament at home because he is about to be clasped to the president's bosom.

Britain's anger over the Adams visit is understandable, although it should not be forgotten that, sooner or later, the Sinn Fein leader will have to shake hands with John Major. The more important point is that we should learn from America's unsentimental attitude. In the Clinton scheme of things it would have been much more convenient had Britain, in Mr Major's phrase, been at 'the heart of Europe'. But as we are seeing, with the latest currency crisis engulfing Europe, such a course would not have served Britain's interests. The United States may be tilting its foreign policy axis towards the Asia–Pacific region, but there is no reason why Britain should not do so, too.

In economic terms, Britain's special relationship with Japan (which is exceptional among European countries) is becoming as important as that with the United States. All foreign policy relationships are up for grabs. Our relationship with Washington has never been as special as we once hoped it was, but it has served us well and better than any other affair of state. The lesson of the Adams episode, however, is that if we expect too much from the United States we are bound to be disappointed.

'Our one-sided relationship', *Sunday Times* leading article. *The Sunday Times*, 12 March 1995.

9.9 'A friendship made of solid stone': Douglas Hurd on Anglo-American relations

At a conference organised by the Royal Institute of International Affairs and supported by the government, and in what was widely seen as an opportunity for Douglas Hurd to sum up his views on Britain's foreign policy prior to his retirement, the Foreign Secretary turned his attention to Anglo-American relations. Despite the differences he reaffirms the importance of the relationship to Britain.

We and the United States share defence and intelligence assets with one another in a way which neither of us does with any other partner. The United States is now our largest overseas market. It is the largest recipient of British investment, and Britain is the largest recipient of US overseas investment. The lives and prosperity of millions of Britons and millions of Americans are tied together. As with all genuinely close friendships, we don't have to aim off when we differ, or trim our convictions in case of damage. A few chips fly from time to time, but it is a friendship made of solid stone, not the dust of sentimentality.

We have always worked side by side with the United States in NATO. There is no longer a major threat to our defence. Russian weapons are no longer targeted on British cities. But the NATO Alliance remains squarely at the centre of our defence in a less threatening but more complex world. We do not know where the next threat to our own security will come from. Whatever it is, NATO will be there to protect its members and uphold the values it stands for – values which are more powerful today than ever and which we hope to share in due course with a wider membership.

The Secretary of State for Foreign and Commonwealth Affairs, the Rt Hon. Douglas Hurd, CBE, MP, speech to the 'Britain in the World' conference, Queen Elizabeth II Conference Centre, London, Wednesday 29 March 1995. Foreign and Commonwealth Office press release.

9.10 Britain is still special

In this article a former Department of State official responds to those who proclaim the death of the 'special relationship' by asserting that the two states still have much in common and that Britain continues to offer crucial support to American foreign policy.

In 1989 the *Sunday Times* of London published a front-page story that pegged me, then serving as an undersecretary of state, as the secret leader of a pro-German cabal within the American government. It was reported that the intent of this cabal was to replace the special Anglo-American relationship with a new Washington–Bonn axis. Almost six years later, commentators are again burying the special relationship. Rumors about strained personal ties between leaders, frictions over the Irish question and frustrations over Bosnia have roused writers on both sides of the Atlantic.

True, Britain is no longer the mother country. Nor are Britons the wise Greeks who must guide the rustic, untutored Roman-Americans. It is even silly to assert that Britain must play the role of translator between continental Europe and the United States, as Americans have had enough experience in European affairs by now to make their own mistakes. So as John Major meets with Bill

243

Clinton tomorrow at the White House, it is fair to ask: Does the special relationship still matter?

The American nation is based on a commitment to a set of ideas, not on race, ethnicity, or creed. These ideas shape Americans' views about the state and government and our role in the world. These ideas have deep British roots. Ideas matter a great deal in this post-Cold War world. We face problems that transcend traditional boundaries; shared reference and even conviction make it easier for nations to act in concert.

To be more specific, the US and Britain share an abiding commitment to the rule of law. In diplomacy, this means that words matter a great deal to both nations. I recall many occasions when others were bemused by American and British reluctance to sign agreements that we worried we could not sustain.

The special relationship has roots, however, in more than a common ideology and political culture. The US and Britain are both maritime nations that are simultaneously interested in, but slightly separated from, the great landmass of Eurasia. In the nineteenth century, this coincidence of interests enabled the young United States to pronounce a Monroe Doctrine against European involvement in Latin America, knowing the British Navy would make it so. Throughout the twentieth century, our combined geopolitical outlook has been that no single power should dominate Europe.

As maritime nations, we also share certain perspectives on international politics. Neither nation believes, as some continental powers have been prone to believe, that geographical propinquity is the sole organizing criterion for nations. Given this outlook, it was natural for the US and Britain to recognize a strategic interest in the Gulf when Iraq invaded Kuwait. If there are threats in the future, Britain is one of a few powers with the capability and will to help.

Our maritime history, in combination with our familiarity with Scottish texts written by Adam Smith and David Hume, also creates strong constituencies in both nations for international trade. Both of us have experienced prosperity from free trade and calamities from protectionism. We also both became significant overseas investors and developed sophisticated capital markets that serve the world. These conditions led us to become the largest direct investors in one another.

The major foreign policy challenge for Britain today is to help determine the future shape of the European Union and Britain's place within it. As a general matter, Britain's preferences for the European design, if it engages, are likely to be positive for the US. Britain tends to favor open trade, competition instead of cartels and a more limited role for the state in the economy. It recognizes the ongoing importance of trans-Atlantic security structures. Britain's outward orientation will seek to preclude any European foreign policy from becoming self-absorbed or paralyzed by elaborate, unresponsive structures.

The US, however, has other close allies in Europe, and one of them, Germany, appears committed to channeling its power through the European Union. Given this dynamic, the US should work with Britain and with Germany and others in Europe, to ensure that the future EU is enlarged to embrace Eastern Europe, open to trade and investment, and attentive to its partnership with North America.

Indeed, the special relationship will be most effective in the future, as it has been in the past, when the US has a firm grasp of its European and global objectives. In the 1980s, the US had a clear concept of confronting Soviet threats and then easing the Soviet Union out of Eastern Europe. Britain provided strong support, even on issues where it had qualms, such as the INF zero option, the Strategic Defense Initiative and German unification. Working together, we strengthened trans-Atlantic ties, not just the US–Britain relationship.

Similarly, when addressing the first post-Cold War challenges, such as forging the Gulf War coalition and completing the Uruguay round of GATT, the US acted with constancy according to its strategic purposes, and Britain played vital roles in each as a European partner.

So perhaps the special relationship, for reasons of ideology and realism, has upended Viscount Palmerston's caution: nations can have perpetual friends and allies as well as interests. But relationships and friends require the commitment of both sides. If the special relationship seems to be fraying, the US should be examining whether it is signaling clear and constant purposes. And the US should recognize that all its relationships might be at risk if it fails to do so in the future.

245

Anglo-American relations

'Mother country no more, Britain is still special', by Robert Zoellick, an Under-Secretary of State and White House deputy chief of staff in the Bush administration. *Wall Street Journal*, 3 April 1995.

9.11 Clinton revives the 'extraordinary relationship'

Following difficulties in Anglo-American relations over Northern Ireland and Bosnia, a new, closer relationship once again began to develop in late November 1995. In an address to both Houses of Parliament President Clinton revived the term 'the extraordinary relationship', used by Mrs Thatcher in the 1980s. The President looked back to the close partnership which developed in World War II and the Cold War and emphasised the need for a continuation of Anglo-American cooperation in 'winning the peace' in the new post-Cold War era.

Today the United States and the United Kingdom glory in an extraordinary relationship that unites us in a way never before seen in the ties between two such great nations. It is perhaps all the more remarkable because of our history; first, the war we waged for our independence, and then, barely three decades later, another war we waged in which your able forces laid siege to our capital. Indeed, the White House still bears the burn marks of that earlier stage in our relationship. And now, whenever we have even the most minor disagreements, I walk out on the Truman Balcony and I look at those burn marks, just to remind myself that I dare not let this relationship get out of hand again.

In this century, we overcame the legacy of our differences. We discovered our common heritage again. And even more important, we rediscovered our shared values. This November, we are reminded of how exactly the bonds that now join us grew. There are three great trials our nations have faced together in this century.

A few weeks ago, we marked the anniversary of that day in 1918 when the guns fell silent in World War I, a war we fought side by side to defend democracy against militarism and reaction. On this Veterans Day for us and Remembrance Day for you, we both paid special tribute to the British and American generation that 50 years ago now, in the skies over the Channel, on the craggy hills of Italy, in the jungles of Burma, in the flights over the Hump, did not fail or falter. In the greatest struggle for freedom in all of history, they saved the world.

Our nations emerged from that war with the resolve to prevent another like it. We bound ourselves together with other democracies in the West and with Japan and we stood firm throughout the long twilight struggle of the Cold War – from the Berlin airlift of 1948 to the fall of the Berlin Wall on another November day just six years ago.

In the years since, we have also stood together, fighting together for victory in the Persian Gulf, standing together against terrorism, working together to remove the nuclear cloud from our children's bright future, and together preparing the way for peace in Bosnia, where your peacekeepers have performed heroically and saved the lives of so many innocent people.

I thank the British nation for its strength and its sacrifice through all these struggles, and I am proud to stand here on behalf of the American people to salute you.

Ladies and gentlemen, in this century democracy has not merely endured, it has prevailed. Now it falls to us to advance the cause that so many fought and sacrificed and died for. In this new era we must rise not in a call to arms but in a call to peace.

The great American philosopher John Dewey once said the only way to abolish war is to make peace heroic. Well, we know we will never abolish war or all of the forces that cause it, because we cannot abolish human nature or the certainty of human error. But we can make peace heroic, and in so doing we can create a future even more true to our ideals than all our glorious past.

To do so we must maintain the resolve in peace we shared in war when everything was at stake. In this new world our lives are not so very much at risk, but much of what makes life worth living is still very much at stake. We have fought our wars. Now let us wage our peace.

This time is full of possibility. The chasm of ideology has disappeared. Around the world the ideals we defended and advanced are now shared by more people than ever before. In Europe, and many other nations, long-suffering people at last control their own destinies. And as the Cold War gives way to the global village, economic freedom is spreading alongside of political freedom, bringing with it renewed hope for a better life, rooted in the honorable and healthy competition of effort and ideas.

America is determined to maintain our alliance for freedom and peace with you, and determined to seek the partnership of all like minded nations to confront the threats still before us. We know the way. Together we have seen how we succeed when we work together.

When President Roosevelt and Prime Minister Churchill first met on the deck of the HMS *Prince of Wales* in 1941, at one of the loneliest moments in your nation's history, they joined in prayer, and the prime minister was filled with hope. Afterwards he said the same language, the same hymns, and more or less the same ideals. Something big may be happening – something very big.

Well, once again, he was right: something really big happened. On the basis of those ideals, Churchill and Roosevelt and all of their successors built an enduring alliance and a genuine friendship between our nations. Other times and other places are littered with the vows of friendship sworn during battle and then abandoned in peacetime. This one stands alone, unbroken, above all the rest – a model for the ties that should bind all democracies.

To honor that alliance, and the prime minister who worked so mightily to create it, I am pleased to announce here, in the home of British freedom, that the United States will name one of the newest and most powerful of its surface ships, a guided missile destroyer, the United States Ship *Winston Churchill*. When that ship slips down the waves in the final year of this century, its name will ride the seas as a reminder for the coming century of an indomitable man who shaped our age, who stood always for freedom, who showed anew the glorious strength of human spirit.

I thank the members of the Churchill family who are here today with us – Lady Soames, Nicholas Soames, Winston Churchill. And I thank the British people for their friendship and their strength over these many years.

After so much success together, we know that our relationship with the United Kingdom must be at the heart of our striving in this new era, because of the history we have lived, because of the power and prosperity we enjoy, because of the accepted truth that you and we have no dark motives in our dealings with other nations. We still bear a burden of special responsibility.

In these few years since the Cold War, we have met that burden by making gains for peace and security that ordinary people feel everyday. We have stepped back from the nuclear precipice with the definite [sic] extension of the Nuclear Non-Proliferation Treaty and we hope next year a Comprehensive Test Ban Treaty.

For the first time in a generation, parents in Los Angeles and Manchester and, yes, in Moscow, can now turn off the lights at night knowing there are no nuclear weapons pointed at their children. Our nations are working together to lay the foundation for lasting prosperity. We are bringing down economic barriers between nations, with the historic GATT agreement and other actions that are creating millions of good jobs for our own people, and for people throughout the world. The United States and the United Kingdom are supporting men and women who embrace freedom and democracy the world over – with good results – from South Africa to Central Europe, from Haiti to the Middle East.

In the United States, we feel a special gratitude for your efforts in Northern Ireland. With every passing month, more people walk the streets and live their lives safely – people who otherwise would have been added to the toll of the troubles.

Tomorrow I will have the privilege of being the first American president to visit Northern Ireland, a Northern Ireland where the guns are quiet and the children play without fear. I applaud the efforts of Prime Minister Major and Irish Prime Minister Bruton, who announced yesterday their new twin-track initiative to advance the peace process – an initiative that provides an opportunity to begin a dialogue in which all views are represented and all views can be heard.

This is a bold step forward for peace. I applaud the prime minister for taking this risk for peace. It is always a hard choice, the choice for peace, for success is far from guaranteed and even if you fail, there will be those who resent you for trying. But it is the right thing to do, and in the end, the right will win.

Despite all the progress we have made in all these areas and despite the problems clearly still out there, there are those who say at this moment of hope we can afford to relax now behind our secure borders. Now is the time, they say, to let others worry about the world's troubles. These are the siren songs of myth. They once lured the United States into isolationism after World War I. They counseled appeasement to Britain on the very brink of World War II. We have gone down that road before. We must never go down that road again. We will never go down that road again.

Though the Cold War is over, the forces of destruction challenge us still. Today they are armed with a full array of threats, not just the single weapon of frontal war. We see them at work in the spread of weapons of mass destruction, from nuclear smuggling in Europe to a vial of sarin gas being broken open in the Tokyo subway to the bombing of the World Trade Center in New York.

We see it in the growth of ethnic hatred, extreme nationalism, and religious fanaticism, which most recently took the life of one of the greatest champions of peace in the entire world, the prime minister of Israel.

We see it in the terrorism that just in recent months has murdered innocent people from Islamabad to Paris, from Riyadh to Oklahoma City, and we see it in the international organized crime and drug trade that poisons our children and our communities.

In their variety, these forces of disintegration are waging guerrilla wars against humanity. Like communism and fascism, they spread darkness over light, barbarism over civilization, and, like communism and fascism, they will be defeated only because free nations join against them in common cause.

We will prevail again if and only if our people support the mission. We are, after all, democracies, and they are the ultimate bosses of our fate.

I believe the people will support this. I believe free people, given the information, will make the decisions that will make it possible for their leaders to stand against the new threat to security and freedom, to peace and prosperity.

I believe they will see that this hopeful moment cannot be lost without grave consequences to the future. We must go out to meet the challenges before they come to threaten us.

Today for the United States and for Great Britain, that means we must make the difference between peace and war in Bosnia. For nearly four years, a terrible war has torn Bosnia apart, bringing horrors we prayed had vanished from the face of Europe forever – the mass killings, the endless columns of refugees, the campaigns of deliberate rape, the skeletal persons imprisoned in concentration camps.

These crimes did violence to the conscience of Britons and Americans. Now we have a chance to make sure they don't return, and we must seize it. We must help peace to take hold in Bosnia, because so long as that fire rages at the heart of the European continent, so long as the emerging democracies of our allies are threatened by fighting in Bosnia, there will be no stable, undivided free Europe, there will be no realization of our greatest hopes for Europe. But, most important of all, innocent people will continue to suffer and die.

America fought two world wars and stood with you in the Cold War because of our vital stake in a Europe that is stable, strong, and free. With the end of the Cold War, all of Europe has a chance to be stable, strong, and free for the very first time since nation states appeared on the European continent.

Now the warring parties in Bosnia have committed themselves to peace and they have asked us to help them make it hold, not by fighting a war, but by implementing their own peace agreement.

Our nations have a responsibility to answer the requests of those people to secure their peace. Without our leadership and without the presence of NATO, there will be no peace in Bosnia.

I thank the United Kingdom that has already sacrificed so much for its swift agreement to play a central role in the peace implementation. With this act, Britain holds true to its history and to its values, and I pledge to you that America will live up to its history and its ideals, as well.

We know that if we do not participate in Bosnia, our leadership will be questioned and our partnerships will be weakened, partnerships we must have if we are to help each other in the fight against the common threats we face.

We can help the people of Bosnia as they seek a way back from savagery to civility, and we can build a peaceful, undivided Europe.

Today I reaffirm to you that the United States, as it did during the defense of democracy during the Cold War, will help lead in building this Europe by working for a broader and more lasting peace and by supporting a Europe bound together in a woven fabric of vital democracies, market economies, and security cooperation.

Our cooperation with you through NATO, the sword and shield of democracy, can help the nations that once lay behind the Iron Curtain to become a part of the new Europe. In the Cold War, the alliance kept our nation secure and bound the western democracies together in common cause. It brought former adversaries together and gave them the confidence to look past ancient enmities. Now, NATO will grow and expand the circle of common purpose, first

251

through its Partnership for Peace, which is already having a remarkable impact on the member countries. And then, as we agree, with the admission of new democratic members. It will threaten no one, but it will give its new allies the confidence they need to consolidate their freedoms, build their economies, strengthen peace, and become your partners for tomorrow.

Members of the House of Commons and noble Lords, long before there was a United States, one of your most powerful champions of liberty and one of the greatest poets of our shared language wrote, 'Peace hath her victories, no less renowned than war.' In our time, at last, we can prove the truth of John Milton's words.

As this month of remembrance passes and the holidays approach, I leave you with the words Winston Churchill spoke to America during America's darkest holiday season of the century. As he lit the White House Christmas tree in 1941, he said, 'Let the children have their night of fun and laughter. Let us share to the full in their unstinted pleasure before we turn again to the stern tasks in the year that lies before us.' But now, by our sacrifice and daring, these same children shall not be robbed of their inheritance or denied their right to live in a free and decent world.

My friends, we have stood together in the darkest moments of our century. Let us now resolve to stand together for the bright and shining prospect of the next century. It can be the age of possibilities and the age of peace. Our forebears won the war. Let us now win the peace.

May God bless the United Kingdom, the United States, and our solemn alliance. Thank you very much.

Address to both Houses of Parliament by President Bill Clinton. European Wireless File, 30 November 1995.

Guide to further reading

It is important for students studying Anglo-American relations since 1939 to set their studies in a broader historical context. The most comprehensive histories of Anglo-American relations are H. C. Allen's *Great Britain and the United States, 1783–1952* (London: Odhams Press, 1954) and H. G. Nicholas's *The United States and Britain* (Chicago: University of Chicago Press, 1974). Also recommended is Max Beloff's chapter 'The special relationship: an Anglo-American myth?', in M. Gilbert (ed.), *A Century of Conflict, 1850–1950. Essays for A. J. P. Taylor* (London: Hamish Hamilton, 1966), and Alan Dobson's *US Wartime Aid to Britain* (London: Croom Helm, 1986).

On the relationship during the Second World War see William H. McNeill, *America, Britain and Russia. Their Cooperation and Conflict 1941–1946* (Oxford: Oxford University Press, 1953); Robert E. Sherwood, *The White House Papers of Harry Hopkins* (2 volumes; New York: Harper, 1948); Winston S. Churchill, *The Second World War* (6 volumes; Boston: Houghton Mifflin, 1948–53); and D. Reynolds, *The Creation of the Anglo-American Alliance 1937–41* (London: Europa, 1981). Christopher Thorne's *Allies of a Kind. The United States, Britain and the War against Japan* is particularly good on the difficulties of Anglo-American wartime relations in the Pacific.

The most useful studies of Anglo-American relations in general since the Second World War include C. J. Bartlett, *The Special Relationship. A Political History of Anglo-American Relations since 1945* (London: Longman, 1992); D. Dimbleby and D. Reynolds, *An Ocean Apart* (London: Hodder & Stoughton, 1988); Alan Dobson, *Anglo-American Relations in the Twentieth Century.*

253

Of Friendship, Conflict and the Rise and Decline of Superpowers (London: Routledge, 1995); William Roger Louis and Hedley Bull, *The Special Relationship. Anglo-American Relations since 1945* (Oxford: Clarendon Press, 1986); and D. C. Watt, *Succeeding John Bull. America in Britain's Place 1900–1977* (Cambridge: Cambridge University Press, 1984).

There are also a number of very interesting studies of specific aspects of the Anglo-American relationship. On the economic relationship students should consult Richard N. Gardner, *Sterling–Dollar Diplomacy* (Oxford: Oxford University Press, 1956), and Alan Dobson, *The Politics of the Anglo-American Economic Special Relationship* (Brighton: Harvester Wheatsheaf/New York: St Martin's Press, 1988). Useful studies of the defence relationship include Richard Best, *Cooperation with like-minded Peoples. British Influences on American Security Policy 1945–1949* (New York: Greenwood Press, 1986); John Baylis, *Anglo-American Defence Relations 1939–1984* (London: Macmillan, 1984); A. Pierre, *Nuclear Politics. The British Experience with an Independent Strategic Force, 1939–1970* (London: Oxford University Press, 1972); I. Clark, *Nuclear Diplomacy and the Special Relationship. Britain's Deterrent and America 1957–1962* (Oxford: Oxford University Press, 1994), and S. Duke, *United States Bases in the United Kingdom* (London: Macmillan, 1987).

Little has been written about Anglo-American relations since the end of the Cold War. There is, however, one significant study which provides a distinctive view of the contemporary relationship. This is J. Dickie's book *'Special' No More. Anglo-American Relations: Rhetoric and Reality* (London: Weidenfeld & Nicolson, 1994). As the title suggests Dickie's view is that the special relationship came to an end with the disintegration of the Warsaw Pact and the implosion of the Soviet Union.

Bibliography

Acheson, D., *Present at the Creation* (W. W. Norton, New York, 1969).

Allen, H. C., *Great Britain and the United States. A History of Anglo-American Relations 1783–1952* (Odhams Press, London, 1954).

— *The Anglo-American Predicament* (Macmillan, London, 1960).

Ambrose, S. E., *Rise to Globalism. American Foreign Policy since 1938* (Penguin Books, Harmondsworth, 1988).

— *Eisenhower. Soldier and President* (Simon & Schuster, New York, 1990).

Anderson, T. H., *The United States, Great Britain and the Cold War 1944–47* (University of Missouri Press, Columbia, 1981).

Ball, G., *The Discipline of Power* (Bodley Head, London, 1968).

— *The Past has another Pattern* (W. W. Norton, New York, 1982).

Barlett, C. J., *The Long Retreat. A Short History of British Defence Policy* (Macmillan, London, 1972).

— *The Special Relationship. A Political History of Anglo-American Relations since 1945* (Longman, London, 1992).

Baylis, John, *Anglo-American Defence Relations 1939–84* (Macmillan, London, 1984).

Bell, C., *The Debatable Alliance* (Oxford University Press, London, 1964).

Beloff, M., 'The special relationship: an Anglo-American myth?' in M. Gilbert (ed.), *A Century of Conflict 1850–1950. Essays for A. J. P. Taylor* (Hamish Hamilton, London, 1966).

Beugel, H. E. van de, *From Marshall Aid to Atlantic Partnership. European Integration as a Concern of American Foreign Policy* (Elsevier, Amsterdam, 1966).

Bloc, Marc, *The Historian's Craft* (Manchester University Press, Manchester, 1954).

Bullock, A., *Ernest Bevin. Foreign Secretary* (Oxford University Press, Oxford, 1985).

Bibliography

Byrd, P. (ed.), *British Foreign Policy under Thatcher* (Philip Allan, Deddington, and St Martin's Press, New York, 1988).

Callaghan, J., *Time and Chance* (Collins, London, 1987).

Calleo, David P., *Beyond American Hegemony. The Future of the Western Alliance* (Basic Books, New York, 1987).

Campbell, D., *The Unsinkable Aircraft Carrier. American Military Power in Britain* (Michael Joseph, London, 1984).

Carr, E. H., *What is History?* (Penguin, London 1964).

Carrington, Lord Peter, *Reflecting on Things Past* (Collins, London, 1988).

Catterall, P., and Morris, C. J. (eds), *Britain and the Threat to Stability in Europe 1918–45* (Leicester University Press, Leicester, 1993).

Churchill, W. S., *History of the Second World War. Their Finest Hour* and *The Grand Alliance* (Cassell, London, 1949–50).

Clark, Sir George, *The New Cambridge Modern History* I (Cambridge University Press, Cambridge, 1957).

Clark, I., *Nuclear Diplomacy and the Special Relationship. Britain's Deterrent and America 1957–1962* (Oxford University Press, Oxford, 1994).

Collingwood, R. G., *The Idea of History* (Oxford University Press, Oxford, 1946).

Crockatt, R., *US and the Cold War 1941–53* (BAAS pamphlet, Durham, 1989).

Crossman, R. H., *The Diaries of a Cabinet Minister* 1, *1964–66* (Hamish Hamilton, London, 1973).

Danchev, A., *Very Special Relationship. Field Marshal Dill and the Anglo-American Alliance 1941–44* (Brassey's, London, 1986).

— *Oliver Franks. Founding Father* (Clarendon Press, Oxford, 1993).

Dickie, J., *'Special' No More. Anglo-American Relations. Rhetoric and Reality* (Weidenfeld & Nicolson, London, 1994).

Dimbleby, D., and Reynolds, D., *An Ocean Apart* (Hodder & Stoughton, London, 1988).

Divine, R. A., *Roosevelt and World War Two* (Penguin Books, Harmondsworth, 1970).

Dobson, Alan P., *US Wartime Aid to Britain* (Croom Helm, London, 1986).

— *The Politics of the Anglo-American Economic Special Relationship* (Harvester Wheatsheaf, Brighton, and St Martin's Press, New York, 1988).

— *Anglo-American Relations in the Twentieth Century. Of friendship, Conflict and the Rise and Decline of Superpowers* (Routledge, London, 1995).

Dugger, R., *On Reagan* (McGraw-Hill, New York, 1983).

Duke, S., *United States Bases in the United Kingdom* (Macmillan, London, 1987).

Bibliography

Eden, A., *Full Circle* (Cassell, London, 1960).

Edmonds, Robin, *The Big Three. Churchill, Roosevelt and Stalin in Peace and War* (W. W. Norton, New York, 1991).

Eisenhower, D. D., *Mandate for Change* (Doubleday, New York, 1963).

— *Waging Peace* (Doubleday, New York, 1965).

Elton, G., *The Practice of History* (Fontana, London, 1969).

Ermath, E. D., *Sequel to History. Postmodernism and the Crisis of Representational Time* (Princeton University Press, Princeton, 1992).

Ferrell, R. H., *American Diplomacy. The Twentieth Century* (W. W. Norton, New York, 1988).

— (ed.), *The Eisenhower Diaries* (W. W. Norton, New York, 1981).

Ford, G., *A Time to Heal. The Autobiography of Gerald Ford* (W. H. Allen, London, 1979).

Foucault, M., *Power/Knowledge* (Pantheon, New York, 1981).

Frankel, J., *British Foreign Policy 1945–73* (Oxford University Press, London, 1975).

Freedman, L. (ed.), *The Troubled Alliance. Atlantic Relations in the 1980s* (Heinemann, London, 1983).

Gardner, Lloyd C., *Safe for Democracy. The Anglo-American Response to Revolution 1913–23* (Oxford University Press, New York, 1984).

Gardner, R. N., *Sterling–Dollar Diplomacy in Current Perspective* (Columbia University Press, New York, 1980).

Gelber, Lionel M., *The Rise of the Anglo-American Friendship* (Oxford University Press, London, 1938).

Gibbs, P. (ed.), *Bridging the Atlantic. Anglo-American Friendship as a Way to World Peace* (Hutchinson, London, 1944).

Gilbert, M., *Winston S. Churchill 5, Companion I* (Heinemann, London, 1979).

Giles, S., 'Against interpretation', *British Journal of Aesthetics*, 28, 1, 1988.

Gill, S., *Atlantic Relations beyond the Reagan Era* (Wheatsheaf, Hemel Hempstead, 1989).

Gowing, M., *Britain and Atomic Energy 1939–45* (Macmillan, London, 1964).

Grayling, C., and Langoon, C., *Just Another Star? Anglo-American Relations since 1945* (Harrap, London, 1988).

Harbutt, Fraser, *The Iron Curtain. Churchill, America, and the Origins of the Cold War* (Oxford University Press, Oxford, 1986).

Hinsley, F., *British Intelligence in the Second World War*, 4 vols (Cambridge University Press, Cambridge, 1979–88).

Hitchens, C., *Blood, Class and Nostalgia* (Farrar Strauss & Giroux, New York, 1990).

Hobson, J. A., *Imperialism* (Unwin Hyman, London, 1988).

Bibliography

Hogan, Michael J., *Informal Entente. The Private Structure of Cooperation in Anglo-American Economic Diplomacy 1918–28* (University of Missouri Press, Columbia, 1977).

Hull, C., *The Memoirs of Cordell Hull*, 2 vols (Hodder & Stoughton, London, 1948).

James, R. R., *Winston Churchill. His Complete Speeches, 1897–1963* VII (Chelsea House Publishers, London, 1974).

Jenkins, K., *Rewriting History* (Routledge, London, 1991).

— *On 'What is History?' From Carr and Elton to Rorty and White* (Routledge, London, 1995).

Johnson, L. B., *The Vantage Point* (Holt Rinehart & Winston, New York, 1971).

Kennedy, P., *Realities behind Diplomacy. Background influences on British External Policy 1865–1980* (Fontana, London, 1981).

— *The Rise and Fall of the Great Powers. Economic Change and Military Conflict from 1500 to 2000* (Fontana, London, 1989).

Kimball, Warren, F., *Churchill and Roosevelt. The Complete Correspondence*, 3 vols (Collins, London, 1984).

— *America Unbound. World War 2 and the Making of a Superpower* (St Martin's Press, New York, 1992).

Kissinger, H., *The White House Years* (Weidenfeld & Nicolson/Michael Joseph, London, 1979).

Kitzinger, U., *Diplomacy and Persuasion. How Britain Joined the Common Market* (Thames & Hudson, London, 1973).

Kolko, G., *The Politics of War* (Weidenfeld & Nicolson, London, 1969).

Kyvig, D. E., *Reagan and the World* (Praeger, New York, 1990).

Lafeber, W., *The American Age. United States Foreign Policy at Home and Abroad since 1750* (W. W. Norton, New York, 1989).

Leuchtenberg, W. E., *et al.*, *Britain and the United States. Views to Mark the Silver Jubilee* (Heinemann, London, 1979).

Lincove, D. A., and Treadway, G. R., *The Anglo-American Relationship. An Annotated Bibliography of Scholarship 1945–1985* (Greenwood Press, Westport, 1988).

Louis, William, R., *Imperialism at Bay. The United States and the Decolonisation of the British Empire 1941–45* (Oxford University Press, Oxford, 1978).

Louis, William R., and Bull, H., *The Special Relationship. Anglo-American Relations since 1945* (Clarendon Press, Oxford, 1986).

Lowenthal, D., *The Past is a Foreign Country* (Cambridge University Press, Cambridge, 1985).

McDonald, I. S., *Anglo-American Relations since the Second World War* (David & Charles, Newton Abbot, 1974).

Macmillan, H., *Riding the Storm* (Macmillan, London, 1971).

Bibliography

— *Pointing the Way* (Macmillan, London, 1972).

Manderson-Jones, R. B., *The Special Relationship. Anglo-American Relations and Western European Union 1947–56* (Weidenfeld & Nicolson, London, 1972).

Marwick, A., *The Nature of History* (Macmillan, London, 1970).

Mearsheimer, J., 'The false promise of institutions', *International Security*, 19, 3, winter 1994/5.

Neustadt, R. E., *Alliance Politics* (Columbia University Press, New York, 1970).

McKenzie, F. A., *The American Invaders* (Grant Richards, London, 1902).

McMillan, J., and Harris, B., *The American Take-over of Britain* (Hart Publishing, New York, 1968).

McNeil, W. H., *America, Britain and Russia. Their Cooperation and Conflict, 1941–46* (Oxford University Press, London, 1953).

Morton, H. V., *Atlantic Meeting* (Methuen, London, 1943).

Mowatt, R. B., *The Diplomatic Relations of Great Britain and the United States* (Edward Arnold, London, 1925).

Nicholas, H. G., *The United States and Britain* (University of Chicago Press, Chicago, 1975).

Nixon, R. M., *The Memoirs of Richard M. Nixon* (Book Club Associates, London, 1978).

Northedge, F. S., *Descent from Power. British Foreign Policy 1945–73* (Allen & Unwin, London, 1974).

Nunnerly, D., *President Kennedy and Britain* (Bodley Head, London, 1972).

Ovendale, Ritchie (ed.), *Appeasement and the English Speaking World. Britain, the United States, the Dominions and the Policy of 'Appeasement' 1937–39* (University of Wales Press, Cardiff, 1975).

— *The Foreign Policy of the British Labour Government 1945–51* (Leicester University Press, Leicester, 1984).

— *The English Speaking Alliance. Britain, the United States, the Dominions and the Cold War 1945–51* (Allen & Unwin, London, 1985).

Pierre, A., *Nuclear Politics. The British Experience with an Independent Strategic Force 1939–1970* (Oxford University Press, London, 1972).

Pym, F., *The Politics of Consent* (Hamish Hamilton, London, 1984).

Reynolds, D., *The Creation of the Anglo-American Alliance 1937–41* (Europa, London, 1981).

— 'A "special relationship"? America, Britain and the international order since the Second World War', *International Affairs*, 62, 1, winter 1985/6.

Richelson, J. T., and Ball, D., *The Ties that Bind. Intelligence Cooperation between the UKUSA Countries* (Allen & Unwin, Hemel Hempstead, 1985).

Bibliography

Roberts, H. L., and Wilson, P. A., *Britain and the United States. Problems in Cooperation* (Harper & Bros, New York, 1953).

Rorty, R., *Contingency, Irony and Solidarity* (Cambridge University Press, Cambridge, 1989).

Ryan, Henry, B., *The Vision of Anglo-America. The US–UK Alliance and the Emerging Cold War 1943–46* (Cambridge University Press, Cambridge, 1987).

Sampson, Anthony, *Macmillan* (Penguin, Books, Harmondsworth, 1967).

Sanders, D., *Losing an Empire, Finding a Role* (Macmillan, Basingstoke, 1990).

Schulzinger, R. D., *American Diplomacy in the Twentieth Century* (Oxford University Press, New York, 1984).

Sorensen, T., *Kennedy* (Harper & Row, New York, 1965).

Sprout, Harold, and Sprout, Margaret, *The Rise of American Naval Power 1776–1918* (Princeton University Press, Princeton, 1914).

Stoler, M. A., *The Politics of the Second Front. American Military Planning and Diplomacy in Coalition Warfare 1941–1943* (Greenwood Press, Westport, 1977).

Thatcher, M., *The Downing Street Years* (HarperCollins, London, 1993).

Thorne, Christopher, *Allies of a Kind. The United States, Britain and the War against Japan* (Hamish Hamilton, London, 1979).

Tosh, J., *The Pursuit of History* (Longman, London, 1984).

Truman, H. S., *Years of Decisions* (Doubleday, New York, 1955).

— *Years of Trial and Hope* (Doubleday, New York, 1955).

Von Ranke, L., *Histories of the Latin and German Nations from 1494 to 1514*, extract translated in G. P. Gooch, *History and Historians in the Nineteenth Century* (Longman, London, 1952).

Watt, D. C., *Succeeding John Bull. America in Britain's Place 1900–1977* (Cambridge University Press, Cambridge, 1984).

Weinberger, C., *Fighting for Peace. Seven Critical Years in the Pentagon* (Warner Books, New York, 1990).

Wheeler-Bennett, J., *The Disarmament Deadlock* (Routledge, London, 1934).

Wilson, H., *The Labour Government 1964–70* (Penguin Books, Harmondsworth, 1974).

Wilson, T. A., *The First Summit. Roosevelt and Churchill at Placentia Bay* (Houghton Mifflin, Boston, 1969).

Woods, R. B., *A Changing of the Guard. Anglo-American Relations 1941–45* (University of North Carolina Press, Chapel Hill, 1990).

Young, K., *Churchill and Beaverbrook. A Study in Friendship and Politics* (Eyre & Spottiswoode, London, 1966).

Index

Acheson, Dean 74–5, 129, 185, 186, 233
Acton, John E. E., Lord 3
Adams, Gerry 223, 229–30, 231, 232, 238–42 passim
Aden 151
Adenauer, Konrad 136, 141, 233
Admiralty (UK) 140
Adriatic 43
Afghanistan 202, 212
Africa 56, 141, 175
Crown colonies 65
see also South Africa
Agreement for Cooperation on Civil Uses of Atomic Energy (1955, amdt 1956) 111
Agreement for Cooperation Regarding Atomic Information for Mutual Defence Purposes (1955) 111
aid 61
air bases/ports 23, 43, 50, 78
Air Ministry (UK) 115–16
aircraft
F-111, 197
V-bombers 118, 123, 124, 130, 134, 137, 148
Albright, Madeleine 226
Alexander, Gen. Harold 31
Alexandra, Princess 210
Allen, H. C. 5, 8
Alsace Lorraine 19
American Revolution 54
ANF (Atlantic Nuclear Force) 146–50
Anglo-Soviet Treaty (1942) 35
Angola 209
anti-Americanism 69
appeasement 72, 249
Appropriation Bill see Marshall Plan
Aqaba, Gulf of 91

Arabs 41
Arcadia Conference (1941) 18
Argentina 200–1
arms control 153, 197
see also SALT
Asia 141, 230
non-communist 70
social upheavals 70
South-East 56, 155, 157
Aspen (Colorado) 225
Atlantic Alliance 128, 137, 151, 153, 173, 185
advantage to strength of 195
America and the future of 202
thrown into state of disarray 190
Atlantic Charter (1941) 25
Atlantic Community 90
Atlantic Ocean 24
Atomic Energy Act (UK, 1946) 80
Atomic Energy Act (US, 1954) 79, 80, 81, 92, 94, 97, 105
Atomic Energy Authority (UK) 104, 113
Atomic Energy Commission (US) 107
atomic energy field 110
co-operation 18
fears of the bomb 73
information transfers/exchanges 80–2, 104–13
military applications 105
weapons 28, 104, 105, 106, 112
Attlee, Clement R. (1st Earl Attlee) 72, 73, 126
Austin, Gen. Hudson 208
Australia 157
authoritarian regimes 232
Axis powers 18

Baghdad Pact (1955) 68, 90, 95

261

Index

Bahamas 23, 130
  see also Nassau Conference
Balfour, Sir J. 47
Balkans see Bosnia; Greece; Serbia
Ball, George 9, 12, 119, 153
Baltic 43, 206
Bangladesh 171
Barbados 208, 210, 213
Basle 167
Becker, Carl 4
Beirut 210
Belgium 175
Belgrade 43
Beloff, Max 11
Bengal 171
Berlin 43
  Corridor 151
  crisis (1948) 125, 247
  fall of Wall 247
  joint Three Power responsibility
    128
Bermuda 23, 171, 172, 173–4
Bermuda Conference (1957) 84,
    89–91
Bevin, Ernest 38, 74
  document to British embassy in
    Washington 39–41
  thoughts on American criticisms
    levelled at British 47–9
bilateralism 123–5, 143
Bishop, Maurice 208, 209, 214
Black Sea 206
Blair, Tony 241
Blue Streak rocket 118, 130, 132
Bohlen, Charles E. 46, 63, 64
Bohr, Niels H. D. 37
Bomber Command (UK) 138
Bosnia 225–7, 228, 229, 230, 247,
    251
  NATO future placed at risk over
    232
  policy vacuum 240
Boston 232
Brandt, Willy 170, 172
Bretton Woods 56, 171, 175
Brezhnev, Leonid I. 194
British Empire 59, 129
British Guiana 23, 151
British Navy 244
Brown, George (Baron George-Brown)
    162
Brown, Harold 195
Bruce, David 63–4
Bruce, Heather 229
Brussels Pact (1948) 38
Bruton, John 238, 249

Bucharest 43
Budapest 43
Bulganin, Nikolai 95
Bundy, McGeorge 122, 125
Buraimi 101
Bush, George 224–5, 231, 241
Bush, Vannevar 29

Caccia, Sir Harold 85, 86–9
Callaghan, James (Lord) 168, 187,
    191–6
Camp David 132
Campbell, John 173
Canada 29, 35, 52, 125, 183
Canning, George 75
Cape Canaveral 116, 195
capitalism 60, 188
CARICOM (Caribbean Communities)
    208
  see also Barbados; Cuba; Grenada;
    Jamaica; St Lucia
Carrrington, Peter, Baron 215
Carr, E. H. 7–8
Carter, Jimmy 191, 192, 193, 194–5,
    196, 198
Carter, Rosalynn 193
Castro, Fidel 209
Central America 201, 202, 217
Central Europe 236, 249
Chad 216
Channel ports 21
Chiang Kai-shek 70
China 150, 172, 180
  American policy in 53
  American relations with 168
  British views toward 70
  detonation of nuclear device 153
  difficulties over recognition of 68
  economic opportunities for America
    230
  hopeless war with 69
  nuclear programme 192, 194
  UN Moratorium on the question of
    representation 92
  vying for political influence in third
    world 151
Churchill, (Sir) Winston S. 8, 26, 34,
    78, 126, 132, 252
  address at Harvard 31, 35
  asks Roosevelt for assistance 19, 22
  exclusion from secret Yalta meeting
    240
  famous speech at Westminster
    College 9
  first meeting with Roosevelt 248
  Fulton speech 41–5, 150–1, 152

Index

letter to Eisenhower about Suez 82–3
opposition to appointment of Supreme Commander 32
publication of histories of Second World War 10
quoted by Reagan 204, 206, 207
reference to 'special relationship' 164
reservations about co-ordination of military policy 32
Roosevelt's criticism of de Gaulle and pledge to liberate France, in correspondence 27
tackles Roosevelt on Quebec agreement 36
updates Roosevelt on Britain's position 23–5
Churchill, Winston (grandson of above) 248
CIA (Central Intelligence Agency) 214
City of London 234
Clark, Sir George 4
Clark, Ian 10
Clarke, Kenneth 241
Clinton, Bill 223, 226, 227, 229–32, 235, 241–2, 244
address to both Houses of Parliament (1995) 246–52
Irish peace process 238–9, 240
Cold War
access to nuclear information 2
British step-by-step approach too leisurely for pace of 62
emblem of 41
end of era 223–52
gathering of momentum 38
new 197
new technological intensity 92
special relationship created by 188
tempo not such as to permit leisure 60
Collingwood, R. G. 4
Colonies 49
Combined Chiefs of Staff 30–1, 52
appointment of Supreme Commander 32, 33
forces assigned by 34
Combined Wartime Boards 18, 38
common culture/language 9, 42, 50, 52–3, 74, 116, 155, 161, 228
and Clinton's eastward-looking strategy 232
common-law alliance 25–7, 117, 165, 238

egalitarianism 234
Hollywood and television 233
special relationship reflected in 163–4, 190
Thatcher and 197
Common Market see EEC
Commonwealth 42–3, 44, 50, 52, 53, 59, 67, 78, 95, 120, 165
American suspicion that UK is exploiting 55
Britain's role as head 129
continued solidarity 70
dependence on US 58
Grenada invasion 208–21
no future in economic isolationism 62
sentimental allegiance shelved 169
tentative exploration of relations 34
world-wide interests 66
communism 43
aggression in Korea 92
anti Americanism 69
Chinese 70
danger of despotism 96
fifth columns 44
guerillas 72
resistance to 49
resistance to expansion 58
struggle against 38
threat of 14, 88, 94, 96
trade unionist 188
Comprehensive Test Ban Treaty 249
Conant, James B. 29
Connally, John 171
Conservative Party (UK) see Tory Party
Continental Powers 63, 66
Coolidge, Calvin 55, 179
Council of Foreign Ministers 40
Crossman, Richard 161–2
Cuba 151, 209
missile crisis (1962) 125–9, 135, 220, 224
currencies
convertible 64–5, 180
reserves 175, 178
Czechoslovakia 212

Daily Telegraph 214
Danchev, Alex 13
Declaration of Common Purpose (1957) 92–6, 101
Declaration of Independence (1776) 42

263

Index

defence 49, 80, 90, 119, 142, 175, 176–7
British GNP allocated to 72–3
burden should be shared more equitably 154, 184
classical information 81
common interests 168
free world 173
freedom from a few commitments 189
Hong Kong 97, 101
international, Western alliance 199
mutual/joint 79, 104, 105, 110, 113, 205
NATO squarely at the centre 243
nuclear 150, 153
parallel 238
shared 242
US effort 73, 233
Defense White Paper (1962) 121
De Gasperi, Alcide 141
demobilisation 48
democracy 207, 251
ideals 50
strength of 206–8
Department of Commerce (US) 143
Department of Defense (US) 140
Dependencies 49
destroyers 20–2
détente 166, 168, 202
Dewey, Johhn 247
Dickie, John 14, 223
Dill, Field-Marshal Sir John 29
diplomacy (American)
creative 186
methods have to be changed 176
shortcomings 71
three major objectives 235
very adult 156–7
weaknesses 70
diplomacy (British) 71, 234–5
'special relationship' as a tool of 11, 12–13, 198
disarmament 94, 153, 166, 241
Disarmament Conference (1932–4) 36
Dixon, Sir Pierson 75, 76–7
Dominica 210
Dominions 35, 49
Douglas, Lewis 64–7
Dulles, John Foster 88, 114, 116–17, 143
Dunkirk 75, 134

Eastern Europe 90, 232, 245
economic policy/relations 52, 54–5

Eden, Sir Anthony (1st Earl of Avon) 82, 126–7
EEC (European Economic Community) 90, 95, 123, 124, 132, 147, 173
Britain's attempts to join 146, 168, 169
plans treated with contempt 13
relations with the rest of the world 174–82
Thatcher's confrontational approach to 197
US interest/support in UK involvement 119, 120, 141, 142, 161, 163, 171
US relationship with 123, 182–7
Egypt 48, 78
conflict with Israel (1956) 86
disapproval of Anglo-French intervention 85
Eisenhower, Dwight D. 10, 27, 84, 116, 132, 157, 203
communiqué on talks between Macmillan and (1957) 89–91, 125
Declaration of Common Purpose (1957) 92–6
letter from Churchill about Suez (1956) 82–3
Mediterrranean HQ 31
memorandum on conversation with Eden (1953) 126–7
personal prestige 85
El Salvador 217
ERP (European Recovery Programme) 55, 56
Ethiopia 209
EU (European Union) 234, 235, 237, 241, 245
European Cooperation 90
European Defence Community 68
European Free Trade Area 90, 95, 103
European integration 119–22, 164, 178, 181

Falkland Islands 200–2, 203
War (1982) 197, 241
Far East 10, 11, 44, 97
British withdrawal from 161–2
common problems concerning 90
Heath's Five-Power Defence Pact 171
maintenance of peace and stability 154
regional alliance 153
resistance to Communist expansion 58

Index

US policy in 69, 70, 74
see also China; Hong Kong; Japan;
  Korea; Singapore
FBI (Federal Bureau of Investigation)
  229
Fechteler incident 76
Feltwell 115
fleets 20, 21
Fletcher, Martin 225
Florida 210
Force Reductions in Central Europe
  195
Ford, Gerald 190
Foreign Office (UK) 34, 38, 74, 125–
  9, 154–7, 162, 213, 214
  memoranda: 'Tactics with US
    Administration' (1947) 47–9;
    'Third World Power or Western
    Preponderance' (1949) 51
  senior officials' sensitivity to
    'relationship' 75–7
  telegram from British embassy,
    Washington (1947) 45–7
foreign policy (American) 52, 61, 63,
  69, 70–1, 78, 142, 219
  Clinton 229, 230
  combined, basis for 64
  common interests 168
  economic 176
  Europe 57
  most difficult to face 226
  reflection of ethnic profile 237
  tilting towards Asia-Pacific region
    242
  toward Britain 49–50, 169
foreign policy (British) 13, 38, 71–2,
  78, 176, 234
  Adams outflanking 241
  basic 73–4
  combined, basis for 64
  common interests 168
  major challenge 245
  new tone regarding US 187–91
  revolution in 170
Formosa 70
Fortress America' policy 100
France 57, 58, 59, 150
  danger of nuclear cooperation with
    Germany 121
  destroyers lost 20
  former colonies 175
  impact of ANF on 147
  nuclear programme 192, 194
  planned opening of second front
    32
  pledge to liberate 28

resentment of US-UK nuclear
  monopoly in NATO 121
resistance to Germany 19, 21
review of US relationship with UK
  and 91
rogue elephant policies 152
Skybolt and 133, 134
strength 43
troops available to stand by US 235
US sentiment reserved for 75
see also Gaulle; Mitterrand
Franks, Sir Oliver 75–6, 77
fraternal association 41–5
Freedom of Information Act (1966) 2

Gairloch 132
Gamelin, Gen. Maurice G. 134
Gandhi, Indira 171
GATT (General Agreement on Tariffs
  and Trade) 245, 249
Gaulle, Charles de 27, 132, 134, 164,
  233
  nuclear ambitions 136
  reaction to Macmillan's nuclear deal
    with Kennedy 169, 189
  rejection of Britain's attempts to
    join Common Market 146, 189–
    90
Gaza Strip 91
Gemayel, Amin 216
Geneva conference (1954) 156, 158
Germany 18, 57, 124, 224, 225, 243
  appears committed to channelling its
    power through EU 245
  balance of power 10
  Britain's prospect of standing alone
    against 19
  danger of nuclear cooperation with
    France 121
  demand for nuclear status 152
  expansion 233
  growth in economic power 240
  impact of ANF on 147, 150
  Jews 40
  last Russian soldier to leave 236
  rearmament 71, 72
  reunification 90, 91, 95, 241, 245
  Russians' need to be secure from
    renewal of aggression 43
  Skybolt and 133, 134
  support costs 104
  trade with US 234
  U-boat fleet 21
  withdrawal of troops from 103
  see also Adenauer; Brandt; Schmidt
Gettysburg 204

Index

Gibraltar 34
Gifford, Walter 68–74
Giles, Steven 5
Gore-Booth, A., Lord 154–7
Gort, Gen. John 134
Great Depression (1930s) 176
Great Powers 55, 77
Greece 67, 79
  British withdrawal from 45–7, 48
'Greeks' 12
Grenada 208–21
Grimond, Jo (Baron) 125
Group of Ten 167
Guadeloupe 191–6
Guatemala 217
Gulf War (1991) 224–5, 235, 241,
  244, 247

Habash, George 232
Haig, Gen. Alexander 200, 203, 204
Haiti 228, 249
Hankey, H. A. A. 85–6
Harlech, David 157
Harriman, Averill 63, 64
Harrison, Earl 40
Hartley, Anthony 232, 236
Hawaiian Islands 64
Hawley-Smoot tariff (1930) 36
H-bomb 125
Healey, Denis (Lord) 153, 212–17,
  218, 219, 221–2
Heath, (Sir) Edward 168, 169–74,
  182–5
Heren, Louis 188, 191
Heseltine, Michael 211
Hiroshima 132
Hitler, Adolf 19, 20
Ho Chi Minh 158–9
Hoff, Philip H. 161
Holy Alliance 75
Holy Loch 126, 132, 188
Hong Kong 70, 97, 101
Hoover, J. Edgar 72
Hound Dog missile 137
Howard, Sir Michael 13
Howe, C. D. 29
Howe, Sir Geoffrey (Baron Howe of
  Aberavon) 211, 217–18
Hume, David 244
Hungary 90
Hunt, Sir John 193
Hurd, Douglas 226, 237, 242–3

IMF (International Monetary Fund)
  54, 167
Independence (USS) 209–10

India 70, 171–2
Indian Ocean 24, 171
Indochina 68, 151
industry 20
interdependence 96–104, 116–17, 132,
  134, 179
  America's desire for 136
international law 212
international relations 181
IRA (Irish Republican Army) 197,
  229, 240
Iraq 224, 225, 244
Irish Americans 54, 230, 232, 237
'Iron Curtain' 41, 43, 65, 251
Islamabad 250
isolationism 241, 249
  danger of retreat into 56–7
  economic, no room for 62
  neo- 72
Israel 53, 250
  conflict with Egypt (1956) 86
Italy 20, 70, 133
  communist party 43
  withdrawal of troops from 46–7
ITO (International Trade
  Organisation) Charter 54

Jamaica 23, 208, 210
Japan 18, 19, 20, 171, 183, 186, 224,
  225
  American treatment of 53
  economic opportunities for America
  230
  expected length of war 44
  growth in economic power 240
  investment in US 234
  proposed nuclear bombing of 37
  see also Pearl Harbor
Jebb, Sir Gladwyn 76
Jefferson, Thomas 206
Jenkins, Keith 6
Jessup, Phillip 63–4, 74
Jewish Agency 40
Jews
  American 39, 53
  German 40
  number in world 53
Johnson, Lyndon B. 146, 150, 153–
  4, 155–6, 158–60, 162, 166,
  170
  attempt to involve Britain in
  Vietnam 172
  special relationship 189
Joint Chiefs of Staff 144
Joint Framework Document (Northern
  Ireland) 238, 239

266

Index

Joint Staff Mission 46
Joint Steering Task Group (Polaris) 140
Jones, Jack 188
Jordan 40–1

Kennedy, Edward 230
Kennedy, John F. 118, 122, 126, 127, 157, 190
  attempt to involve Britain in Vietnam 172
  lack of enthusiasm for Defense White Paper 121
  Macmillan's avuncular relationship with 188
  view on US-European relations 141–2
  see also Nassau Conference
Kennedy, Joseph 20
Kerner, Otto 161
Khrushchev, Nikita S. 95, 135
Kissinger, Henry 162–4, 169–70, 171–2, 180, 190
  address before Pilgrims of Great Britain (1973) 185
Korea 92, 230
  War (1950–53) 68–74, 78, 197
Kosygin, Alexei N. 158, 159, 160
Kuwait 224, 225, 244

Labour Party/Government (UK) 50, 59, 121, 144
  see also Callaghan (James); Wilson (Harold)
Lamb, Charles 165
Laos 156
Latin America 141–2, 155, 201, 216, 244
Lebanon 216
left-wingers 69
Lend Lease arrangements 38
Lewis, Bernard 225
Liberal Party (UK) 121
Libya 151, 197, 241
Lincoln, Abraham 204
Llewellin, Col. J. J. 29
Lloyd, Selwyn 86–9
Loan Agreement 48, 52
Louis, J. J. 210

Maastricht Treaty (1991) 231, 235, 237
MacArthur, Gen. Douglas 70,
McCall, Tom 161
'McCarthyism' 72
McDonald, Ian 189, 190

McElroy, Neil H. 114–15
McMahon Act (1954) 68, 79, 87, 92, 132
  repeal 92, 104–13
Macmillan, Harold (1st Earl Stockton) 83, 84, 115, 116, 157, 190
  communiqué on talks between Eisenhower and (1957) 89–91, 125
  Declaration of Common Purpose (1957) 92–6
  institutionalizing 143, 145
  preparation for his visit to Washington (1962) 119–22
  special relationship kept alive by 188
  see also Nassau Conference
McNamara, Robert 123–5, 130, 131, 153
Major, John 223, 227, 231, 232, 233, 235, 242, 243–4
Makins, Sir Roger 75, 76, 77, 87
Malaya 72
Malaysia 151, 154
Manchuria 36, 44
Manhattan Project 18, 28
Marshall, Gen. George C. 18, 48
Marshall Plan (1947) 67, 73, 76
Marxism 209
Mason, Sir Roy 195, 196
Mayhew, Sir Patrick 239, 240
Meany, George 188
Mearsheimer, John 15
Mediterranean 21, 32, 56, 175, 209
  British Command 33–4
  Eisenhower's HQ 31
Menzies, Sir Robert 157
Mexico 216
Middle East 39, 54, 56, 58, 68, 155, 232, 249
  Australians have very little say in 157
  Churchill's expectation of Soviet control 83
  common problems concerning 90
  maintenance of peace and stability 154
  regional alliance 153
  see also Aden; Bangladesh; India; Pakistan; Suez Canal
military policy 32, 52
Minuteman missile 135
missiles 100, 115–16
  air-launched 118
  ballistic 118, 121, 192
  cruise 197, 212

mixed-manned 148
'Moss Bros' 222
see also Blue Streak; Hound Dog;
   Minuteman; Polaris; Skybolt;
   SS20; Thor; Trident; TSR-2
Mitterrand, François 216
MLF (Multilateral Nuclear Force) 145,
   147, 148, 149, 150
monetary matters
   American dominance of world
      system 179–80
   dollar crisis (1971) 177, 178, 179
   exchange rates 173–4
   financial policy 178
   financial union 57
   post-war dollar shortage 52
   reform 184
   see also currencies
Monroe Doctrine (1823) 75, 244
Moscow 136
Moynihan, Daniel Patrick 230
MRBMs (medium-range ballistic
   missiles) 121, 124
'muddling through' 60
multilateralism 119–22, 123–5
multinational enterprises 187
Munich 72
munitions factories 24

Nassau Conference (1962) 12, 119,
   131–9, 169, 232
Nasser, Gamal Abdel 83, 86
NATO (North Atlantic Treaty
   Organisation) 13, 89, 114, 122,
   127, 143, 152, 155, 205, 219
belief that Europe should shoulder a
   larger role within 169
bilateral consultation 91
collective responsibility of North
   Atlantic Council for the Alliance
   128
Commanders consider forces below
   strength 150
expansion 251–2
French resentment of US-UK nuclear
   monopoly 121
future placed at risk over
   Bosnia 232
ground forces in Europe 184
hostile attitude of French to 136
joint commitment 218
leadership from Washington 235
non-nuclear members 147
nuclear force 138
Nuclear Planning Group 166
Partnership for Peace 252

special importance for both
   countries 90
squarely at the centre of UK/US
   defence 243
Trident II force assigned to 199,
   200
US interest in UK involvement
   119
naval bases/ports 23, 43, 50
Nazis 236
Near East 58, 65, 74
Nehru, Jawaharlal (Pandit) 70
Neustadt, Richard E. 143–5
New Republic 225
New York
   bombing of World Trade Center
      250
   Irish lobby 232
   Jews 53
New York Times, The 224, 229
New Zealand 157
Newfoundland 23
Nicholas, H. G. 5
Nixon, Richard M. 162–3, 164–5,
   169–72, 171–4, 180
North America Free Trade Area
   234
North Atlantic Council 93–4, 114,
   127, 128
North Atlantic Treaty (1949) 38, 72,
   95, 127
Northern Ireland 238–9, 249
Norway 20
NSC (National Security Council, US)
   209, 226
Policy Directive (1961) 123
nuclear issues 220, 221, 222, 248–9
   access to information during Cold
      War 2
   Americans impatient with British
      pretensions 189
   Britain's experience and expertise
      166
   challenges to partnership 118–45
   challenges to the partnership 118–
      45
   collaboration 36–7
   joint declaration on policy regarding
      tests 91
   management of the Alliance 151–2
   non-proliferation 235
   outside detection of tests 167
   parity 186
   possession of power 95
   preferential treatment in the form of
      information 84

Index

safeguards on the use of weapons
153
submarine propulsion plant and
materials 106–7, 109, 110–11,
113
sufficiency and American reliability
113–15
unilateral ending of cooperation 38
see also ANF; missiles; MLF; SALT
Nuclear Non-Proliferation Treaty 249
Nunnerly, David 154–7

OECD (Organization for Economic
Cooperation and Development)
167
OECS (Organization of Eastern
Caribbean States) 208, 210, 213–
14
Official Secrets Act (UK, 1911–39) 2,
80
Ogilvy, Angus 210
oil reserves/resources 34, 235
Oklahoma City 250
Operation Overlord 32, 33
Organisation of American States 95
Ottawa 89

Pacific Ocean 24, 53, 56, 238
Pacific Rim 230, 234, 240
Pakistan 171, 172
PAL (permissive action link) 148, 149
Palestine 38, 39–41, 54
Paris 48, 250
Summit (1972) 182, 183
Pearl Harbor 18, 23, 74
Persian Gulf 92, 162, 189
see also Gulf War
Peterson, Peter G. 176
Pierre, Andrew 12–13
Pilgrims of Great Britain 185
Polaris 12, 118, 119, 123, 126, 130,
132, 134
alleged difference between Skybolt
and 135
Americans impatient with British
nuclear pretensions but made
amends by providing 189
Britain's 'inheritance' as trading-
stock 144
commitment of force 148
HMS Repulse 195
replacement of 191, 192–3, 194,
196, 198
US agreement to supply UK 136,
137, 138, 139–41, 233
policy see foreign policy

political collaboration 52–3
Pompidou, Georges 169, 170
ports 21
poverty 151
Powell, J. Enoch 218–19
Prague 43
Prince of Wales (HMS) 248
proliferation 153
propaganda 50, 240
Puerto Rico 210
Pugwash Conferences 167

Quebec agreement (1943) 28–30, 36
Quemoy 85

Rambouillet 134
Rampton, Calvin 161
Ranke, Leopold von 3
reactors 112–13
Reagan, Nancy 205
Reagan, Ronald 197, 198, 234, 241
Grenada invasion 210, 211, 213,
214–16
'hemispheric' strategy 209
relationship with Thatcher 202–5,
231
speech to both Houses of Parliament
205–8
Renwick, Sir Robin 227–9, 240
Repulse (HMS) 195
resistance 19, 21
Reynaud, Paul 19
Reynolds, Albert 239
Reynolds, David 10, 11
Rhee, Syngman 70
Riddell, Peter 227
Rio Treaty (1947) 201
Riyadh 250
rockets 116, 135
see also Blue Streak
'Romans' 12
Roosevelt, Franklin D. 19, 26, 34, 72,
73, 75, 132
exclusion of Churchill from secret
Yalta meeting 240
first meeting with Churchill 248
response to Churchill's request for
assistance 22–3
stinging criticism of de Gaulle and
pledge to liberate France 27–8
tackled by Churchill on Quebec
agreement 36
update from Churchill on Britain's
position 23–5
Rose, Sir Clive 195, 196
Royal Air Force 115, 137

Index

Royal Institute of International Affairs 242
Rusk, Dean 74, 123–5, 153, 162
Russia 228, 230
  even chance of authoritarian regime 232
  probability of serious strife between Ukraine and 232
  see also Soviet Union

SACEUR (Supreme Allied Commander Europe) 134, 135, 150
SACLANT (Supreme Allied Command Atlantic) 150
St Lucia 23
Salerno, Battle of (1943) 32
SALT (Strategic Arms Limitation Talks) 166, 172
SALT III, 192, 194, 195
sanctions 226
Sandys, Duncan 114, 115–16
Scanlon, Hugh 188
Schmidt, Helmut 193–4
Schuman, Robert 141
sea power 20, 24
SEATO (South-East Asia Treaty Organization) 89, 166
secrecy 111
security 42, 175, 237
  Britain 39, 51
  collective 70, 93
  Eastern Europe 232
  establishment of a permanent system 26
  Europe 69, 91, 141, 194
  future 70, 72
  international 94
  mutual 43, 79, 80–1, 104, 105
  NATO 200
  overwhelming assurance of 45
  trade routes 24
  trans-Atlantic 245
  unwillingness of officials to take risks 2
  US 22, 69, 141
Seitz, Raymond 236–8
Serbia 226, 229
Shepard, Taz 122
Shepherds Grove 115
Shonfield, Andrew 182
Shuckburgh, Evelyn 129
Shultz, George 216
Singapore 162
Sinn Fein 223, 229, 240, 241–2
Skybolt missile 118, 123, 124, 137, 143–5, 189, 222

cancellation 130–1, 189
Smithsonian Agreement (1971) 171
Smith, Adam 244
Soames, Lady 248
Soames, Nicholas 248
socialism
  British: no inconsistency between state and expanding world trade 59–60; suspicions in US 38, 55, 59
Society of Pilgrims 75
Sofia 43
Somalia 228
South Africa 171, 228, 249
South-East Asia Collective Defence Treaty (1954) 95
South Korea 230
Soviet Union 49, 70, 83, 180, 236
  Afghanistan aggression 202
  American relations with 168
  balance of power 10
  break-up/disintegration 223, 241
  Britain's ideological opposition to 51
  Britain's relations with 35
  communist penetration 53
  defiance of relevant UN resolutions 90
  expansion 43, 44, 53, 59
  fear of war with 69
  formidable material accomplishments 93
  impact of ANF on 147
  India regarded as a puppet of 172
  need to stand firm against 121
  new Cold War between US and 197
  nuclear programme 192, 194
  perceived threat 51, 233, 245
  propaganda 50
  proposals for neutralisation of Europe 103
  Rio Treaty and 201
  Sputnik launch 113
  technological advances 97
  threat in Indian Ocean 171
  unofficial scientists 167
  US accommodation with 57
  US dialogue with successor states 235
  US expectation of support from UK in dealings with 91
  violation of international law 212
  vying with China for political influence in third world 151
  Yalta agreement favourable to 44

270

Index

see also Brezhnev; Bulganin;
    Khrushchev; Kosygin; Stalin
Spaak, Paul-Henri 93, 95
'special relationship' 9, 11, 12–13, 14,
    16, 18–37
    (1945–50): new, search for 38–67
    (1950–56): cooperation and friction
        68–83
    (1957–59): rebuilding 84–117
    (1960–63): challenges to nuclear
        partnership 118–45
    (1964–70): 'close' 146–67
    (1970–79): 'natural' 168–96
    (1979–89): restored 197–222
    (1990s): post-Cold War 223–52
Spring, Dick 239
SS20 missile 194
Stalin, Joseph V. 43, 72, 240
standard of living 73
sterling 56, 57, 61, 62
Stettin 43, 206
Strang, Sir William 75, 77
Strategic Air Command (US) 134
Strategic Defense Initiative 245
Straw, Jack 218
submarines 21
    hunter-killer nuclear-powered 124–5
    see also Polaris; Trident
Suez Canal 91, 155, 156
    British withdrawal from 162
    crisis (1956) 13, 82–6, 91, 189
Sunday Times, The 115, 231, 239–42,
    243
superiority 11, 12

Taft, Robert A. 72
Taft-Hartley Act (1947) 188
terrorism 197, 247
Terry, Charles 161
Tet truce 159
Thatcher, Margaret (Baroness) 197–
    200, 215, 224–5, 226, 234, 241
    relationship with Reagan/US 202–5,
        231, 235–6
    views on US invasion of Grenada
        208–11, 212
'Third Power' grouping 38–9
Thompson, William H. 74
Thor missiles 89, 114, 116
Thorne, Christopher 5, 10, 11
Thorneycroft, Peter, 124, 130–1
Times, The 161, 189, 212, 220, 226
Tito, Josef Broz 43
Tokyo 250
torpedo boats 22
torture 208

Tory Party/Government (UK) 119,
    121–2, 231, 241
    empire-fired 69
    idiocy of Central Office 233
    totalitarianism 206, 207
trade 233, 237
    trade barriers 174
    trade security of routes 24
    world/universal/international 59–60,
        176, 178, 183, 184, 204, 244
    see also European Free Trade Area;
        ITO
trade unions 188
Trident 193, 195, 196, 197, 198–200,
    221, 222
    implementation of agreement 223
Trieste 43
Trinidad 23
Tripartite Technical Cooperation
    Program 125
Truman, Harry S 38, 39, 48, 126,
    129, 222
TSR-2 missiles 148
Tube Alloys project 28–30, 37, 131
Turkey 48, 95
Tyler, Bill 125
tyranny 45

U-boats 21
Ukraine 232
Ulster 229
    see also Northern Ireland
unemployment 25
United Nations 39, 49, 50, 56, 58,
    83
    American ambassador to 226
    Charter 44, 94, 212
    General Assembly 91
    Moratorium on the question of
        Chinese
        representation 92
    Security Council 86, 91, 94, 212
    Soviet defiance of relevant
        resolutions 90
United States of Europe 20
uranium 113, 106–7
US Air Force 115
USSR see Soviet Union

Varna 206
V-bombers 118, 123, 124, 130, 134
    commitment of force 148
    improving and extending the
        effective life of 137
Vienna 43
Vietnam 168, 170–1

Index

British initiative on the war (1967)
158–60
British refusal to help 155, 158, 189
economic opportunities for America
230
North 159
South 154, 156, 158, 159
violence 208

Waldegrave, William 2
Walker, Gordon 153
Wall Street 234
Wall Street Journal 224, 235
warheads 116, 138
Warsaw 43
Warsaw Pact 223
Washington, George 220
Washington Conference (1957) 84,
97–8
Washington Post, The 225
Western European Union 38, 50
Wilson, Harold (Baron Wilson of
Rievaulx) 125, 146–7, 153–4,
156, 168, 170, 191

Anglo-American relations' speech
(1971) 165–7
Kosygin and 158, 159, 160
new tone to British foreign policy
regarding US 187–9
'Strategy for Washington' briefing
(1964) 150–2
Wilson, Woodrow 164–5
Winston Churchill (USS) 248
World Bank 167
world powers 39, 175
dominant 71
major 59
question of a third 51, 52

xenophobia 190

Yalta agreement (1945) 44, 240
Yom Kippur War (1973) 219
Yugoslavia *see* Bosnia; Serbia

Zionists 40, 53
Zoellick, Robert 246
Zuckerman, Sir Solly 148